MODERN JEWISH MASTERS SERIES
General Editor: Steven T. Katz

1. Shlomo Avineri: *Moses Hess: Prophet of Communism and Zionism*

2. Joseph Dan: *Gershom Scholem and the Mystical Dimension of Jewish History*

3. Arnold Band: *Franz Kafka*

4. David Singer: *Rabbi Joseph Soloveitchik*

5. Steven T. Katz: *Martin Buber*

6. David Roskies: *Scholem Aleichem*

7. Steven Schwarzschild: *Hermann Cohen*

8. Pinchas Peli: *Abraham Joshua Heschel*

GERSHOM SCHOLEM

AND
THE MYSTICAL DIMENSION OF
JEWISH HISTORY

Joseph Dan

 New York University Press
New York *and* London
1987

Library of Congress Cataloging-in-Publication Data

Dan, Joseph, 1935–
Gershom Scholem and the mystical dimension of
Jewish history.

(Modern Jewish masters series ; 2)
Bibliography: p.
Includes index.
1. Mysticism—Judaism—Historiography.   2. Scholem,
Gershom Gerhard, 1897–   I. Title.   II. Series.
BM723.D36   1986   296.7'1   86-21760
ISBN 0-8147-1779-9

Book designed by Laiying Chong.

CONTENTS

Chapter 1   THE MAN AND THE SCHOLAR   1
Chapter 2   THE EARLY BEGINNINGS OF
             JEWISH MYSTICISM   38
Chapter 3   FROM THE ANCIENT EAST TO
             THE EUROPEAN MIDDLE AGES   77
Chapter 4   THE ASHKENAZI HASIDIC
             MOVEMENT   92
Chapter 5   THE ENIGMATIC BOOK *BAHIR*   127
Chapter 6   THE EARLY KABBALAH   147
Chapter 7   FROM GERONA TO THE *ZOHAR*   188
Chapter 8   THE *ZOHAR*   203
Chapter 9   FROM THE *ZOHAR* TO SAFED   230
Chapter 10   THE SAFED SCHOOL OF THE
             KABBALAH   244
Chapter 11   THE SABBATIAN UPHEAVAL   286
Chapter 12   HASIDISM AND THE MODERN
             PERIOD   313
             Index   329

CHAPTER 1

THE MAN AND THE SCHOLAR

I

THREE BOOKS should be written about Gershom Scholem. This is intended to be one of them. One book should describe Scholem and the twentieth century: his background, his approach to Zionism, and his immigration to Jerusalem (subjects dealt with in his autobiography, *From Berlin to Jerusalem*),[1] his activity in Jerusalem and at the Hebrew University, his friendships with Agnon[2] and other great Jerusalem figures, his relationship with Walter Benjamin,[3] his social and political views, his impact upon Israeli culture and outlook concerning its past, and all other aspects of a long, fruitful, and extremely active and influential life.

Another book should deal with Scholem the phenomenologist. How did Gershom Scholem understand the meaning of "religion," "mysticism," "symbolism," "mythology," the relationship between mysticism and language, his concept of the scholarly field of history of religions and history of ideas, his attitude toward the Freudian and Jungian schools in psychology, his understanding of Gnosticism, his concept of Judaism and Zionism, and many other similar subjects.[4]

And one book should be dedicated to Scholem's scholarship. He worked for 63 years on a history and bibliography of Jewish mysticism and the integration of this history with the general development of Jewish history and culture. The present book intends to be this third book. It does not deal with Scholem the man and his times, nor does it deal with Scholem's views on the general phenomenological problems which he encountered. It deals only with content, the major outlines of Scholem's history of the kabbalah, and its integration into Jewish history.

Gershom Scholem published over 40 volumes and nearly 700 studies. About 95 percent of these pertain to the subject of this book. Readers may disagree concerning the question of what Scholem's importance is. (They also may disagree over where his main contribution to contemporary Judaism is to be found, whether in his relationship and presentations concerning current affairs, or his contribution to the understanding of mysticism and symbolism in general, or his efforts as a historian. But there can be no doubt that Scholem spent his life being a historian in the fullest sense of the term and concentrated all his efforts in this field. It is very rare to find a young man outlining his scholarly career and then following it without deviation for nearly 60 years; but Scholem did just this. His letter to Bialik, written soon after his arrival in Jerusalem, gives the outline for almost all his subsequent work.[5] Scholem considered that his biographical and bibliographical studies concerning various kabbalists and their works were important. He once said: "All I found were scattered, shabby pages, and I transformed them into history."[6] This is an accurate statement, without any qualifications. He saw himself as a historian, he understood his work as being historical work, he dedicated all his efforts to the study of kabbalistic texts as historical documents. There may be different views concerning what is important in his work; there can be no doubt what, in his labor, was important to him.

It is impossible to summarize in one volume the years of scholarship and publications and articles.[7] All this book intends to bring before the reader are the broadest outlines of the contents of Jewish mysticism and its impact on Jewish religion and history. I have concentrated exclusively on Scholem's work, but often, undoubtedly, the presentation is influenced by the works of Scholem's disciples and subsequent work done on the same subjects. The notes, for the most part, are limited to primary sources, besides pointing out some details and comments. I have also included cases of disagreement and controversy. One can consider this work in its entirety as a survey of the current state of the study of the field as a whole.

Before we turn to a general review of Scholem's scholarly work, a few paragraphs about his biography and his attitude toward Judaism and Zionism are in order. As stated above, there is no intention to present in this framework anything approaching either a full biography or an appreciation of his intellectual response to the main ideas with which his life brought him into contact. These are just bare outlines, to facilitate the understanding of the background of his scholarship.

3

II

There can be no doubt that the young Gershom Scholem was a rebellious intellectual. Nothing in the background in which he was born could explain this, however. If we compare the spiritual world in which he was born and was raised to the one he created for himself in his young manhood, only contradictions emerge. It is as if Scholem had not preserved in his later life anything from his childhood atmosphere except, most probably, a clear resolution never to return to the same values.

Scholem was born in Berlin in 1897 to a family that was a typical Jewish-German assimilationist one. In later years he used to tell the story (included also in his autobiography), that when his parents wanted to please him, they would do something like hang a picture of Herzl on their Christmas tree. There was nothing in that home that would give any basis or impetus to a stirring of a Jewish interest. Hebrew was unknown and unspoken, and the young, emerging Jewish national movement, Zionism, was completely outside the family's realm of interest. German nationalism was the accepted norm of thinking, and the first hints of an interest in socialism were apparent. In short, it is impossible to study Scholem's family to understand what caused him to turn to Judaism and Zionism. Nor is the paradox, like many others, clarified by Scholem's autobiography, which one would expect to throw some light on his early development.

Scholem's autobiography is an unusual book. While most autobiographies tend to serve their authors as a vehicle to reveal their innermost thoughts and feelings, Scholem's *From*

4

Berlin to Jerusalem concerned itself almost exclusively with external facts. That is, he gives detailed information concerning his family, relatives, studies, teachers, books he read, people he met and their background but reveals little about himself. He relates his decisions to study Hebrew, his quest for a teacher in the field of Talmud, his meetings with scholars, and similar incidents, but the natural questions arise: Why did he choose this and not that? What were his motives? What was his attitude toward the various alternatives that stood before him? On these questions there is hardly a word. The reader acquires from reading the autobiography an impressive amount of detailed information, but not a glimpse of the soul of its author, and almost no answer to the basic questionmarks surrounding his early life.

Scholem was no different even in private conversation. He enjoyed talking about his early life, about people he met, and about things he had done. Those who met him frequently and talked with him a great deal recognized most of the events included in *From Berlin to Jerusalem,* because they served as the basis for anecdotes he related in his conversations. However, the motives, the reasons, the emotions—these Scholem kept hidden in his book as well as in his conversations.

It was not known, until after his death in 1982, that Scholem left a large number of personal letters in his files. His widow, Fania (a relative of Freud), is working now to sort them out, arrange them chronologically and by subject, and prepare a selection for publication. There is a possibility that these letters may shed some light on the questions which we are discussing here.

If Scholem did not leave us with a statement of his motives

5

concerning his major decisions in his early life, to some extent his actions speak for themselves. All his actions point in one direction: an intense, extreme sense of rebellion.

Not only in his early life, but throughout the 65 years of his career, Scholem was and remained a fierce foe of German nationalism. He expressed it in the most difficult circumstances during the First World War, when he belonged to the tiny minority among German Jews who opposed the war wholeheartedly and without reservation (without, however, joining the communists, who also opposed the war). He never forgave some of his friends and teachers who were carried away by the German nationalistic spirit and in one way or another supported, even if halfheartedly, the war effort. When called to army service, Scholem successfully persuaded the doctors that he was mentally unbalanced and therefore should be exempt from army service. This act never gave him any qualms nor did he express any misgivings. The war was nothing of a Jew's concern, and he expressed in this way his complete and resolute negation of the spirit of German nationalism that prevailed in his home and toward which he felt nothing but alienation and hatred.

This basic attitude is reflected in his response in later years to the horrible questions of the Holocaust and subsequent relationships with Nazi and post-Nazi Germany. His resolute answer to Hannah Arendt concerning the evil of Nazi Germany is a clear example, but only the best-known one. In one of his essays he deals with the problem of the role of Jews in modern German culture, and points out, like nobody else before him, the stark asymmetry in the description of this process. Scholem pointed out that only Jewish writers

6

and historians had stressed the Jewish contribution to German culture in the nineteenth century and the first third of the twentieth, when the Nazi regime took over. He asked: Where are the German historians who accept the thesis that Jewish spiritual force was integrated into modern German culture? Where is the German who will admit that there was a meeting (Scholem even used a sexual expression to describe such a meeting) between Judaism and Germanism in the modern period? The love affair between Jews and German culture that began in the middle of the eighteenth century was a completely one-sided one, Scholem explained; there was no expression of any German appreciation of the Jewish contribution. Nazi anti-Semitism, one may infer, was for Scholem a deep expression of the German-Jewish relationship, a far truer expression than the idyllic picture of an "interrupted love affair" that could have been resumed were it not for the brutal intervention of the Nazis.

How much of this did the young Scholem understand before he decided to repudiate his home and turn to Jewish nationalism and Hebrew studies? We cannot know, but it is possible to imagine that the fierceness of his rebellion reflected a deep-seated aversion toward the assimilationist world in which he was raised and that he remained steadfast and committed throughout his life to the values he adopted in his adolescent years when he rebelled against those which governed his family and his education.

It should also be noted that Scholem chose, when adopting Judaism and Zionism, the least popular alternative among those he could have followed, and probably the most difficult one. Young Jews at that time were joining various socialist and leftist groups, and the young Scholem was aware of their ideology and politics. Socialism never appealed to him, even though a great and important friendship in his life was with Walter Benjamin, a profound (though an unorthodox) socialist thinker.

To become a socialist, one did not have to study a forgotten, neglected language like Hebrew, and certainly could study texts easier to follow than the Talmud. Yet Scholem chose the most difficult way and followed it with a dedication which would characterize his attitude to every subject he would deal with throughout his life.

What came first—Zionism or Judaism? Did Scholem adopt Jewish nationalism first, and then, in order not to appear hypocritical, begin to study Jewish history, Hebrew, and the Jewish classical texts, or was it the other way round—first the interest in Hebrew and Judaism, and only later the awakening of Jewish nationalism, followed by Zionist activity? It seems from Scholem's statements on this subject that adherence to nationalism came first, but that his cultural interest was never separated from his Zionist ideology. The two were fused together very early in his life.

It is clear that Scholem did not choose to be a student of mysticism first, and then of Jewish mysticism second. His road toward the study of the kabbalah began with the repudiation of German nationalism and of Jewish assimilationism. This brought him to the Hebrew language, to Jewish history, and to the study of the Talmud and Midrash. Only much later did he choose the neglected field of the kabbalah as the subject to which he would dedicate over 60 years of scholarly work. That is, often one reads descriptions of Scholem depicting him as a great mystic, who used scholarship as a vehicle to express his innermost feelings toward God and the creation, toward history and divine revelation. Nothing could be farther from the truth. As has been intimated above, Scholem was first and foremost a Jewish nationalist. Then he studied Jewish culture thoroughly. Only then did he become a scholar of the history of the kabbalah.

It is interesting to note how seldom the term "Jewish mysticism" appears in Scholem's writings in the 1920s. He dedicated himself (as we shall see below) to the study of the history of kabbalistic texts but without characterizing them as revelations of Jewish mystical creativity. It was not until his series of lectures in New York, after which his first book in English appeared (*Major Trends in Jewish Mysticism* in 1941, when Scholem was 44 years old and had written nearly a hundred studies) that the subject of the relationship between the kabbalah and mysticism began to be central to his work. Scholem did not become a scholar of the kabbalah because he was a kabbalist or a mystic. He chose it after choosing Jewish nationalism over German nationalism, Hebrew culture over German culture; from among the possible Hebrew subjects to which he could have dedicated his scholarly enterprise he chose the kabbalah. Why?

Again, Scholem's autobiography, like Scholem's conversation, does not give a clear answer. However, when analyzing his writing on the subject, one is immediately faced with Scholem's sense of outrage, outrage at the treatment that the kabbalah had received from previous generations of scholars who had dealt with it. It was not only the sense of following a neglected field that inspired him but also the thought that he could correct the mistakes of those who had published on the kabbalah. One example was the scholar who wrote extensively on the kabbalah. When Scholem admired his vast library and asked: "You undoubtedly have read all these books?" Scholem received the following answer: "What? Do I also have to read this junk?"

Modern scholars, too, reflected the ignorance Scholem found in the writings of his predecessors, the historians and scholars of the nineteenth century. They not only neglected the kabbalah, but they hated it and expressed this hatred in emotional terms in their putatively scholarly analyses. Several statements of Scholem's, describing his early career in the field of kabbalah, express his sense of indignation at this attitude, an attitude for which he could find no justification whatsoever. When reading kabbalistic texts he felt as if he were the first scholar to ever read them. Accordingly his researches gave him a sense of pioneering adventure, a feeling akin to the discovery of an unknown continent. To a dedicated historian, experienced in the study of subjects on which whole libraries have been written and for whom the chance of making a really significant discovery is slim, this sense of discovery provided a most unusual experience and one which caused Scholem great satisfaction.

How can we explain the various reasons that caused Scholem to choose Jewish mysticism as a subject of his scholarship? Did his rejectionist mood carry him away from Jewish assimilationism and German nationalism to Zionism and Jewish culture? Was he reacting in the same way toward those previous Jewish historians and scholars who treated the kabbalah with such disdain? Did he select the works that historians had mistaken or brushed aside with the conviction that a meaningful life of intellectual adventure waited for him there? And was there an element of empathy toward forgotten mystics, who brought out a mystical spark in his soul?

The last cannot be denied, but should not be overemphasized, at least when trying to understand Scholem's initial choice of the book *Bahir* as a subject for his Ph.D. thesis. When we actually read his thesis, and follow it up by reading his published scholarly monographs produced in the first years of his stay in Jerusalem, we do not find much of a sense of empathy and connectedness, certainly not when compared to that found in his later works. The enthusiasm of his essay on Sabbatianism, "Redemption Through Sin," is completely lacking. Most of the work on the *Bahir* consists of notes and references, and very little revelation of the mystical gnostic spirit of the *Bahir* can be gleaned from these pages. The same is true concerning his long papers in the first numbers of the Israeli journals *Tarbiz* and *Kiryat Sefer,* which were the fruit of the first ten years of his scholarly career, nor in his first books to be written after the thesis, his bibliography of kabbalistic works, *Bibliographia Kabbalistica,* and a second volume of bibliography, *Kitvey Yad be-Kabbalah,* which was a list of the Hebrew kabbalistic manuscripts in the possession of the National and University Library in Jerusalem.

Did the young Scholem successfully hide his innermost empathy with mysticism in these early studies, or is it that it developed somewhat later in his scholarly career? We cannot really know. It is my belief that both alternatives are at least partially correct. Scholem's early works are written in a strict—too strict—conformity to historical-philological norms, covering details in great length, presenting before the reader the writer's reasoning, doubts, and contradictory alternatives to his own interpretations in a way which he was to follow in later years, but with much greater emphasis and a heightened sense of importance. It is as if Scholem were trying to prove that "this, too, is history," and to convey this fact by the literary style and organization of his articles. If this was indeed his attitude, it is understandable that he forbade himself from revealing his subjectivity in any way, trying instead to present the material as if it were completely remote from his feelings. It is, therefore, possible that he had an intense feeling of empathy, but that he concealed it completely.

To the contrary, I believe that it is evident that as the years passed, with material accumulating and knowledge growing, Scholem became more and more fascinated and, one might even say, "conquered" by the material with which he was dealing. In the early studies one hardly finds expressions which define the general historical meaning of the kabbalistic sources. In the period after 1935, such expressions are increased greatly, and Scholem's conviction of the meaningfulness and relevance of his field of study to every aspect of Jewish culture increased dramatically. The enormous interest evoked by his first publications concerning Sabbatianism demonstrated that he was correct in pointing out the rich spiritual values hidden in the kabbalistic texts. With this reinforcement, Scholem's subjective acceptance of the symbols of the kabbalah also increased. That is, unlike some of my colleagues and Scholem's friends, I do not believe that Scholem was inclined toward mysticism in general when he chose the field of kabbalah around 1920. It seems to me that if Scholem, as a person, had been mystically inclined, he would have revealed more interest in mysticism in general throughout his academic career. It is a fact, however, that Scholem strictly confined himself to Jewish mysticism, and strayed to generalizations concerning religion, mysticism and the history of ideas only when he was writing brief introductions to the study of a Jewish idea or symbol. Mysticism per se, as a generalization within which Jewish mysticism is a detail, did interest him only tangentially. As stated above, it is very difficult to know whether he was involved with anything except the truth beyond kabbalistic symbolism as a 20-year-old. Also, as has been discussed above, no mystical tendency is revealed in his early papers, and very little can be gleaned about it in his later ones. Yet because Scholem did not present the kabbalistic texts just as history and nothing more, he most probably did believe that they (not all, of course, but the best and most profound) contained a transcendent spark, something beyond the mere literary and religious expression of a particular cultural attitude.

It is important to emphasize that Scholem's involvement with the texts he was studying never influenced his historical analyses. Scholem did not choose—or neglect—the subjects he discussed and dissected according to his preference, nor according to his belief in the transcendent spark of truth he believed they contained. One example demonstrates this fact.

It would be difficult to find anything that Scholem wrote with more enthusiasm, empathy and keen historical analysis than his study of the career of Moshe Dobrushka, a follower of the great Sabbatian radical heretic, Jacob Frank (to be discussed in Chapter 12). Yet Scholem's repugnance of Frankist

13

anarchistic and destructive attitudes and their anti-Jewish activity is evident in many of his works, including his first programmatic essay, "Redemption Through Sin." His interest in Dobrushka's career is purely the consequence of a deep satisfaction gained from the study of hundreds of documents in half a dozen languages. There is no identification with the "hero," and certainly no inclination to embrace his political or theological views, nor is there any ethical acceptance of his bizarre actions.

It is sometimes stated that Scholem was interested in the heretical, anarchistic movements among Jewish mystics, thus revealing his own tendencies. This does not have any basis in the facts. Scholem did not dedicate more energy and interest to the Frankist movement, for instance, than to the rather conservative and moderate circle of kabbalists in Gerona (northern Spain) in the first half of the thirteenth century. He did not dedicate more space or time to the study of the Sabbatian movement than he did to the book *Bahir* and the early kabbalah. Why, therefore, this persistent impression, found in so many descriptions of Scholem's outlook?

The answer is rather simple. This impression is not based on what Scholem actually did, but on what his readers preferred to study. Few people read his books on the early kabbalah, while his studies on Sabbatianism and Frankism have, since the 1950s, become part of Israeli culture. The questions, therefore, should not be directed toward Scholem, but rather toward our generation: Why are we so interested in the anarchic and unorthodox in the Jewish past? Is it because we feel ourselves to be, in relation to our forefathers, anarchistic and revolutionary, and hence we seek justification for our own efforts at anarchy from previous examples?

Scholem did not cover every subject, nor did he exhaust many that he did concern himself with in the history of Jewish mysticism, even though he did seek to present at least an outline of every phase and phenomenon and chose which to enlarge upon according to their intrinsic historical and cultural significance. His own preferences and beliefs remained very far in the background of his scholarly efforts, contrary to the preferences of some who read his work.

Reading through Scholem's scholarly books and articles may give an incorrect impression. Scholem was very careful to publish only the things he understood, and not the things he did not know. When one reads his publications, there is an impression of clarity and conclusiveness, as if everything were now clear and all problems solved. But this impression is completely mistaken. Scholem, for instance, kept a copy of each of his publications bound with empty pages intervening between every two pages of printed text, and used these inserted pages to write down notes, additions, changes, and added information. In some of his works the added pages include more material than the printed ones. He never regarded any of his studies as complete; the publication was the report of the situation as he viewed it at that time, but he intended to rewrite and reformulate large parts of his publications. In later years he republished, in corrected and enlarged form, several early studies to which he had a great deal to add, like those on kabbalah and alchemy,[8] on Rabbi Joseph dela Reina,[9] on the early concept of the *kavvanah* in prayer and others.[10] Every new edition or translation of his books included new material, new information and sometimes even changes of point of view.[11]

III

Scholem's preoccupation with bibliography is legendary, and it is another side to the intensity with which he collected and built his own library. It must be stressed, however, that in the first fifteen years of Scholem's work in Jerusalem there was an inherent unity in his work and achievements in the three fields: the study of kabbalah, his work in Jewish bibliography, with emphasis on kabbalah, and the building of his library, the core of which is the collection of kabbalistica.

Bibliography, for Scholem, was the basic, and sometimes even the final, product of scholarship. It is not an accident that the first two major works he prepared and published after his Ph.D. thesis were bibliographies: *Bibliographia Kabbalistica*[12] and *List of Kabbalistic Manuscripts at the National and University Library in Jerusalem*.[13] He began his academic career in Jerusalem as a Judaica librarian at the National and University Library, a chapter vividly described in his autobiography. He did not describe the enormous accomplishment of preparing a directory for the adaptation of the Dewey Decimal System to the needs of Judaica, a directory that was updated several times and serves to this day for the classification of Judaica books in the National Library and many other Judaica libraries in Israel and abroad.

Scholem's intensity regarding the study of books was apparent in his scholarship in the twenties and early thirties. Many of his articles were published in *Kiryat Sefer,* the bibliographical publication of the National library, which lists all books pertaining to Judaica to arrive at the Library, and allots some of its space to scholarly studies related to Judaica bibliography. Scholem published his major articles in *Kiryat Sefer* under the common title *Studies in the History of Kabbalistic Literature.*[14]

Meanwhile Scholem was building his private library. The emphasis was on everything connected to Jewish mysticism.

In various editions of his famous brochure "Alu le-Shalom," ("Ascend to Scholem") he listed his bibliographical desiderata. When a book appeared on that list, its price immediately tripled. It became obvious to Scholem that his modest means would never enable him to collect kabbalistic manuscripts, so instead he helped the National Library build a comprehensive collection in the field. After his death, his collection became an integral part of the National and University Library's Gershom Scholem Center for the Study of Kabbalah.

IV

Scholem's studies in 15 years from 1921 to 1936 covered all periods in the history of Jewish mysticism and most of its main subjects, from the ancient *Hekhalot* mysticism of the Talmudic period to ninth-century Hasidism, a span of a millennium and a half.[15]

During this time, Scholem attempted to absorb and organize the vast material of Jewish mysticism, to master it, and to allot each work, treatise, and writer its proper slot in the history of kabbalah. At the same time he began to publish works intended to cover all major areas of kabbalistic creativity and to present a coherent picture of the development of kabbalistic literature. Scholem's main comprehensive achievement of this period was his extensive article on kabbalah in the German *Encyclopaedia Judaica*—the first scholarly history of Jewish mysticism ever written.[16]

V

Between 1921 and 1936, Scholem concentrated on finding, copying, and analyzing every kabbalistic manuscript he could reach. Scholem travelled from library to library in Europe (and later in the United States) and collected information from scholarly catalogues and from bookseller's lists. By the comprehensive study of the manuscripts, and by the mastery of the printed kabbalistic texts, Scholem achieved a full, comprehensive knowledge of the history of the kabbalah. His published papers in this period reflect this.

Judging from his publications, one group of kabbalists interested him more than others in this period: the brothers Jacob and Isaac, sons of Rabbi Jacob ha-Cohen, who flourished in Castile in the second half of the thirteenth century. His first major publication after his arrival in Jerusalem was a book which described their works and main ideas.[17] This was immediately followed by a second volume, published as a series of articles in *Tarbiz*,[18] which added important material concerning the Cohen brothers and studied the works of their disciple, Rabbi Moses of Burgos. Scholem was especially attracted to them because of the gnostic character of some of their texts, especially Rabbi Isaac ha-Cohen's *Treatise on the Emanations of the Left,*[19] which is the first kabbalistic work which reveals a clear dualistic attitude concerning good and evil, and which subsequently had great impact on the *Zohar* and the later development of kabbalistic theology. His conclusions concerning this circle of Jewish mystics were incomplete, because, while he described the close connections between the ideas of this circle and those of the *Zohar,* he could not clearly state which was the source and which came later, for at that time he had not yet arrived at a decision concerning the date of the *Zohar*'s composition.[20] The possibility that Rabbi Isaac ha-Cohen used zoharic sources seemed to Scholem at that time a real one. Only in the next decade did Scholem present his conclusions concerning Rabbi Moses de Leon's authorship of the *Zohar,* and then, of course, the independent thought of the Cohen brothers and their original contribution to the development of kabbalah was clearly apparent. It is a curious fact, however, that while Scholem dedicated much time and effort to the study of this school of kabbalists in the 1920s and early 1930s, he did not return to this subject in later years. He did, however, dedicate a memorable seminar to the Cohen brothers in the early 1960s.

Another kabbalist central to Scholem's interests between 1921 and 1936 was Rabbi Abraham be-Rabbi Eliezer ha-Levi, who flourished at the end of the fifteenth century and the beginning of the sixteenth.[21] The intense, messianic, and mythological works of Rabbi Abraham signified a change in the attitude of kabbalists toward messianic redemption.

Scholem investigated him against the traumatic background of the expulsion of the Jews from Spain, to which Rabbi Abraham was a witness. The works of Rabbi Abraham were central to the understanding of the emergence of kabbalistic messianism in the land of Israel in the sixteenth century and as a background to the development of the Lurianic school of kabbalists in Safed later in that century.

While the Cohen brothers and Rabbi Abraham be-Rabbi Eliezer ha-Levi were the principal subjects in Scholem's publications at that time, his subsequent books and papers prove that he was also working intensely on the problems of the emergence of the kabbalah in the twelfth and thirteenth centuries, on the *Zohar,* its authorship and its theology, on the Lurianic literature, and on the Sabbatian movement. This became apparent with the publication of "Mitzvah ha-Ba'ah be-Averah" ("Redemption through Sin") in 1936.[22]

VI

Until 1936, Scholem thought the kabbalah should be studied along with other areas of Jewish religious creativity to arrive at a comprehensive picture of this vast culture. He was regarded—and the image was supported by the nature of his published material—as a historian of kabbalistic literature, interested in establishing the various stages in the development of Jewish mysticism. After 1936, however, Scholem set out to rewrite major chapters in Jewish history as a whole.

Scholem's presentation of the Sabbatian movement in

"Mitzvah ha-Ba'ah be-Averah," although revolutionary, was accepted as signalling a major change in the attitude of Jewish scholars toward Jewish history, as well as in Scholem's own career. He showed that the Sabbatian movement, although neglected by many historians (but not by all, as he was the first to insist),[23] actually provided the key to understanding Jewish history from the exile from Spain in 1492 to Jewish emancipation in the late eighteenth century. Suddenly scholars and readers were brought to the realization that the symbolism of the kabbalah was not just a curious, mildly interesting, marginal aspect of Jewish culture but was a source that could supply many answers to basic, perplexing problems of Jewish history.

After publishing his paper on the Sabbatian movement, Scholem delivered a series of lectures in New York. These were published as Scholem's first major book—and the first one in English—*Major Trends in Jewish Mysticism.*[24] There can be no doubt that its publication has been and will remain one of the major turning points in the history of Jewish scholarship. In this book Scholem presented the first analysis of ancient Jewish mysticism, the *Hekhalot* and *Merkabah* mysticism, and described it as Jewish gnosticism; it was the first time this literature was not treated as an insignificant, late collection of incomprehensible texts with no bearing on the development of Jewish culture. In this book Scholem presented the first comprehensive discussion of the Ashkenazi Hasidic movement, its sources, development, mystical element, ethical teachings, and historical impact. Here too we find the first study of the fascinating career and teachings of Rabbi Abraham Abulafia. But above all, in this book Scholem presents his conclusions concerning the authorship of the *Zohar,* dating it to the late thirteenth century. In addition, it was in this work that the teachings of Isaac Luria (1534–1572) with their intense messianism and mythology, were first presented and connected with the history and ideas of the Sabbatian movement, while the chapter on the Sabbatian movement is a more detailed and more comprehensive presentation than the one in his 1936 paper. Finally, the chapter on Hasidism, which concludes the book, signalled a new approach to this movement, based on a detailed analysis of its mystical symbolism, and viewed it as a modern continuation of kabbalistic mysticism. As a result of this book, the study of Jewish mysticism began to be included in general works about mysticism in world religions, and Scholem began to be accepted as an authority.

Major Trends in Jewish Mysticism did not describe the beginnings of the kabbalah. Scholem was working intensely on the subject, and published a paper on it in 1943[25] and a short book in 1948.[26] Scholem continued to work on the subject and in 1962 he published his most comprehensive and detailed discussion of the origins of the kabbalah under the title *Ursprung und Anfänge der Kabbala.*[27] He also gave a lecture series at the Hebrew University on the same subject, which was published in four volumes starting in 1962.[28]

The third achievement of this period was the publication in 1957, in Hebrew, of a two-volume history of the Sabbatian movement during Sabbatai Zevi's lifetime.[29] Here the generalizations offered in previous publications were documented in minutest details.

Scholem's fourth important achievement in this period was

the series of lectures he gave at the annual meetings of the Eranos society in Zurich. This society, dedicated to the study of Jungian psychology, religion, and history, invited Scholem year after year to deliver major papers in its meetings although he could by no means be regarded as Jungian psychologist, philosopher, or religious historian. Scholem used the opportunity to prepare and publish a series of studies of various subjects in Jewish mysticism: the role of the mystic in religious society, the mythological element in kabbalah, the anthropomorphic image of God in Jewish mystical symbolism, the concept of good and evil in kabbalah, the symbol of the *shekhinah* in Jewish mysticism, and many others.[30] These were the first monographs on kabbalistic subjects presented from the point of view of general scholarship in the fields of mysticism, religion, and the history of ideas. In these papers Scholem employed comparisons between Jewish phenomena and parallels which he perceived to exist in human religious experience everywhere.

By 1962 Scholem had covered all the major subjects that he had begun to deconstruct. He then became interested in presenting very detailed studies of Sabbatianism as it existed in later periods, that is, after Sabbatai Zevi's death and on into the eighteenth century, and in the beginning of Hasidism, especially as represented by the life of its founder, Israel ben Eliezer, also called the Besht. In the next 20 years, up until his death, Scholem published many papers and collections of papers on these and other subjects. He repeatedly returned to ancient *Hekhalot* mysticism, the study of which became more important after the discovery of the Dead Sea Scrolls and the Nag Hamadi gnostic library.[31] He rewrote many of his early papers and assembled his papers into volumes with revisions.[32]

VII

Scholem was one of the "founding fathers" of the Institute of Jewish Studies and the Hebrew University. This enabled him to influence the character of the university as a whole. He insisted on high-quality scholarship. His insistence did not bring him only friends; often his sharp tongue and uncompromising adherence to his own views aroused resentment. Thus, Baruch Kurzweil, Scholem's bitterest critic, for example, argued that nobody of Scholem's stature could busy himself in the study of Jewish mysticism and Sabbatianism just because these subjects were interesting, challenging, and historically significant. There must be some selfish motive behind it all,[33] and as such it should be seen as an allegory concerning contemporary movements within Judaism. It is interesting to note that in some of these disputes an identification was made between Scholem and the Hebrew University. Scholem came to represent the values held by the Hebrew University. Enmity toward the university was transformed into enmity toward Scholem, and vice versa. Scholem did not bother to answer the critics.[34]

The most important characteristic of Scholem's teaching style was that he never underestimated his listeners; he always presented his studies in the depth and detail necessary to make his case understandable. Thus, Scholem's lectures were intended for undergraduate students (though many non-students participated, these lectures being some of the most interesting intellectual events in Jerusalem). In them he presented subjects which he had also described in detail in his published or forthcoming books.

Not so in his seminars. He usually chose difficult texts for seminars, ones he believed that a student could not read alone and understand. In these seminars the discussion was closely connected to the text. Scholem seldom moved away from it to present a more general picture.[35]

Scholem had a different attitude toward his graduate seminars. As subjects for these seminars Scholem used to choose those which he thought had not yet been sufficiently investigated. In these seminars, for example, the book *Bahir* was studied for two years. Every sentence was to be interpreted. One year the seminar was dedicated to the enigmatic *Iyyun* circle of early kabbalists; another year it was devoted to reading the quotations from Rabbi Isaac Sagi Nahor's teachings, all of which are very cryptic and difficult. Another year was dedicated to the works of the Cohen brothers from Castile, and another to the study of the relationship between the works of Rabbi Joseph Gikatilla and those of Rabbi Moses de Leon, still to be clarified, which has some implications concerning the authorship of the *Zohar*.

In his graduate seminars Scholem presented the structure and outlines of the development of Jewish mysticism, pointing out that most subjects awaited exhaustive scholarly review. Scholem never resented a student's correction concerning something he had published, and incorporated the correction or modified view in a subsequent publication. He was always ready to help, in fact, insisting that any difficulty that a younger scholar encountered be brought to him for discussion.

It seems to me that Scholem's most fascinating characteristic as a teacher was his deep, sincere belief in the importance and significance of his work and Jewish mysticism. Nothing was trivial; everything necessitated serious, thorough investigation. Every fact or idea was expressed with a deep conviction of its relevancy to historical truth as a whole. His belief in that was catching, and his students followed him in this sense of the integrity and relevance of their work in this field.[36] Further, he insisted on detailed analysis and a philological approach; he insisted that detail is the basis of everything.

When Scholem began his scholarly work, the concept of Jewish studies was not yet clear. He probably contributed more than any other contemporary scholar to its clarification and to the establishment of Jewish studies as a true discipline within the humanities. Scholem vehemently rejected any apologetic tendency, whether it was of the nineteenth-century variety, which tried to satisfy the prejudices of non-Jews as Jewish scholars saw them (often erroneously), or of the twentieth-century variety, which tried to incorporate nationalistic or socialist elements. That is, the texts had to speak, and the scholars had to understand them in a philological manner and then proceed to interpret history on its own terms, to the limit of their ability. He was not susceptible to the fashion of doubting whether "there is really historical truth," but put this truth as the ultimate target, probably never to be reached, but to be approached by every scholar in his analysis of detail after detail.

Many scholars in Jewish studies seek the meaning of their work in the context of the humanities as a whole. Some try to achieve this by pointing out parallels and meanings that could connect their subject to other fields in the humanities. Scholem did not do this. He started his studies from a neglected corner of a neglected field, the kabbalah within Jewish studies, and he contributed significantly to the integration of Jewish studies into the humanities as a whole as well as of Jewish mysticism into the general fields of religion and mysticism. He did not accomplish this by drawing parallels between Jewish mystics and Christian and Moslem ones; in fact, he very seldom did that. Rather, he interpreted the works of the Jewish mystics within the framework of Jewish culture and religion. He studied the influences of historical circumstances upon them and the historical consequences of their ideas and symbols. He always emphasized the specific, the unique, and resisted categorizing phenomena. Thus, the meaning of *mysticism* is different in his conception of "Jewish mysticism" from some accepted notions concerning mysticism in general; he insisted more on showing what was unique to Jewish mysticism and in what way it was different from Christian mysticism than on pointing out parallels between Jewish and non-Jewish mystical phenomena.

It is because of this, because of his intensive insistence on understanding the unique character of every phenomenon, that Scholem achieved the universal meaning of his studies. Only when presenting the unique does one avoid any limitation in achieving the full range of the meaning of the subject being considered, and only this full meaning has significance concerning the study of Man as a whole. By ruthlessly dedicating

27

himself to the comprehensive study of a historical phenomenon in its fullness Scholem presented a conclusion which is meaningful and relevant to any scholar in any field of study. His message to scholars in Jewish studies everywhere is, therefore, that it is their duty to exhaust the significance of the detail under study and present it in its many-sided uniqueness. It is from this insistence on the particular that the universal meaning arises.

VIII

The death of Gershom Scholem on February 21, 1982 caused a renewed discussion of his achievements, assessments of his role in contemporary Jewish thought and his contribution to the study of Jewish history. The most important contribution to this reassessment so far has been made in a book by E. Schweid.[37] Several other papers and articles have appeared. However, it is too early to present an accurate appraisal of Gershom Scholem's contribution to Jewish intellectual life in the twentieth century. The remarks below, therefore, are not intended to serve as an assessment, but a personal view concerning the most important ways in which Scholem helped shape contemporary Jewish self-awareness and self-image, and contributed to the new, emerging Jewish identity of the late twentieth century, which might continue to develop in the next century.

As the title of this book suggests, I believe that Scholem's most important achievement was the redemption of Hebrew mystical literature from neglect and oblivion, and its integra-

tion into the broader parameters of Jewish history and literature. The obstacles Scholem had to overcome in order to
achieve this were two: first, ignorance, and, second, a dis-
torting, apologetic attitude. Mystical literature was not known.
Most of the manuscripts and books were unknown and un-
read, and no one was interested in studying them because the
prevailing intellectual atmosphere in Jewish scholarship demanded that Judaism be presented before the non-Jewish world
in terms acceptable to non-Jews, and not first and foremost
as it really was. For Scholem, historical veracity and accuracy
were the most cherished values, and he believed that only the
authentic image of Judaism could be accepted by the intellectual world as legitimate, respected, and culturally equal.
His instincts as a historian and his liberal, humanistic views
combined in this belief to produce a vehement resistance to
ignorance and apologetics and a consistent struggle for
knowledge and truth.

Scholem took on the task of demonstrating the richness
and profundity of the mystical dimension in Jewish history.
Some writers (such as E. Schweid) misunderstand Scholem
and maintain that he wanted to demonstrate that mysticism
was the only source of Jewish religious vitality and renewal.
This is not true; Scholem did not magnify the role of the
Jewish mystics beyond the results of his careful, systematic,
historical assessment. What misled many readers of his books
into believing that he saw in Judaism mysticism and nothing
else was his historian's insistence on working and publishing
only in his own field, trying not to stray from his subject
and staying close to the texts he was discussing. Schweid and
others contended as well that what Scholem did not write

about was unimportant to him, when all he was doing was mastering his own special field while straying as little as possible into other fields. The claim that Scholem disregarded the *halakhah* and relegated it to second place in the hierarchy of the most important Jewish areas of creativity is unfounded. He was not a specialist in the *halakhah* and therefore did not publicly air his views regarding it. We do not find in his works superlatives concerning the role of Jewish mysticism which may preclude other sources of Jewish spirituality. We do find clear statements concerning the previous neglect of this literature and its importance in order to achieve a complete and coherent view of Jewish culture as a whole.

It is important to note how careful Scholem was when making his rare statements concerning the role of mysticism in the further development of Judaism. He was most skeptical concerning the possibility of a future mystical awakening that would bring to the Jewish people new answers to religious and national questions. One has the feeling that Zionism was much more important to him in contemporary Jewish ideology than mysticism. He opposed the combination of the two. Zionism was for him a political movement, but one which could also contribute to spiritual development.

When assessing historical developments Scholem was careful not to be carried away by his enthusiasm for the kabbalistic texts and to overestimate their historical importance. He insisted that ancient Jewish mysticism, *Hekhalot* and *Merkabah* literature, should be regarded as one aspect of traditional, rabbinic Judaism and not as a later trivial aberration. But he did not claim that *Hekhalot* mysticism was the spiritual source of the Mishnah, the Talmud, and the Midrash.

He was discovering and presenting an added dimension, not a substitute for previous ones. The same is true concerning the mystical element in Ashkenazi Hasidism and the impact of the kabbalah on Jewish culture in medieval Spain, France, and Italy. He believed only that mysticism should not be ignored, not that it should be regarded as the source and fountain of everything, disregarding other major cultural and religious forces.

Scholem's main demand was a search for the totality of Jewish culture, which cannot be achieved if Jewish mysticism is ignored; but it cannot be achieved either if other aspects are not taken into consideration. Scholem was not a historiosoph, and did not present a coherent, complete picture of all aspects of Judaism; he was a specialist publishing constantly in one area, waiting for others to do the same in their fields, and hoping for a balanced picture to emerge.

Scholem occasionally published his opinions on subjects outside his area of specialization. That these have become well-known and are republished and discussed frequently is the result of the readers' interest rather than the intention of the author to make them the central concern of his work. Subjects like Jewish-German relations, the characteristics of the *Wissenschaft des Judentums* movement, Walter Benjamin, and others, were never very important to Scholem. He published such articles because he was an interested, observant intellectual aware of his times, not because he wanted to encompass all modern developments into one systematic history.

Scholem advanced the thesis that Jewish mysticism in its later development in the Lurianic kabbalah in Safed, in the

Sabbatian movement of the seventeenth and eighteenth centuries, and in modern Hasidism of the eighteenth and nineteenth centuries, had an enormous impact on shaping modern Jewish history. Scholem believed that modern Judaism cannot be understood without the correct assessment of the mystical elements in these three major spiritual upheavals, and the influence that these had on the major developments in mysticism in modern Judaism. The study of the Jewish mysticism of ancient times and the Middle Ages is important both because it gives an added dimension to the history of these periods, and because it helps explain the later eruption of mystical influence into the center of Jewish life from the sixteenth to the nineteenth centuries.

NOTES

1. See Gershom Scholem, *Von Berlin nach Jerusalem: Jugenderinnerungen* (Frankfurt am Main: Suhrkamp, 1977). [English translation: *From Berlin to Jerusalem: Memories of My Youth,* translated by Harry Zohn (New York: Schocken, 1980)]. Cf. the Hebrew version, completely rewritten with many changes: *Me-Berlin le Yerushalayim: Zikhronot Neʿurim* (Tel Aviv: Am Oved, 1982).

2. Some remarks concerning this unique relationship were included in *From Berlin to Jerusalem.* Scholem revealed a little more about this friendship in his interview with Professor David Miron of the Hebrew University, Jerusalem. The interview was shown, in part, on Israeli television, and the text published in the literary supplement of the daily newspaper *Ha-ʾAaretz,* 29 Jan. 1982, p. 19.

3. Scholem published a lecture and a volume of his correspondence with Benjamin under the title *Walter Benjamin: die Geschichte einer Freundschaft* (Frankfurt am Main: Suhrkamp, 1975). The work was translated into several languages including English. See G. Scholem, *Walter Benjamin: the Story of a Friendship,* translated by Harry Zohn (Philadelphia: The

Jewish Publication Society, 1981). The story of this friendship, however, is still awaiting a biographer.

4. An attempt to write such a work is to be found in David Biale, *Gershom Scholem: Kabbalah and Counter-History* (Cambridge: Harvard University Press, 1979). My remarks concerning this book were published in *Kiryat Sefer*, 54 (1979), pp. 358–62.

5. This letter written in 1925, was reprinted in G. Scholem, *Devarim Be-Go* (Tel Aviv: Am Oved, 1976), vol. 1, pp. 59–63. In the letter Scholem made a list of desiderata in the field of Jewish mysticism and announced his intention to fulfill most of them. It is most interesting to compare this list with his accomplishments. It is evident that at that time he was most interested in the publication and study of texts, and in the *Zohar* dictionary, while the historical aspect of his studies is almost completely absent.

6. G. Scholem, *Devarim Be-Go*, vol. 1, pp. 64–68. The quote is included in a speech that Scholem delivered on the occasion of acceptance of the Rothschild prize. It was first published in the literary monthly *Molad*, 20 (1963), pp. 135–37.

7. Two editions of Scholem's bibliography have been published. (1) F. Scholem and B. Yaron, eds. and comps., "Bibliography of the Published Writings of Gershom G. Scholem," in *Studies in Mysticism and Religion presented to Gershom Scholem on his Seventieth Birthday* (Jerusalem: Magnes Press, The Hebrew University, 1967), pp. 199–235 (of the Hebrew section). (2) Moshe Catane, ed. and comp., *Bibliography of the Writings of Gershom G. Scholem presented to Gershom G. Scholem on the Occasion of his Eightieth Birthday* (Jerusalem: Magnes Press, The Hebrew University, 1977). The former covers the years 1914–68, whereas the latter is updated until 1977.

8. See G. Scholem, "Alchemie und Kabbala. Ein Kapitel aus der Geschichte der Mystik," *Monatsschrift für Geschichte und Wissenschaft des Judentums*, 69 (1925), pp. 13–30, 95–110. See also ibid., "Nachbemerkung," pp. 371–74. The new version was based on a lecture delivered in Switzerland before the Eranos society. See G. Scholem, "Alchemie und Kabbala," *Eranos Jahrbuch*, 45 (1977).

9. See G. Scholem, "Le-ma aseh R. Yosef delah Reina," in *Meʾasef Zion*, 5 (1933), pp. 124–30. For the fuller version, see Siegfried Stein and Raphael Loewe, eds., *Studies in Jewish Religious and Intellectual History Presented to Alexander Altmann on the Occasion of His Seventieth Birthday*

(University, Ala.: The University of Alabama Press, 1979), pp. 101–08 (Hebrew section).

10. See G. Scholem, "Der Begriff der Kawwana in der alten Kabbala," *Monatsschrift für Geschichte und Wissenschaft des Judentums,* 78 (1934), pp. 492–518.

11. The best example of Scholem's rewriting is to be found in the various versions of his book on the beginning of the kabbalah; see below, ch. 6. Even his book on Sabbatai Zevi was changed in several sections when translated into English; see below, n. 29.

12. G. Scholem, *Bibliographia Kabbalistica,* 2nd ed. (Berlin: Schocken, 1933).

13. G. Scholem, *Kitvei Yad ha-Qabbalah* (Jerusalem: The Hebrew University Press, 1930). The book not only describes in great detail the kabbalistic manuscripts which were, at that time, in the collection of the National and University Library, but also includes the publication of several important texts from the collection.

14. Cf. *Kiryat Sefer,* 4 (1927–28), pp. 302–27; 5 (1y. 8–29), pp. 263–77; 6 (1929–30), pp. 109–18, 259–76, 385–419; 7 (1930–31), 149–65, 440–65. The articles were collected and published together in one volume under the title *Peraqim le-Toledot sifrut ha-Qabbalah* (Jerusalem: Azriel, 1931).

15. Cf., e.g., *Kiryat Sefer,* 6 (1930), pp. 62–64, where Scholem published a detailed review of H. Odeberg's edition of *3 Enoch or The Hebrew Book of Enoch* (Cambridge: Cambridge University Press, 1928). At the same time he also worked on modern Hasidism, as well as many other subjects.

16. *Encyclopedia Judaica* (Berlin, 1932), 9: col. 630–732. Only half of this encyclopedia was published. The Nazi persecution made continuing the project impossible. A new *Encyclopedia Judaica* in English was published in Jerusalem in 1972. For this series Scholem wrote many articles on kabbalah, Sabbatianism, and other topics related to Jewish mysticism. The many entries were collected and published together under the title *Kabbalah* (Jerusalem: Keter, 1974).

17. See G. Scholem, "Qabbalot R. Yaʿaqov ve-R. Yiẓḥaq ha-Kohen," *Maddaʿei ha-Yahadut,* 2 (Jerusalem, 1927), pp. 165–293. This lengthy article was subsequently published as a separate book under the title *Qabbalot R. Yaʿaqov ve-R. Yiẓḥaq* (Jerusalem, 1927).

18. Cf. the series of Scholem's articles, which included the brilliant

THE MAN AND THE SCHOLAR

analysis of the concept of multiple worlds in the early kabbalah, entitled "Le-Ḥeqer qabbalat R. Yiẓḥaq ben Yaʿaqov ha-Kohen" in *Tarbiẓ,* 2 (1931), pp. 188–217, 415–42; 3 (1932), pp. 33–66, 258–86; 4 (1933), pp. 54–77, 207–25; 5 (1934), pp. 50–60, 180–98, 305–23. The series of articles was subsequently bound and published as one volume under the same title (Jerusalem, 1934).

19. G. Scholem, "Qabbalot," *Maddaʿei ha-Yahadut,* 2, pp. 244–64.

20. Concerning the problem of the dating and the authorship of the *Zohar,* see below, ch. 8.

21. See G. Scholem, "Ha-Mequbal R. Avraham b. Eliʾezer ha-Levi," *Kiryat Sefer,* 2 (1925–26), pp. 101–41, 269–73. Idem, "Ḥaqirot had-ashot ʿal R. Avraham b. Eliʾezer ha-Levi," *Kiryat Sefer,* 7 (1930–31), pp. 149–65, 440–56. The last-mentioned articles formed part of Scholem's *Peraqim le-toledot ha-Qabbalah* (see n. 4). See also Abraham b. Eliezer ha-Levi, *Maʾamar Meshare Qitrin,* introduction by G. Scholem revised by Malachi Beit-Arie (Jerusalem: Jewish National and University Library Press, 1978).

22. G. Scholem, "Miṣvah ha-Baʾah baʿaverah: Toward an Understanding of Sabbatianism" (Hebrew), *Keneset,* 2 (1937), pp. 347–92. Reprinted in G. Scholem, *Studies and Texts Concerning the History of Sabbatianism and Its Metamorphoses* [Hebrew] (Jerusalem: Mosad Bialik, 1977), pp. 9–67. [Translated into English by Hillel Halkin as "Redemption Through Sin," in *The Messianic Idea in Judaism* (New York: Schocken, 1971), pp. 78–141.]

23. Scholem often expressed his debt to the studies on Sabbatianism by Zalman Rubashov, later Zalman Shazar, the third president of the state of Israel. Shazar's most important article was on R. Abraham ha-Yachini who served as a secretary to Sabbatai Zevi. A bibliophilic printing of this article was published by the Bialik Institute, Jerusalem, 1975.

24. G. Scholem, *Major Trends in Jewish Mysticism,* 3rd rev. ed. (New York: Schocken, 1954). The book has been reprinted many times and has also been translated into several other languages, e.g., German, French, Spanish, and Japanese. It is a curious fact that no complete Hebrew translation of the book exists. Scholem rejected all suggestions to have it translated insisting all the while that the Hebrew reader has no need for such a general work for he should be able to read the texts in their original version. Only recently work has begun on the preparation of a Hebrew edition of the book.

25. G. Scholem, "Hathalot ha-Qabbalah," *Keneset,* 10 (1947), pp. 179–228.

26. G. Scholem, *Reshit ha-Qabbalah* (Jerusalem: Schocken, 1948). The book, which has been out of print for many years, included three important appendices which were not published elsewhere.

27. G. Scholem, *Ursprung und Anfänge der Kabbala* (Berlin: Walter de Gruyter, 1962).

28. The four volumes include: R. Shatz, ed., *Reshit ha-Qabbalah ve-Sefer ha-Bahir* (Jerusalem, 1962); R. Shatz, ed., *Ha-Qabbalah be-Provans* (Jerusalem, 1963); J. Ben Shlomo, ed., *Ha-Qabbalah be-Gerona* (Jerusalem, 1964); J. Ben Shlomo, ed., *Ha-Qabbalah shel Sefer ha-Temunah ve-shel Avraham Abulafia* (Jerusalem, 1965).

29. G. Scholem, *Shabbatai Sevi veha-tenuʿah ha-shabbethaʾit bi-yemei hayyav,* 2 vols. (Tel Aviv: Am Oved, 1957); a revised and augmented translation of the Hebrew edition by R. J. Zwi Werblowsky: *Sabbatai Sevi—The Mystical Messiah 1626–1676* (Princeton: Princeton University Press, 1973).

30. In German two volumes of these lectures were published under the title *Zur Kabbala und ihrer Symbolik* (Zurich: Rhein-Verlag, 1960), and others were included in the three volumes of *Judaica* (Frankfurt am Main: Suhrkamp, 1963–73). One volume of these lectures was published in English: *On the Kabbalah and Its Symbolism,* translated by Ralph Manheim (New York: Schocken, 1965). Most of these essays were translated into Hebrew by J. Ben Shlomo and published as *Pirqei Yesod be-havanat ha-Qabbalah u-semaleha* (Jerusalem: Mosad Bialik, 1976).

31. Of special importance is G. Scholem, *Jewish Gnosticism, Merkabah Mysticism and Talmudic Tradition,* 2nd rev. ed. (New York: The Jewish Theological Seminary, 1965).

32. Amongst the most important of such collections in Hebrew one should mention *Devarim Be-Go* (Tel Aviv: Am Oved, 1976), and *Studies and Texts Concerning the History of Sabbatianism and Its Metamorphoses* (Jerusalem: Mosad Bialik, 1977). In English the most important collection is *The Messianic Idea in Judaism and Other Essays on Jewish Spirituality* (New York: Schocken, 1976).

33. A summary of the controversy is to be found in D. Biale, *Gershom Scholem: Kabbalah and Counter-History,* esp. pp. 172–74, 192–93. Biale, in fact, accepts Kurzweil's essential attitude.

34. The controversy, however, was carried on by some of Scholem's colleagues. See the dialogue between Kurzweil and Jacob Katz in *Ha-*

'*Aretz*, 16 April 1965, p. 5; 14 May 1965, pp. 10–11; and 28 May 1965, pp. 10–11. See also Isaiah Tishby in *Davar*, 15 January 1965.

35. These seminars, though reasonably popular in his last years of teaching, were not always popular. See G. Scholem, *Abraham Cohen Herrera—Leben, Werk und Wirkung* (Frankfurt am Main: Suhrkamp, 1974). In the introduction to the book the author himself notes that the study was based on material he presented to a seminar in Jerusalem in 1937 in which a single student participated. The student, as Scholem noted, was Mr. Perlmuter (Anat) who later wrote, under Scholem's guidance, a doctorate concerning the Sabbatian elements in the works of Rabbi Jonathan Eibeschutz, published in Jerusalem, 1953.

36. Three generations of Scholem's disciples are teaching in Israeli universities and abroad, and publishing in this field. Their names are often quoted in the notes to this volume. Among those most frequently mentioned are I. Tishby, Scholem's first Ph.D. graduate (1945), and the late Professor E. Gottlieb who died prematurely in 1973.

37. Eliezer Schweid, *Mysticism and Judaism According to Gershom Scholem: A Critical Analysis* (Hebrew), *Jerusalem Studies in Jewish Thought, Supplement II* (Jerusalem: Magnes Press, The Hebrew University, 1983).

CHAPTER 2

THE EARLY BEGINNINGS OF JEWISH MYSTICISM

I

A JUDGMENT CONCERNING the beginning of a religious phenomenon depends on its definition. If mysticism is defined only as the individual's religious quest for union with the Godhead, the investigation of the beginning of a mystical trend becomes, in fact, a problem in literary analysis, i.e., can certain verses or chapters in the Bible, for instance, be interpreted as expressing mysticism? It is possible that several chapters in the Psalms, and some prophetic visions, can be perceived as an expression of a mystical trend. If one follows this method, it is possible to trace mystical inclinations throughout Jewish religious literature, from the Bible through the Apocrypha and Pseudepigrapha, the apocalyptic literature, Philo, the Dead Sea Scrolls, the works of the early Christian writers, and so on; indeed no period in the development of Jewish religious expression could be excluded.

While it is possible to find some scattered mystical expressions in ancient Jewish literature, it is impossible to characterize any group of Jewish writers, or even a single extensive work, as being completely mystical. Neither the books of Isaiah and the Psalms, nor the Enoch literature or the Gospels, can be described as mystical works, even though one may maintain that they contain certain mystical elements. In order to find a whole body of literary works which can be described as mystical, representing the spiritual cravings and achievements of a mystical group, one has to turn to the *Hekhalot* and *Merkabah* literature, written by the Jewish mystics of the Talmudic period, sometime between the end of the second century C.E. to the fifth or sixth centuries.

Gershom Scholem was first and foremost a historian concerned with the effect of mysticism on Jewish culture. Scholem first turned to a group which had produced a whole body of literature that can be characterized as mystical: he began his investigations with the *Hekhalot* and *Merkabah* schools of mysticism. Scholem found a good example of the beliefs and practices of all mystical cults here. Scholem used this historical approach in his first survey of Jewish mysticism, the article on kabbalah in the first *Encyclopaedia Judaica* (published in the 1930s)[1] and in his many subsequent writings, such as *Major Trends in Jewish Mysticism*[2] and articles on the subject in the new *Encyclopaedia Judaica*[3] and the *Hebrew Encyclopaedia*.[4] Scholem removed the history of Jewish mysticism from the sphere of speculative analysis and based it on the rock of historical fact.

Once the starting point had been defined, the gathering of historical facts could begin. But Scholem encountered many difficulties. Many works in later kabbalistic literature are anonymous; *Hekhalot* literature is completely anonymous. There is not even one text whose chronology can be fixed with any degree of certainty to assist the dating of others. The linguistic element is of very little assistance, because the texts have undergone a long process of editing and re-editing during which many interpolations were introduced. Many of the *Hekhalot* texts seem to be anthologies and collections of materials of many kinds without apparent structure or order.[5] If the origins of this literature go as far back as the period of the *tannaim*—the second century C.E.—then the first manuscripts which contain portions of them were written at least six or seven centuries later, and in many cases even later than that. Some material concerning this literature reached us through the works of early Jewish philosophers in the tenth century and contemporary Karaitic literature;[6] some fragments were found in the Cairo genizah.[7] Most of these works were preserved by the Ashkenazi Hasidic movement in the twelfth and thirteenth centuries, and many manuscripts contain interpolations and commentaries added by members of this medieval school.[8] Thus, much of the material on which we can base a historical study of the early Jewish mystics of the Talmudic period has reached us through sources written a millennium after the emergence of the mystical school itself. Scholem had to reconstruct the history of the whole kabbalistic literature through quotations and copies made by the later Hasidic movement and other sources. He succeeded in this daunting task.

Another complicating factor concerning the history of early Jewish mysticism is the need to understand its relationship to previous and contemporary major religious movements, both within Judaism and outside of it. Strong links between *Hekhalot* mysticism and some parts of the apocryphal and apocalyptic literature are evident. This is doubly interesting, as the Talmudic and Midrashic literature chose not to preserve and not to develop these earlier ideas. There are especially close relationships between the Enoch literature and *Hekhalot* mysticism, which are almost unmentioned in the ancient Talmudic sources.[9]

Close contact between *Hekhalot* mysticism and the earlier Jewish body of religious works is revealed by the Dead Sea Scrolls. There are definite linguistic and ideological similarities between them, elements which in most cases are also absent from Talmudic literature. The relationship between the Hekhalot texts and some ideas and terms found in a parallel way in the early Christian literature, the Gospels, and the early Church fathers raises some interesting historical and ideological problems concerning the place of both groups in Jewish society and in the framework of Jewish thought in antiquity.[10]

Hekhalot and *Merkabah* mysticism also shows a relationship to early gnostic literature and its vast body of radical images, visions, and myths.

Scholem used the term "gnostic" to describe *Hekhalot* mysticism, following the terminology used by the great nineteenth-century Jewish historian Heinrich Graetz.[11] Although Scholem opposed Graetz's attitude toward Jewish mysticism, which he regarded as a reactionary, destructive element within Jewish culture, Graetz's works were also at that time the only significant, serious, and comprehensive scholarly studies of the subject. However, Scholem used the term "gnostic" in a

completely different way. For Graetz, the term was a derog-
atory appellation, signifying non-Jewishness and a degener-
ating element in religious thought. Scholem saw in it an
imaginative, mythological outburst of creative energy that
might have Jewish sources.

None of Scholem's many suggestions concerning ancient
Jewish mysticism was so severely criticized as this one. Scholars in Jewish studies, as well as experts in the history and
thought of the gnostics,[12] rejected Scholem terminology. They
apparently had no difficulty in refuting Scholem by listing
the differences they found between classical Gnosticism and
Hekhalot literature. If a strict definition of Gnosticism could
be offered, it would be easy to decide whether it is appropriate to designate ancient Jewish mysticism as gnostic.[13] But
we do not have such a definition.

Therefore, Scholem presented a long series of quotations,
parallels, and analyses which seem to indicate a connection
between *Hekhalot* mysticism, its terminology and imagery,
and ancient Gnosticism.[14] Scholem also was impressed by early
twentieth-century scholarship concerning the Mandaic sect of
Gnosticism, a heterodox Jewish sect which claimed to have
migrated from the Transjordan to Babylonia early in the
Christian era. It preserved an ideology and a mythology closely
connected to classical Gnosticism, in works written in a language close to Aramaic and using terminology very similar
in some cases to the terminology of the *Hekhalot* texts.[15] Other
gnostic symbols and myths resemble terms and visions found
in Jewish mystical works. There are references in Jewish literature which can be explained as anti-gnostic polemic, prov-
ing that gnostic ideas were known in rabbinic circles.[16] Scho-

lem never doubted that ancient Jewish mystical texts were written at the same time and in the same religious and cultural environment as some (mainly ophitic) gnostic works. He insisted that a proper understanding of each of them should be based on constant comparison between the two groups of texts. However, Scholem did not decide to call *Hekhalot* literature "Jewish gnosticism" because of these parallels; this point is missed by many critics. He never claimed that *Hekhalot* literature was a part of the ancient gnostic literature and movement.

Scholem did think, however, that the religious phenomenon represented by *Hekhalot* and *Merkabah* mysticism was a Jewish counterpart to the gnostic phenomenon.[17] He believed that the same type of religious drives, the same mystical attitude, inspired the creators of both *Hekhalot* mysticism and classical Gnosticism. Scholem concluded that Gnosticism was a certain type of mystical expression and believed that *Hekhalot* mysticism belonged, as a special Jewish variant, to it. He did not designate this mystical Jewish literature as "Gnosticism," but as "Jewish gnosticism" because of the major variations and differences between them. The critics complained that *Hekhalot* literature does not include this or that gnostic element—especially the dualistic mythology of the struggle between good and evil—and therefore should not be treated as "gnostic." This did not impress Scholem. Dualistic mythology, for him, was a characteristic of several Christian-gnostic sects (though not all of them), while Jewish Gnosticism had its own characteristics, which did not happen to include this mythological element. What was important to him was the thesis that the same urge which brought forth the concepts of *pleroma* (the totality of the powers and emanations of the Divine) and *aeons* (emanations of the Divine) in gnostic Christian mythology, brought forth in Judaism the system of the seven palaces and the various divine forces surrounding the throne of glory in the descriptions of the *Merkabah*. Differences in many details, even central ones, can only be expected and are necessary. They reflect the vast difference between Jewish and Christian Gnosticism. To some extent this can be compared to Scholem's designation as "mystical" many Jewish religious ideas which, in a Christian context, would not be called mystical but rather theosophical or philosophical. Scholem set out to describe Jewish mysticism, and defined its characteristics and boundaries within the framework of Jewish religion and religious literary expression. He did not follow the Christian examples of calling "mystical" only those portions of Jewish religious experience which resembled Christian mystical experiences.[18]

Scholem insisted that every religion has the autonomy to express universal religious attitudes (of which, according to Scholem, Gnosticism was one), in its own unique way, differing from all other religions. Of course, Scholem's understanding of Gnosticism as one form of mystical expression can be disputed, but his critics have to go somewhat deeper into the nature of the gnostic mystical experience; they cannot merely claim there is no dualistic mythology in the Hebrew texts when comparing *Hekhalot* literature and Gnosticism.

One of the reasons for the turmoil surrounding Scholem's designation of ancient Jewish mysticism as Jewish Gnosticism was that when he published his opinion the controversy concerning the origins of Gnosticism was reaching its peak.

Then, as today, scholars were divided between those who believed Gnosticism to be a heretical Christian group of sects, as it was presented by the Church fathers who supply the most important sources for its history, and those who believe Gnosticism to be a "third religion," independent of Christianity in its origins and probably preceding it, only later accepting many Christian elements while at the same time influencing some of the emerging Christian ideas.[19] Many of those who hold the second view look for the pre-Christian or non-Christian roots of Gnosticism within Judaism. Therefore, if there was a "Jewish Gnosticism" before the emergence of Christianity, the movement assumes an enormous historical importance concerning the early history of Christianity.[20] It seemed to some that by designating *Hekhalot* mysticism as Jewish Gnosticism, Scholem was claiming that this group of Hebrew texts was not only a parallel to Christian Gnosticism but also the root and source for the vast gnostic phenomenon.

Scholem did not mean anything of the kind. While he may have seen a source of gnosticism independent of Christianity, he never claimed that *Hekhalot* literature was that source. The hypothetical "Jewish Gnosticism" from which non-Christian Gnosticism developed is a completely different concept from that presented by Scholem when he designated *Hekhalot* mysticism as Jewish Gnosticism. However, he clearly expressed the view that early Jewish mysticism had an impact on the symbolism and terminology of Christian Gnosticism. He never meant the term "Jewish Gnosticism" to denote that the source of Gnosticism as a whole was within Judaism (as some Christian historians of Gnosticism do), nor to be used as a chronological statement, defining Jewish Gnosticism as preceding classical Gnosticism. On the historical level Scholem pointed out the parallels between Christian Gnosticism and Jewish mysticism, explaining that the Christian gnostics received material from heterodox Jewish sects;[21] on the phenomenological level he claimed that both Christian Gnosticism and *Hekhalot* mysticism derived their spiritual force from the same universal religious drives.

II

Scholem's studies of the *Hekhalot* literature abound with discussions of the relationship between the mystical terms, symbols, and ideas found in this literature and in the corresponding material in the Apocrypha, the Pseudepigrapha, the Dead Sea Scrolls, early Christian sources, and gnostic literature. However, his main purpose was to define the relationship between *Hekhalot* and *Merkabah* mysticism and Talmudic and Midrashic sources, thus defining the place of this mystical movement within the framework of rabbinic Judaism.

According to Scholem, ancient Jewish mysticism was created by the same culture which created classical rabbinic Judaism, the Mishnah and the Talmud. This statement itself seemed heretical when Scholem began his work, and even today some scholars find it very difficult to accept because of the profound rethinking that it brings to the image of classical rabbinic Judaism, which for generations was described as completely rational, legalistic, and logical.

Heinrich Graetz was the spokesman for the traditional view of Talmudic Judaism, which claimed that *Hekhalot* literature must be placed chronologically in the late Gaonic period in Babylonia, and that the great Jewish sages who created the Mishnah were "pure of mind" and rational in attitude. They could never have produced or even tolerated around them such "degenerate" literature as the *Hekhalot* texts, with their long lists of strange names for angels, their magical formulas, and their stories of ascensions to heaven. As guardians of what was regarded as the true nature of Judaism, which Graetz and his followers equated with rationalism, they ascribed the appearance of mysticism within Judaism to the influence of foreign sources, especially to Moslem influences. Since in their view this foreign intrusion could not have occurred during the classical Talmudic and Midrashic periods, it therefore must be very late, belonging to the late Gaonic period. Scholem, who fiercely opposed the apologetic attitude of nineteenth-century scholars and their modern followers, found ample proof of the antiquity of the early Jewish mystical texts. He analyzed the relationship between them and Talmudic literature, which was created at the same time. In this he was assisted by other scholars, most notably by Saul Lieberman, the outstanding Talmudic scholar of our age. Their studies made meaningful contributions to the understanding of the mystical dimension of classical rabbinic works.[22]

Scholem demonstrated that rabbinic references to mystical, cosmological, and magical matters can be elucidated and understood only when taken together with the material presented in *Hekhalot* and *Merkabah* texts. The ancient tradition of Midrashic exegesis of the first chapter of the Book of Ezekiel, which describes the holy chariot, the *merkavah,* is referred to in Talmudic sources as *ma'aseh merkavah,* or "the work of the chariot." It was developed by the early mystics, and the old traditions and the new additions to them are to be found together in the *Hekhalot* mystical texts. At the same time the Talmudic sources treated this subject as esoteric, and devised laws concerning the specific circumstances under which the subject could be studied.[23]

A similar mystical exegetical tradition developed around the interpretation of sections from the Song of Songs, which was regarded as a revelation of the innermost secrets of the Godhead. This was veiled in the Talmudic sources, but it is presented in relative clarity in the book *Shiur Komah (The Measurement of the Height)*, and in some other sections of the *Hekhalot* texts.[24]

Talmudic sources tell, in a most cryptic manner, a parable about four Mishnaic sages, among whom were Rabbi Akiba and Rabbi Elisha ben Avuya (known as *aḥer,* "the alien"),[25] who attempted to ascend to the divine realm in the famous parable of the "Four Who Entered the Pardes [Garden]." The full story, with the details of the successful mystical achievement of Rabbi Akiba and the failure of his three comrades (one went mad, one died, and *aḥer* became a heretic), is told in the text of the book *Hekhalot Zutarti (The Lesser Book of Hekhalot).*[26] The ascension of Rabbi Ishmael is the main subject of the most detailed mystical work that reached us from this period, *Hekhalot Rabbati (The Greater Book of Hekhalot.)*[27] The hymns which form a great part of the mystical literature of the period have left their mark in certain aggadic segments in the Talmud,[28] and in the traditional liturgy, especially the *kedusha.*[29] The figures of the divine realm, only hinted at in the Talmud and Midrash, like Metatron and Akhatriel, are described in detail in the works of the mystics.[30] Scholem proved that in order to understand the spiritual life of the Jews in a period that shaped traditional Judaism for centuries to come, and created its normative works in the fields of law, exegesis, and theology, one has to combine the study of the Talmud and Midrash with that of the contemporaneous works of mysticism.

III

The many mystical and esoteric works included in the *Hekhalot* and *Merkabah* literature can be divided into several subjects. Although almost no work is dedicated solely to one subject, and most of them constitute anthologies and collections, each subject is dealt with in a way unique to this literature.

The first major theme is the description of the holy chariot, the *merkavah*, and all that is associated with it, following the visions of Ezekiel. According to the mystics, there are seven heavens. In each of them there is a throne of glory on which the Divine Glory sits. The thrones are surrounded by hosts of angels, ministering angels, angels that carry out the divine commands, as well as many others who bear "angelic" names but are called by divine attributes and can be viewed as secondary divine powers (these are called "archangels" in the Christian tradition). Rivers of fire are described as flowing through the divine realm; there are bridges on these rivers. There are also the holy beasts described by Ezekiel, the various parts of the chariot and its wheels, and the enormous treasuries in the various heavens, treasuries of snow and hail as well as gold and silver. These and other elements make this literature into a colorful, visionary, and vivid description of the divine worlds. Among the works containing these descriptions are the books *Reuyot Yehezkel (The Visions of Ezekiel)*,[31] parts of *Sefer ha-Razim (The Book of Secrets)*,[32] portions of the three *Hekhalot* books, the *Ma'aseh Merkavah (The Work of the Chariot)*,[33] and others.

The second subject, which is also undoubtedly ancient and which the sages of the Mishnah and Talmud treated as esoteric, is that of magic. The magical element is closely interwoven into most of the texts of the mystical literature; there can be little doubt that the *Hekhalot* mystics regarded it as an integral part of their mystical tradition. Many magical elements in this literature were common not only to Jews but also to the syncretistic world of the late Hellenistic period, especially in Egypt. Some formulas found in Hebrew in these texts seem to be nothing but literal translations from the Greek magical literature, often still preserving the names of various gods of Greek mythology and having a distinct pagan character.[34] In other cases, it is possible to show a clear Hebrew influence on Greek magical formulas, especially the use of Hebrew divine names, which were taken over and incorporated into universal magical incantations used by all magicians in late antiquity.

These magical formulas often deal with everyday problems and include incantations for love, relief from pain, success in wars, protection from thieves, and so on. More often, they designate the special status of the mystic, whose knowledge of these secrets protects him from every earthly peril and enables him to achieve his material needs. Sometimes these incantations are used to aid the mystical process, assisting the mystic to ascend to the divine realm, protecting him from the dangers that surround him once he reaches the higher *Hekhalot*, and forcing the celestial powers to supply him with the information he requires. A distinct part of this literature deals with the ways to achieve wisdom, especially divine wisdom, which was given to Moses on Mount Sinai and kept a secret which only the mystic-magician can reach and comprehend.[35] Some formulas help the user achieve without effort a knowledge of the Torah that would normally require arduous years of study.[36]

The major part of *Sefer ha-Razim* is dedicated to such magical formulas, as are both the beginning of *Hekhalot Rabbati* which describes the powers of the mystic, and parts of the *Sar shel Torah (The Prince of the Torah)*, which are usually appended to that work. Portions of *Hekhalot Zutarti* deal with the magical means of the mystical ascent. Some works are dedicated almost exclusively to magic, and some of them may be the works of later esoteric writers in Babylonia, like the *Harba de-Moshe (The Sword of Moses)*[37] and the *Havdalah de-Rabbi Akiba*.[38]

A closely related subject is that of physiognomy and chiromancy, described in one of the earliest Hebrew esoteric works. The main text in this area is called *Hakarat Panim ve-Sidrey Sirtutin, (Discerning the Penance)*[39] an early mystical work which bears some of the characteristics of *Hekhalot* literature, even though it deals with secrets of a living person rather

than those of the hidden Godhead. This "science" was regarded by the *Hekhalot* mystics as an integral part of their
esoteric traditions.

The third major subject is that of cosmology and cosmogony, of which *Sefer Yezirah, (The Book of Creation),* is the
most important work. But besides this ancient enigmatic work
there are several books and chapters in others which reveal
the deep interest these mystics also had in *ma'aseh bereshit,*
"the work of creation." *Seder Rabba de-Bereshit (The Great Order of Creation),* and other works of esoteric literature of the
Talmudic and Gaonic periods combine cosmology and astron-
omy to present a structure of the created cosmos.[40] They
demonstrate the ways in which God governs, and reveal many
secrets. Some astrological elements can also to be found in
these works. Sections dealing with the secrets of the creation
are scattered in many of these texts. They may be connected
with the speculations concerning the divine wisdom as a
creating power, as described in the books of Proverbs and Job
and further developed in apocryphic literature of the second
commonwealth period. It is clear that the Talmudic prohi-
bition on dealing with secrets concerning "what is above and
what is below, what is before and what is after"[41] was neglected by these mystics.

The fourth, and most important, subject is the mystical
process itself, the ascension to the divine chariot and the
meeting with the figure sitting on the throne of glory in the
seventh divine palace, or *hekhal.* This is the main subject in
four books, which form the core of the *Hekhalot* mystical library: *Hekhalot Rabbati* and *Hekhalot Zutarti,* the *Shiur Komah
(Measure of the Divine Stature)* and *Sefer Hekhalot,* also known

as the *Hebrew Book of Enoch* or *3rd Enoch*.[42] The main mystical ideas of this school describe the process of ascension and the perception of the divine figure in the center of the seventh palace.

IV

The texts describing the mystical ascension to the celestial palaces are divided into those in which Rabbi Akiba plays the central role, those in which both Rabbi Akiba and Rabbi Ishmael appear but Rabbi Ishmael is usually the main figure, and others in which all the traditions transmitted are attributed to Rabbi Ishmael. *Hekhalot Zutarti* belongs to the Akiban tradition; in *Hekhalot Rabbati* both appear, while the text of the *Shiur Komah* seems to be a combination of texts. In some Rabbi Akiba is the speaker and in others both Rabbi Akiba and Rabbi Ishmael transmit the esoteric traditions and visions. In *Sefer Hekhalot* Rabbi Ishmael is the spokesman of the esoteric information given to him by Metatron.

The two central stories of mystical ascension are told as part of a narrative. In *Hekhalot Zutarti* the story is that of the "Four Who Entered the Pardes." It mainly reveals the way in which Rabbi Akiba succeeded in "entering in peace and coming out in peace,"[43] and briefly describes the tragic results of the failure of his three companions. The ascension of Rabbi Ishmael is connected in *Hekhalot Rabbati* with the story of the ten martyrs. According to this work, when the circle of mystics in Jerusalem, which included Rabbi Akiba but whose leader was Rabbi Nehunia ben ha-Kanah, heard that the Roman emperor planned to execute ten (in one chapter the number is four) of the greatest sages, the pretext being punishment for the sin of Joseph's brothers in selling their brother to captivity in Egypt, the gathered mystics doubted whether this decision was a divine decree or just the whim of the evil emperor. Rabbi Nehunia then asked his "youngest disciple," Rabbi Ishmael ben Elishah, to ascend to the divine realm and determine the origin of this decree.[44] The center of the work is the description of Rabbi Ishmael's ascension and the secrets revealed to him, along with the answer that indeed it was a divine decree. However, the result of the sacrifice of the ten martyrs (which included both Rabbi Akiba and Rabbi Ishmael), would be the complete destruction of Rome. Thus, these two central works are not presented as theological or mystical manuals. Rather, they are the stories of particular events and "historical" ascensions of the two great sages, even though in many parts of these works the descriptions are given in a generalized form, as if they were abstract instructions given to anyone who wishes to participate in this mystical process.[45]

The basic cosmological picture given in the Talmudic sources and in mystical texts such as the *Sefer ha-Razim* and the *Reuyot Yehezkel*, in which the celestial world is composed mainly of the seven heavens, is replaced in *Hekhalot Zutarti, Hekhalot Rabbati*, and other works by the detailed description of the seven celestial palaces, the *hekhalot*, which is the major subject of speculation. Each of the divine palaces is full of hosts of angels of various kinds; leading into and out of every palace there is a *petah*, or "gate," which is guarded by battalions of angels, commanded by major figures in the *Hekhalot* angelology and other divine powers. To pass each gate the mystic must show the guards a special *hotam* (probably a secret sign or a holy name), which gives him permission to continue on his mystical journey. The guards at every gate, especially those at the sixth gate, do everything they can to prevent the entrance of the mystic, to dissuade him from continuing, or even to harm him physically, using both force and trick questions. Only the most accomplished mystics, both in their knowledge and in their ethical behavior, cleanliness, and ascetic life can hope to ascend successfully. Sometimes even their family and racial descent is checked. They must answer trick questions to prove that their ancestors were not among those who kissed the golden calf in the desert after the exodus from Egypt. They have to beware of trick situations, like mistaking the pure, bright marble of the floors of the heavenly palaces for water or waves.[46] After overcoming the trials and dangers, they approach the seventh palace and face the "king in his beauty," the divine figure described in anthropomorphic detail in the *Shiur Komah,* probably the central theological work of ancient Jewish mysticism.

Scholem described the *Shiur Komah* as a work "based on the descriptions of the beloved in Song of Songs 5:11–16.[47] This supplied the basis for understanding this enigmatic work. The essential part of the work (which also includes hymns, prayers, and other material, as do both the *Hekhalot Rabbati* and the *Hekhalot Zutarti*) is a description of the creator, who is consistently called *yotzer bereshit* or *yotzrenu,* meaning "the creator of genesis" or "our creator."

The emphasis in this description, as in other parts of *Hekhalot* literature, is on the image of God as a supreme king.

Scholem studied the hymns scattered in this literature, which are directed to the "king of kings," who is depicted as sitting on the celestial throne in his celestial palace. All the ministering angels and the princes of the nations and those in charge of various tasks are gathered around him, praising him and praying to him. This element of kingship in the aspect of God can be the result of the influence of the Song of Songs. The king image can thus be combined with the anthropomorphic picture of God presented in the *Shiur Komah*. The deep religious and mystical reverence for this divine image is manifest throughout the *Hekhalot* literature, especially in the *Shiur Komah*.

The central part of the *Shiur Komah* consists of two combined lists. One is the list of the esoteric names of the various limbs of the divine figure, from the head to the feet. Each limb is given a name or a series of names, some of them consisting of dozens of letters. These names are completely incomprehensible to us. They are composed either of a series of vowels (especially those in which the holy name of God is written in Hebrew), or a series of Hebrew letters that seldom are combined to create a word. The second list, which is contained within the first, gives the measurements of each limb. These measurements are given in units of thousands or tens of thousands *(alfey revavot)* of parasangs *(parsaot)*. Each such parasang consists, according to the *Shiur Komah,* of thousands of smaller units, the smallest being the little finger *(zeret),* which is God's little finger and stretches from one end of the world to the other.

This description of the enormous figure in the *Shiur Komah* is the classical Jewish text of the anthropomorphic conception

56

of God,[48] which has confused and perplexed later Jewish philosophers from Rav Saadia Gaon in the tenth century[49] to Heinrich Graetz in the nineteenth century. This text was, however, enthusiastically embraced by many kabbalists in the Middle Ages who used it as the cornerstone of their mythological descriptions of the various powers comprising the divine realm. This visionary picture of the divine beloved in the Song of Songs became one of the most problematical, but also the most profound, elements in the structure of Jewish mystical symbolism.

Saul Lieberman, in his study of the *Shiur Komah* published as an appendix to Scholem's *Jewish Gnosticism*,[50] analyzed the rabbinic texts concerning the esoteric meaning of the Song of Songs. Much of the material presented in the Mishnah and in the Midrash concerning this aspect of the Biblical book is presented as taught by Rabbi Akiba, and at least some of these sayings could indeed be his historically.

Rabbi Akiba stated that the Song of Songs was the "holy of holies," the most sacred among the Biblical books.[51] He argued against Rabbi Eliezer concerning the time that this book was "given" (*nitan*) to Israel, using the same term frequently mentioned concerning the "giving" of the Torah in the Mount Sinai theophany. Rabbi Eliezer claimed that the book was given to Israel when they crossed the Red Sea, while Rabbi Akiba held the view that it was given on Mount Sinai.[52] Thus the book was not "written," and certainly not composed, by King Solomon son of David, but given, like the Torah, in a theophany by "the King of Peace" (*melech she-ha-shalom shelo*),[53] thus homiletically explaining the attribution to King Solomon as referring to God himself. When

Rabbi Akiba entered the "pardes" it was said of him, in the words of Song of Songs 1:6, that "the King has brought him into his chambers."[54] Even Rabbi Akiba's death as a martyr was connected by the early homiletical authors of the Midrash to a verse.[55] Lieberman concluded his analysis by showing the unity between the Midrash on Song of Songs, the *Shiur Komah* and the mysticism of *ma'aseh merkavah*.[56]

Rabbi Akiba is the hero of the mystical ascension in *Hekhalot Zutarti*, a work which includes some portions of the *Shiur Komah*.[57] The king sitting on the throne in the seventh palace is named in this work by verses 5:6–11 from the Song of Songs,[58] not by accident the same verses which describe the body of the beloved. The physical appearance of God as described in the Biblical text was regarded by the mystics as an esoteric group of names of the Godhead, revealed to Rabbi Akiba when he ascended to the seventh palace. The story of the four who entered the "pardes" is a brief and cryptic parable, alluding to the developed mystical myth of the ascension of Rabbi Akiba from the first palace to the seventh. He overcame all the dangers in his way, saw the elements of the divine chariot, the throne of glory, and the hosts of angels surrounding them, heard their hymns and added to them his own hymns of praise, until finally he faced the figure on the throne, the enormous figure described in the *Shiur Komah*, which is based in turn on the description of the king in the Song of Songs.

The mysticism surrounding the divine palaces is a fusion of several elements, some of them old and some relatively new in the Talmudic period. The most important old elements are those of the ancient homiletical speculation concerning the visions of Ezekiel, the traditional *ma'aseh merka-vah*. This tradition was known in tannaitic circles and was practiced in some of their schools, especially that of Rabbi Yohanan ben Zakkai and his disciples in the period immediately following the destruction of the second temple.[59] Another old element was the tradition of the ascension to heaven, clearly described in the Enoch literature, whose Hebrew and Aramaic original versions were discovered recently in the Judean desert.[60] It comes most probably from the second century B.C. This myth, almost completely ignored or excluded by the editors of Talmudic literature, obviously survived in the circles of the mystics in one form or another, and was used to describe the celestial journeys of the ancient sages.

To these traditional elements a new one was added, which served as a focal point for *Hekhalot* mysticism: a new interpretation of the Song of Songs as a description of the creator. The *Hekhalot Zutarti* describes the mystical journey toward this divine figure, and the *Shiur Komah* is a detailed picture of the limbs of this divine being, including the names and measurements of each limb. Whether the creator in this theology was identical with the supreme Godhead, or whether it was conceived as a second, demiurgic power besides the Godhead, is very difficult to ascertain.[61] Several sources can be interpreted as distinguishing between them and seeing them as parts of a whole in the divine realm.[62] There is no doubt, however, that no element of the dualism of good and evil, which is often found in gnostic mythology, can be found in these texts.[63]

The central work of this mystical school, the *Hekhalot Rabbati,* includes many paragraphs taken verbatim from the *Hek-*

halot Zutarti, and it also includes a section from the *Shiur Komah.* In the *Hekhalot Rabbati* the description of the ascension from palace to palace is repeated, but it is attributed to Rabbi Akiba's colleague, Rabbi Ishmael ben Elishah, who is described as a High Priest and the son of a High Priest.[64] The head of the "mystical academy" to which these two sages belong, and which is reported to be centered around the temple in Jerusalem, is Rabbi Nehunia ben ha-Kanah, a relatively obscure *tanna,* who is mentioned once as the teacher of Rabbi Ishmael. (It is interesting to note that Rabbi Shimeon bar Yohai, the second-century *tanna* who was believed by the medieval mystics to be the great teacher of mysticism and the author of the *Zohar,* does not appear on the lists of this circle. The earliest mystical work attributed to Rabbi Shimeon is probably from the Gaonic period.)[65]

Hekhalot Rabbati is the most detailed description of the ascension to the chariot and the divine palaces[66] (including a description of the ascent of Rabbi Nehunia).[67] It is also an anthology of the mystical and esoteric traditions of the *Hekhalot* mystics. It includes a major anthology of hymns of praise, some of them chanted by the ministering angels and others by the mystical ascenders to the divine realm. It includes detailed lists of the various powers in the celestial palaces, some of them clearly angelic but others referred to by the names of God himself.[68] It includes significant magical elements, and descriptions of the special status of the mystic in the world and his magical powers over his fellow men. It is the most detailed description we have concerning the circle of mystics, their behavior and their status in their society.[69] All these are conveyed through two integrated narratives, one of the martyrdom of the ten sages to atone the sin of selling Joseph to Egypt, and that of the ascension and the journey of Rabbi Ishmael in the celestial realm. (His guide in these travels, and the one disclosing to him the secrets of the divine world, is a celestial power called Soria, the "Prince of the Divine Face," or "of the Countenance," *sar ha-panim*.)

The problem of the demiurgic power besides God, i.e., the problematic issue of dualism, of a cosmic power operating in the Universe other than God, is the background of another major work of *Hekhalot* mysticism, the *Sefer Hekhalot*, which was published in a modern edition by Hugo Odeberg in 1928 under the title *3rd Enoch or the Hebrew Book of Enoch*.[70] (This edition was the subject of one of Scholem's earliest book reviews, published in *Kiryat Sefer* in 1929.)[71] The *Sefer Hekhalot* describes the ascension of Rabbi Ishmael to the celestial world and his meeting with Metatron, who is called here the "Prince of the Countenance," the *sar ha-panim*. Rabbi Ishmael transmits all the secrets in this book, but its hero is undoubtedly Metatron. His biography is told in the first part of the book. In a detailed myth, the story of Metatron, who was originally a human being, Enoch son of Yared (the hero of the ancient Enoch literature), unfolds and reveals a creative fusion between the ancient Enoch literature and *hekhalot* mysticism.[72]

God selected Enoch from among all humanity of his age, which was the age to be destroyed by the deluge. He was to be the witness to the sins of his contemporaries, which caused the deluge. The divine messenger who brought Enoch to heaven was Anafiel, a divine power very similar to Metatron himself.[73] Over a long period Enoch lost all his human appearance, clothes, and intellectual limitations. He became the chief power in the divine world, second only to God himself. His body became one of fire; he rode a chariot of fire drawn by fiery horses. His dimensions increased until they became similar to those described in the *Shiur Komah;* he acquired 24 enormous wings and 70 eyes. God transmitted to him all revealed and secret knowledge, including the secrets of the creation, and made him the ruler of all the celestial hosts, his jurisdiction covering the princes of all nations. He was even seated on a throne of glory. This set him apart from the world of the angels, who cannot sit because they cannot bend their legs, as attested, according to the common homiletical interpretation, by Isaiah's vision.[74]

Metatron became so great that when Elishah ben Avuyah, "Aḥer," who entered the "pardes" with Rabbi Akiba, saw Metatron when he ascended to the palaces, he mistook him for a divine figure equal to God. He declared that there were two powers in heaven, and thus became a heretic. In order to prevent such a mistake from happening again, Anafiel was sent to Metatron, who punished him with 60 lashes of fire, making clear who was the master and who the slave.

Scholem dedicated several studies to the figure of Metatron.[75] Even his name is not sufficiently understood, and there are many unclear elements in the myth of the Prince of the Countenance. Scholem discovered that many attributes which belonged originally to the divine powers Michael and Yahoel were transferred to Metatron.[76] Several indications suggest that there was an early, heterodox concept of Metatron (either under this name or another name) as demiurgic in character, a creator or co-creator beside God.[77] The myth concerning the human origin of Metatron and his identification as Enoch son of Yared might be a later myth, contradicting Metatron's first exalted status.

Hekhalot mysticism should not be seen as a completed, comprehensive theological and mystical system. Rather, it underwent a long process of development, coming into conflict with other schools of thought and usually incorporating some of the ideas of its opponents. It flourished for several centuries in different forms and emphases, and had an enormous impact on subsequent developments in the Jewish mystical literature of the Middle Ages. Scholem drew the outlines of the historical and cultural circumstances of the development of *Hekhalot* mysticism, analyzed its main works and ideas, and clearly demonstrated that it was not a separate entity unrelated to Talmudic and Midrashic literature but the product of the same cultural environment in which rabbinic literature and thought were formulated.

V

Another dimension of ancient Jewish mysticism and esotericism is found in the brief but profound *Sefer Yezirah (The Book of Creation)*, attributed to the patriarch Anraham (and, later in the Middle Ages, also to Rabbi Akiba). This short work, which "could be learned by heart in two hours," as Scholem used to say, is the most important to reach us from ancient times concerning *ma'aseh bereshit*, "the secret of creation." This is coupled in tannaitic traditions with the *ma'aseh merkavah*,[78] and refers to the esoteric traditional doctrines concerning the process of the creation.

Sefer Yezirah discusses the process of creation in a completely different manner than the book of Genesis. It describes the underlying principles used by God in the process of creation. According to the first chapter of the book, God used thirty-two "paths of mystery." This number is a combination of two elements: the twenty-two characters of the Hebrew alphabet and the ten *sefirot,* which probably here refer to the ten elementary numbers.

The combination of letters and the number ten is not new to Jewish cosmogonical speculations. Tannaitic literature already incorporated the idea that the world was created by God's ten utterances in Genesis.[79] The power of creation resides, therefore, in the pronunciation of Hebrew words, and ultimately in the Hebrew alphabet, which is the basis of these words. This power is regulated by the number ten.

The first chapter of *Sefer Yezirah* is dedicated to the description of these *sefirot.* They are defined in one of the key paragraphs as the ten dimensions of the infinity of God: his infinity toward the east, west, north, and south; upward and downward—the dimensions of space; his infinity toward the beginning and the end of all—the dimension of time. The last two are his infinity toward good and evil (often interpreted as a reference to paradise and to hell, but there is no basis for that interpretation in the ancient text itself).[80] The latter parts of the work concentrate on the letters and other elements.

Later in the first chapter of *Sefer Yezirah* the *sefirot* are given a completely different description. They represent the stages by which the elements of the world emerged. The first *sefirah* is the holy spirit, *ruah elohim hayim,* from which emerged the second, the air or earthly wind, also called in Hebrew *ruah*. The third *sefirah* is the emergence of water from this air or wind, and the fourth is the fire that came from that elementary water. Obviously the author of this work held the view that there were only three elements, while earth, following a homiletical interpretation of a biblical verse, was nothing but the product of water, snow being the intermediary substance between water and earth.[81] This list stops after the fourth stage and does not include the full ten *sefirot*. It is evident that for the author of this work the *sefirot* were not only numerical principles but also the stages by which creation progressed from the spiritual divinity down to the elements of which material creation is comprised. It is also possible that the *sefirot* had a mystical, visionary aspect, connected with Ezekiel's vision of the holy chariot, and that they were the subject of mystical contemplation.[82]

The richness, as well as the obscurity, of the descriptions of the *sefirot* in this work led many historians of Jewish mysticism to regard the *Sefer Yezirah* as a kabbalistic work—indeed, as the first book of the kabbalah—and start the history of kabbalistic literature with it. Scholem opposed this view, claiming that the *sefirot* of this book are completely different from the divine hypotheses described by the medieval kabbalists as dynamic, mythological powers within the Godhead. In the *Sefer Yezirah* none of these basic elements is to be found. The book does not describe the processes going on within the Godhead. The emergence of creation from the Holy Spirit is dealt with in a scientific way, according to the basic beliefs of the time and the circle of Jewish mystics. It is a book of cosmogony and cosmology, not a book of theology. Any mystical elements found in it resemble not the medieval kabbalah but the *Hekhalot* mysticism of the Talmudic period. The mystical attitude toward the Hebrew alphabet is typical for this period, though it was continued and developed by medieval mystics.

Sefer Yezirah should be regarded as one of the most important works of ancient Jewish mysticism. Its impact on later Jewish mystical sects was enormous. This influence is obvious as far as terminology is concerned. The obscure, yet suggestive, unique terminology of this ancient work, which includes terms never before used in any Hebrew text, fascinated the medieval Jewish mystics who used it consistently (and thus gave the false impression that the book originated in their schools). From this work the basic concept of ten *sefirot*, ten divine powers, ("ten and not nine, ten and not eleven," as *Sefer Yezirah* insisted),[83] which is a basic characteristic of the kabbalah, was derived. The mystical aspect of the Hebrew language, developed in various ways in the Middle Ages,[84] was based on the cryptic linguistic statements of this work. Another aspect of Jewish mysticism based on this book is the belief that a homunculus, a *golem,* could be created by man. This belief derived from the description of the creation by the alphabet. If God created the world and man by the power of the letters of the Hebrew alphabet, and if the power of creation is inherent within the letters, then it should be possible to repeat this process and create an artificial man by the proper use of several groups of Hebrew letters. One of Scholem's most important articles was dedicated to a detailed history of this belief from Talmudic times to the twentieth century.[85]

NOTES

1. See *Encyclopedia Judaica* (Berlin, 1932), 9: col. 630–732.

2. See Gershom Scholem, *Major Trends in Jewish Mysticism,* 3rd rev. ed. (New York: Schocken, 1954) [henceforth cited as *Major Trends*], pp. 40–79, the notes on pp. 355–69, and the bibliography on pp. 425–27. In the 1954 edition, and all subsequent editions, the bibliography was updated; see p. 438.

3. See *Encyclopedia Judaica* (Jerusalem, 1972), 10: pp. 489–653. Scholem wrote several articles dealing with ancient Jewish mysticism for this encyclopedia, including such topics as "Merkabah Mysticism," "Metatron," and "Chiromancy." These articles, together with all those which dealt with topics in Jewish mysticism, were published as one volume entitled *Kabbalah* (Jerusalem: Keter, 1974).

4. See *Hebrew Encyclopedia* (Jerusalem and Tel Aviv, 1977), pp. 71–136.

5. Peter Schaefer, for instance, when publishing the main manuscripts of these texts, did not separate them into specific works, claiming that we cannot even be certain about the beginning and end of some of them. He claimed, moreover, that textual study of these documents should begin from the manuscripts as they are not from preconceived notions about the scope of individual works and titles. See P. Schaefer, *Synopse zur Hekhalot Literatur* (Tübingen: Mohr, 1981). One of the more important of these texts, viz. *The Alphabet of Rabbi Akiva,* has not been studied at all and its relationship to the field is obscure. See G. Scholem, *Kabbalah,* p. 223. An edition of this text is being prepared now in a project supported by the Israeli Academy of Sciences.

6. The Karaite polemicist, Salmon ben Yeruhim, the great opponent of Rav Saadia Gaon in the first half of the tenth century, wrote a satirical version, in verse, of the *Shiur Komah,* in order to ridicule rabbinic tradition. This constitutes one of the earliest versions of any Hekhalot text that we have. See Salmon ben Yeruhim, *Sefer Milḥamot ha-Shem,* I. Davidson, ed. (New York: Jewish Theological Seminary, 1934).

7. The Genizah fragments of the Hekhalot literature are being prepared for publication by P. Schaefer. Concerning these fragments, see Ithamar Gruenwald, "New Fragments from Hekhalot Literature" (Hebrew), *Tarbiz,* 38 (1969), pp. 354–72; 39 (1970), pp. 216–17; 40 (1971),

pp. 301–19. The *Shiur Komah* fragment is included in Martin Cohen, "The Si'ur Qomah: A Critical Edition of the Text with Introduction, Translation, and Commentary" (Ph.D. thesis, Jewish Theological Seminary, 1982), pp. 533–631; English translation and commentary, pp. 434–526. [The English translation and commentary have now been reproduced in M. Cohen, *The Shi'ur Qomah: Liturgy and Theurgy in Pre-Kabbalistic Jewish Mysticism* (Lanham, Md.: University Press of America, 1983) pp. 187–265.]

8. Concerning the attitude of the Ashkenazi Hasidim to the Hekhalot, see J. Dan, *The Esoteric Theology of Ashkenazi Hasidim* [Hebrew] (Jerusalem: Mosad Bialik, 1968), pp. 24–28.

9. The relationship between Jewish apocalyptic and apocryphal literature, especially the Enoch books and the Hekhalot, was studied in detail by I. Gruenwald in his *Apocalyptic and Merkabah Mysticism* (Leiden: E. J. Brill, 1980). One of the most interesting links between the Hekhalot texts and apocalypticism, the *Book of Zerubavel,* has not been studied yet. The text has been published in J. Even-Shmuel (Kaufman), *Midreshei Geʾulah* (Jerusalem: Mosad Bialik, 1954), pp. 55–88.

10. See, for instance, my review of this problem in "Mysticism in Jewish History, Religion and Literature," in J. Dan and F. Talmage, eds., *Studies in Jewish Mysticism* (Cambridge: Association for Jewish Studies, 1982) pp. 1–14.

11. Graetz's first and most comprehensive study of this subject was his *Gnosticismus und Judenthum* (Krotoschin: Monasch, 1846).

12. See esp. D. Flusser's review of Scholem's *Jewish Gnosticism, Merkabah Mysticism and Talmudic Tradition* [henceforth cited as *Jewish Gnosticism*] in *Journal of Jewish Studies,* 2 (1960), pp. 59–68. See also I. Gruenwald, "Knowledge and Vision," *Israel Oriental Studies,* 3 (1972), pp. 63–107. Hans Jonas, the great historian of gnosticism, adopted the same attitude. See also E. Yamauchi, *Pre-Christian Gnosticism: A Survey of the Proposed Evidences* (Grand Rapids: Eerdmans, 1973), pp. 149–51. Cf., however, my remarks in "The Concept of Knowledge in the *Shi'ur Qomah,*" in S. Stein and R. Loewe, eds., *Studies in Jewish Religious and Intellectual History Presented to Alexander Altmann,* pp. 63–73.

13. The most serious collective effort to define gnosticism was made in the 1966 conference in Messina dedicated to the subject. The papers and discussions of the conference were edited by Ugo Bianchi and published under the title *Gnosticismo Colloquio di Messina 13–18 Aprile 1966*

(Leiden: E. J. Brill, 1967). It is a fact, however, that to this very day, not only every book, but every article on the subject defines or redefines the term according to a given tendency. While most definitions insist on a dualistic posture between good and evil divine forces as characteristic of gnosticism, some of the major gnostic sects, especially the Valentinian school, did not accept such a position.

14. In many of the chapters of *Jewish Gnosticism* Scholem dealt with this subject. See, e.g., pp. 66–70, concerning his remark about the concept of the *ogdoas* and the Hebrew *Azbogah, shem shel shmini'ot*, the "name of the eightfold," i.e. every two letters of this name equal eight numerically. See also Scholem, "Jaldabaoth Reconsidered," *Mélanges d'histoire des religions offerts à H. C. Puech* (Paris: Presses Universitaires de France, 1974), pp. 405–21. See Francis T. Fallon's critique in *The Enthronement of Sabaoth Jewish Elements in Gnostic Creation Myths* (Leiden: E. J. Brill, 1978), pp. 32–34. It seems to me that there can be no doubt that Yaldabaoth originated in the Hebrew Hekhalot texts, and is the abbreviation of the frequent formula which describes divine powers: *Ya'Elohim 'Adonai Zeva'oth*. See J. Dan, "Anafiel, Metatron and the Creator," *Tarbiz*, 52 (1983), pp. 447–57, and esp. p. 448, n. 5.

15. For instance, the Mandaic use of the term *Shechinta*, usually in the plural, is indicative, even though it often denotes evil powers. The Mandaic theology and mythology served as a major source for Hans Jonas's description of the gnosis in his major work *The Gnostic Religion* (Boston: Beacon Press, 1958), esp. pp. 98–99. Some basic studies of Mandaic texts are to be found in K. Rudolph, *Die Mandaer,* 2 vols. (Göttingen: Vandenhoeck & Ruprecht, 1961), and E. Yamauchi, *Mandaic Incantation Texts* (New Haven: American Oriental Society, 1967). An anthology of Mandaic sources is to be found in W. Foerster, ed., *Die Gnosis,* 2 (Zurich, 1972).

16. See, e.g., I. Gruenwald, "The Problem of the Anti-Gnostic Polemic in Rabbinic Literature," *Studies in Gnosticism and Hellenistic Religions Presented to Gilles Quispel,* ed. by R. van der Broek and M. J. Vermaseren (Leiden: E. J. Brill, 1981), pp. 171–89.

17. See, e.g., Scholem's statement in *Kabbalah,* pp. 12–13.

18. An example of a different attitude is to be found in L. Jacob, *Jewish Mystical Testimonies* (New York: Schocken, 1977), where the criterion for including texts was the similarity to Christian personal expressions of mystical visions.

19. An excellent summary of the scholarship on this problem is to be found in E. Yamauchi, *Pre-Christian Gnosticism: A Survey of the Proposed Evidences*.

20. The subject of the relationship between gnosticism and Judaism, both in general and in particular concerning the Nag Hammadi texts, has been central to several detailed studies. See R. M. Grant, *Gnosticism and Early Christianity* (New York: Columbia University Press, 1959). Grant postulated that gnosticism was the result of Jewish despair after the failure of apocalyptic hopes. See also F. T. Fallon, *The Enthronement of Sabaoth*, and A. Segal, *Two Powers in Heaven: Early Rabbinic Reports about Christianity and Gnosticism* (Leiden: E. J. Brill, 1977). Segal, who analyzed the concept of a demiurgic power in rabbinic and gnostic literature, neglected the Hekhalot sources.

21. The most detailed comparisons are those of I. Gruenwald, "Jewish Sources for the Gnostic Texts from Nag Hammadi?," *Proceedings of the Sixth World Congress of Jewish Studies*, 3 (Jerusalem, 1977), pp. 45–56.

22. Saul Lieberman dealt with this subject in many of his books and articles. The portions of the *tosefta* relation to mysticism are studied in detail in his *Tosefta ki-Peshuta*, part 5, *Order Moʿed* (New York: Jewish Theological Seminary, 1962), pp. 1286–96. Of special importance is his appendix, "Mishnat Shir ha-Shirim," in G. Scholem, *Jewish Gnosticism*, pp. 118–26.

23. For a critique of Scholem, see D. Halperin, *The Merkabah in Rabbinic Literature* (New Haven: American Oriental Society, 1980). Cf. my remarks on this book in *Jerusalem Studies in Jewish Thought*, 2 (1983), pp. 307–16.

24. See M. Cohen, "The Siʿur Qomah: A Critical Edition of the Text with Introduction, Translation and Commentary" (Ph.D. thesis), pp. 30–42. [See now M. Cohen, *The Shiʿur Qomah: Liturgy and Theurgy in Pre-Kabbalistic Jewish Mysticism*, pp. 21–27.] Cohen doubted Scholem's conclusion and even tried to claim that the latter changed his mind about it. But cf. Scholem, *Kabbalah*, p. 17, and see my remarks in "The Concept of Knowledge in the *Shiʿur Qomah*," p. 70. It should be noted that Scholem himself prepared the Hebrew translation of his article on *Shiʿur Qomah*, in J. Ben Shlomo, ed., *Pirqei Yesod be-havanat ha-Qabbalah u-semaleha* (Jerusalem: Mosad Bialik, 1976), pp. 153–86, and repeated most forcefully his original thesis.

25. See the detailed study of this enigmatic figure by G. Stroumsa,

"Aḥer: A Gnostic," in B. Layton, ed., *The Rediscovery of Gnosticism: Proceedings of the International Conference on Gnosticism at Yale New Haven, Connecticut, March 28–31, 1978,* 2 vols. (Leiden: E. J. Brill, 1981), pp. 808–18. Stroumsa's bibliography includes all the important studies of the story of the "four who entered the pardes."

26. Concerning this problem, see E. E. Urbach, "The Traditions about Merkabah Mysticism in the Tannaitic Period," *Studies in Mysticism and Religion presented to Gershom G. Scholem on his Seventieth Birthday,* pp. 1–28 (Hebrew section). See R. Elior ed., *Hekhalot Zutarti, Jerusalem Studies in Jewish Thought, Supplement I* (1982), p. 23, and pp. 62–63. Scholem considered the Talmudic story to be an abbreviated remnant of the detailed one preserved in *Hekhalot Zutarti.* It seems, however, more probable that the early mystics developed the Talmudic story in their own manner.

27. Editions of the work are to be found in A. Jellinek, ed., *Bet ha-Midrash* (Leipzig, 1855; rpt. Jerusalem: Wahrmann Books, 1967), vol. 3, pp. 89–120, and in S. Wertheimer, ed., *Battei Midrashot* (Jerusalem: Ketav ve-Sefer, 1968), vol. 1, pp. 67–136. For a partial English translation, see David Blumenthal, *Understanding Jewish Mysticism: A Source Reader* (New York: Ktav, 1978), vol. 1, pp. 56–89. The translation, done by L. Grodner and edited by Blumenthal, contains many mistakes and is therefore not reliable for scholarly use.

28. See G. Scholem, *Jewish Gnosticism,* pp. 20–30, where he analyzes the Talmudic text in *Sanhedrin* 95b.

29. See I. Gruenwald, "The Source of the Angels, the *Qedushah* and the Composition of the Hekhalot Literature" (Hebrew), in *Jerusalem in the Second Temple Period: Abraham Schalit Volume,* ed. by A. Oppenheimer, V. Rappaport, and M. Stern (Jerusalem: Yad Izhak Ben-Zvi, Ministry of Defence, 1980), pp. 459–81. The whole problem of the relationship between Hekhalot hymns and early Jewish liturgy still needs to be studied in detail. See A. Altmann, "Shirei Qedushah be-Sifrut he-Hekhalot ha-Qedumah," *Melilah,* 2 (1946), pp. 1–24.

30. See G. Scholem, *Jewish Gnosticism,* pp. 43–64.

31. A critical edition has been published by I. Gruenwald in *Temirin: Texts and Studies in Kabbala and Hasidism,* ed. by Israel Weinstock (Jerusalem: Mosad ha-Rav Kook, 1972) vol. 1, pp. 101–39.

32. See M. Margalioth, *Sefer ha-Razim: A Newly Discovered Book of Magic from the Talmudic Period, Collected from Genizah Fragments and other Sources* (Jerusalem, 1966).

33. Published by Scholem from Oxford Ms. Bodleiana 1531 in "Appendix C," *Jewish Gnosticism*, pp. 101–17.

34. See M. Margalioth, "Introduction," *Sefer ha-Razim*, pp. 1–16. Scholem frequently gave examples of such parallels in his studies on the subject. See especially *Jewish Gnosticism*, pp. 75–100. See my review of Margalioth's book in *Tarbiz*, 37 (1968), pp. 208–14.

35. The subject is dealt with in special treatises like *Macayan ha-Ḥokhmah (The Spring of Wisdom)*; see A. Jellinek, *Bet ha-Midrash*, vol. 3, pp. 64–67. See also R. Elior, ed., *Hekhalot Zutarti*, p. 61. On the whole subject, see M. Idel, "The Concept of Torah in Hekhalot Literature and its Reflection in the Kabbalah" (Hebrew), *Jerusalem Studies in Jewish Thought*, 1 (1981), pp. 23–49.

36. The text dealing with this subject was printed as part of the *Hekhalot Rabbati*, see A. Jellinek, *Bet ha-Midrash*, vol. 3, pp. 104–08. It is really a separate, later work describing the builders of the second temple acquiring such knowledge from the revelation of the Shekhinah. See I. Gruenwald, *Apocalyptic and Merkabah Mysticism*, pp. 169–73.

37. Published by M. Gaster in *Studies and Texts in Folklore, Magic, Medieval Romance, Hebrew Apocrypha and Samaritan Archaeology* (New York: Ktav, 1971), vol. 3, pp. 69–94. [English translation: ibid., vol. 1, pp. 312–36.]

38. See G. Scholem, *"Havdala de-Rabbi Aqiva*—A Source for the Tradition of Jewish Magic During the Geonic Period" (Hebrew), *Tarbiz*, 50 (1981), pp. 243–91. The text was prepared by Scholem and published posthumously.

39. The text was published by Scholem in *Sefer Asaf* (Jerusalem, 1953), pp. 459–95. For a German translation, see G. Scholem, "Ein Fragment zur Physiognomik und Chiromantik aus der Tradition der spätantiken jüdischen Esoterik," *Liber Amicorum: Studies in Honour of Prof. Dr. C. J. Bleeker* (Leiden: E. J. Brill, 1969), pp. 175–93. Other parts of the text have been published by I. Gruenwald, "Further Jewish Physiognomic and Chiromantic Fragments" (Hebrew), *Tarbiz*, 40 (1971), pp. 301–19.

40. *Seder Rabba de-Bereshit* was published in S. Wertheimer, *Battei Midrashot*, vol. 1, pp. 3–48.

41. A quotation from Ecclesiasticus used in the *Mishnah, Ḥagigah* 11b.

42. Hugo Odeberg's edition, *3 Enoch or The Hebrew Book of Enoch* (see n. 15, ch. 1). See Scholem's review in *Kiryat Sefer*, 6 (1929–30), pp. 62–

64. On this work, see P. S. Alexander, "The Historical Setting of the Hebrew Book of Enoch," *Journal of Jewish Studies*, 28 (1977), pp. 156–80.

43. *Ḥagigah* 14b. Cf. R. Elior, ed., *Hekhalot Zutarti*, p. 23, and P. Schaefer, *Synopse zur Hekhalot Literatur*, sec. 345.

44. This story, which serves as the basis for the piyyut *ʾEleh ʾEzkerah* included in the Jewish liturgy of Yom Kippur, has been studied by several scholars. See S. Kraus, "ʿAseret Harugei Malkhut," *Ha-Shiloaḥ*, 44 (1925), pp. 10–22, 106–17, 221–33; L. Finkelstein, "The Ten Martyrs," in I. Davidson, ed., *Essays and Studies in Memory of Linda R. Miller* (New York: Jewish Theological Seminary, 1938), pp. 29–55; S. Zeitlin, "The Legend of the Martyrs and its Apocalyptic Origins," *Jewish Quarterly Review*, 36 (1945–46), pp. 1–16. Only P. Bloch recognized its close relationship with *Hekhalot Rabbati*. See P. Bloch, "Die Yorde Merkavah, die Mystiker der Gaonenzeit und ihr Einfluss auf die Liturgie," *Monatsschrift für die Geschichte und Wissenschaft des Judentums*, O.S. 37 (1893), pp. 18–25, 69–74, 257–66, 305–11. See also his study in *Festschrift Jacob Guttmann* (1915), pp. 113–24. Cf. J. Dan, *The Hebrew Story in the Middle Ages* [Hebrew] (Jerusalem: Keter, 1974), pp. 62–68.

45. A special version of a combination of *Hekhalot Rabbati* and the legend of the "ten martyrs" was analyzed by me in *"Hekhalot Rabbati* and the Legend of the Ten Martyrs" (Hebrew) in G. Blidstein, R. Bonfil, and Y. Salmon, eds., *ʾEshel Beʾer Sheva: Studies in Jewish Thought* (Jerusalem: E. Rubinstein's, 1980), pp. 63–80. For an edition of the relevant text, see M. Oron, "Merkavah Texts and the Legend of the Ten Martyrs" (Hebrew), ibid., pp. 81–95. In this text, the instructions are presented as R. Ishmael's personal experience.

46. The description of the marble floors of the celestial palace as resembling waves of the sea is not mentioned in the first appearance of the parable of the "four who entered the pardes" in *Tosefta Ḥagigah* 2:1, it is found, however, in the Babylonian Talmud version (*Ḥagigah* 14b) and is developed in the *Hekhalot Zutarti* (see R. Elior's edition, p. 23). The similarity between this description and the riddle that King Solomon presented to the Queen of Sheba, who mistook the floor of his palace for a pool of water and raised her skirt, cannot be overlooked. It is possible that the Song of Songs background is common to both stories and it may denote that the celestial palaces, the *Hekhalot*, are heavenly pictures of

Solomon's palace rather than the temple. The key verse is Song of Songs 1:9, "The king hath brought me into his chambers." See J. Dan, "The Chambers of the Chariot" (Hebrew), *Tarbiz̧*, 48 (1979), pp. 48–55.

47. G. Scholem, *Kabbalah,* p. 17.

48. Scholem presented his views on this problem in "Die mystische Gestalt der Gottheit in der Kabbala," *Eranos Jahrbuch,* 29 (1960), pp. 139–82. [Hebrew translation in J. Ben Shlomo, ed., *Pirqei Yesod be-havanat ha-Qabbalah u-semaleha,* pp. 153–86.]

49. Rav Saadia's most detailed discussion of the *Shiur Komah* is found in one of his responses to the heretic Hivi ha-Balki, preserved in R. Judah ha-Barceloni's commentary on *Sefer Yezirah.* See J. Dan, *The Esoteric Theology of the Ashkenazi Hasidim,* pp. 105–12.

50. G. Scholem, *Jewish Gnosticism,* pp. 118–26.

51. See *Mishnah Yadayim* 3:5.

52. See Epstein and Melamed, eds., *Mekhilta de-Rabbi Shimᶜon bar Yo-ḥai* (Jerusalem: Meqize Nirdamim, 1955), p. 143; S. Lieberman, "Mishnat Shir ha-Shirim," in *Jewish Gnosticism,* pp. 118–19.

53. *T.B. Shevuᶜot* 35b; S. Lieberman, op. cit., p. 126.

54. *T.B. Ḥagigah* 14b. See J. Dan, "The Chambers of the Chariot."

55. See E. E. Urbach, "The Homiletical Interpretations of the Sages and the Expositions of Origen on Canticles, and the Jewish-Christian Disputation," *Scripta Hierosolymitana,* 22 (1971), pp. 247–75.

56. S. Lieberman, "Mishnat Shir ha-Shirim," in *Jewish Gnosticism,* p. 126.

57. See R. Elior, ed., *Hekhalot Zutarti,* p. 24–35.

58. Ms. Oxford 1531; P. Schaefer, *Synopse zur Hekhalot Literatur,* sec. 419.

59. This tradition has been analyzed in detail by D. Halperin in *The Merkabah in Rabbinic Literature,* pp. 107–41. Cf. N. Sed, "Les traditions secrètes et les disciples de Rabban Yoḥanan ben Zakkai," *Revue de l'Histoire des Religions,* 184 (1973), pp. 49–66; J. Neusner, "The Development of the *Merkavah* Tradition," *Journal for the Study of Judaism,* 2 (1971), pp. 149–60.

60. The new discoveries in the Qumran caves concerning the book of Enoch seem to denote an earlier date for this book than previously considered by most scholars.

61. The problem of the term—and concept—of *yozer bereshit* was discussed by Scholem extensively. See G. Scholem, *Reshit ha-Qabbalah* (Je-

rusalem: Schocken, 1948), G. Scholem, pp. 74–75; *Ursprung und Anfänge der Kabbala* (Berlin: Walter de Gruyter, 1962), pp. 184–88.

62. See J. Dan, "The Concept of Knowledge in the *Shi'ur Qomah.*"

63. The material concerning this problem was recently assembled by A. Segal, *Two Powers in Heaven: Early Rabbinic Reports about Christianity and Gnosticism.*

64. See G. Scholem, *Major Trends*, p. 356, n. 3. Cf. J. Dan, "*Hekhalot Rabbati* and the Legend of the Ten Martyrs."

65. See J. Even-Shmuel, ed., *Nistarot R. Shime'on bar Yoḥai* in *Midreshei Ge'ulah*, pp. 162–98.

66. See M. Smith, "Observations on *Hekhalot Rabbati*," in A. Altmann, ed., *Biblical and Other Studies* (Cambridge: Harvard University Press, 1963), pp. 142–60.

67. Cf. G. Scholem, *Jewish Gnosticism*, pp. 9–13, where Scholem analyzed in detail the story of R. Nehuniah's ascension in *Hekhalot Rabbati*. Cf. S. Lieberman's appendix to I. Gruenwald, *Apocalyptic and Merkabah Mysticism*, pp. 241–44.

68. The formula "*Yah 'Elohim 'Adonai Zeva'ot*" or "*Yah 'Adonai 'Elohim Zeva'ot*" is probably the basis for the description found in *T.B. Berakhot* 7a, and frequently in the lists of divine powers found in *Hekhalot Rabbati* and *Zutarti*. Its repetition many have been the source from which the abbreviated form "*Ialdabaoth*" emerged, which was later used by the gnostics to name the demiurge.

69. See I. Chernus, "Individual and Community in the Redaction of the Hekhalot Literature," *Hebrew Union College Annual*, 52 (1981), pp. 253–74.

70. Published by H. Odeberg in 1928 and reissued in 1973 (New York: Ktav) with a new prolegomenon by J. C. Greenfield.

71. See above, n. 42.

72. The most detailed analysis of the sources dealing with Metatron is to be found in H. Odeberg's *3 Enoch*, pp. 79–147. Cf. G. Scholem, *Kabbalah*, pp. 377–81; I. Gruenwald, *Apocalyptic and Merkabah Mysticism*, p. 192–94 and passim; S. Lieberman's appendix, op. cit., pp. 233–41.

73. See I. Gruenwald, op. cit., pp. 167–68, 202–05; cf. J. Dan, "Anafiel, Metatron and the Creator."

74. See *Genesis Rabbah* 65:21 (Theodor-Albeck, ed., p. 738).

75. See G. Scholem, *Kabbalah*, pp. 377–81. Cf. G. Scholem, *Major Trends*, pp. 67–70; G. Scholem, *Jewish Gnosticism*, pp. 43–50.

76. The relationship between Yahoel and Michael is discussed by Scholem in *Jewish Gnosticism*, pp. 43–50.

77. See J. Dan, "Anafiel, Metatron and the Creator," pp. 454–57.

78. *Mishnah Ḥagigah* 2:1. See D. Halperin, *The Merkabah in Rabbinic Literature*, pp. 19–37.

79. *Avot* 5:1.

80. *Sefer Yeẓirah* 1:5.

81. See the various midrashim on Genesis 1:2–8.

82. The mystical aspect of the *sefirot* is hinted at in all probability in *Sefer Yeẓirah* 1:7, "*ẓefiyatan he-mareh ha-bazak*," ("their appearance is like lightening.") The verb "*zfh*" is often connected with mystical visions both in Hekhalot literature and midrashic sources.

83. *Sefer Yeẓirah* 1:4: "Ten *sefirot belimah*, ten and not nine, ten and not eleven."

84. The kabbalistic mysticism of language and its early sources were studied in detail by Scholem in "The Meaning of Torah in Jewish Mysticism," *On the Kabbalah and Its Symbolism*, translated by Ralph Manheim (New York: Schocken, 1965), pp. 32–86. (See also G. Scholem, "The Name of God and the Linguistic Theory of the Kabbala," *Diogenes*, 79 (1972), pp. 59–80; 80 (1972), pp. 164–94.)

85. Scholem decribed the development of this idea, and the legends connected with it, in one of his Eranos lectures later published under the title "Die Vorstellung vom Golem in ihren tellurischen und magischen Beziehungen," *Eranos Jahrbuch*, 22 (1953), pp. 235–90. Reprinted in *Zur Kabbala und ihrer Symbolik* (Zurich: Rhein-Verlag, 1960), pp. 209–59. Cf. the English translation by R. Manheim, "Tradition and New Creation in the Ritual of the Kabbalists," *On the Kabbalah and Its Symbolism*, pp. 158–204; and the Hebrew translation by J. Ben Shlomo in *Pirqei Yesod be-havanat ha-Qabbalah u-semaleha*, pp. 381–424.

CHAPTER 3

FROM THE ANCIENT EAST TO THE EUROPEAN MIDDLE AGES

I

EVERY READER of *Major Trends in Jewish Mysticism* is puzzled that the first chapter of the book is dedicated to *Hekhalot* mysticism of the Talmudic period, up to approximately the sixth century. The following chapter is dedicated to the Ashkenazi Hasidic movement in medieval Germany, in the twelfth and thirteenth centuries. Was there nothing in between? Did Jewish mysticism freeze in its development after the experiences of the "descenders to the chariot" to be resumed only half a millennium or more later in the Christian countries of medieval Europe?

Scholem did not explore the period between *Hekhalot* mysticism and the emergence of the early kabbalah in Provence and Spain and of Ashkenazi Hasidism in the Rhineland in the twelfth century in any major study. His most extensive discussion of the subject is to be found in his article on kabbalah in the new *Encyclopaedia Judaica*, which, because of the limitations of the format of the encyclopaedia, is necessarily laconic and concise.[1] Yet in many of Scholem's studies this gap in time is discussed.

As far as we know, the long period between the sixth and the twelfth centuries did not bring forth a mystical literature comparable to previous or subsequent periods. We cannot discern whether mysticism lost its impetus within Jewish culture, or whether the works of the great mystics of that period, if indeed there were any, have been lost or consciously suppressed by rabbinic Judaism. All we have from this period are a few remnants of the creative surge of the *Hekhalot* mystics, and some early indications of the coming great outburst of mystical creativity by the medieval kabbalists.

One of the most perplexing problems Scholem faced whenever dealing with this barren period was whether or not "underground" schools of Jewish gnostics existed, or if there were other, hidden avenues of transmission of gnostic symbols and speculations. The Gaonic period, which lasted from the sixth to eleventh centuries, should be the connecting link between ancient gnostic mythology and its reappearance in medieval Europe in the book *Bahir* and the works of the early kabbalists. But we do not have any texts from the Gaonic period that suggest the existence of such an "underground." Scholem was quite certain nonetheless that in one form or another there was a series of links between the ancient gnostics and the medieval mystics; he did not rule out the possibility that the circles of the Ashkenazi Hasidim in the late twelfth century received and preserved traditions which reached them from earlier Gaonic sources.[2] Yet there is no historical record today of those circles which could have transmitted these esoteric traditions.

Below is an outline of the main avenues of the transmission of mystical and esoteric creativity in this period.

1. Through the continuation of the creative impetus of *Hekhalot* mysticism in different forms, probably with a greater emphasis on the magical use of the esoteric traditions.

2. Through works in the fields of cosmology and science, written in the Gaonic period but reflecting the approaches and influences of the *Hekhalot* traditions.

3. Through mystical and mythical elements within Midrashic literature, especially in works written after the advent of Islam which incorporated new traditions taken over from Islam.

4. Through traditions concerning the secret names of God, i.e., the names of 12, 42, and 72 characters. These traditions are known to us from medieval European texts, but they probably developed in earlier periods when commentaries were composed on the various names. In their original or edited forms, these commentaries then reached the Middle Ages.

5. Through compilation of anthologies and collections of mystical material, based mainly on *Hekhalot* mysticism but also probably containing later mystical material belonging to the Gaonic period.

6. Through the influence of the *Sefer Yezirah,* through commentaries on it, through cosmological and cosmogonical speculations based on it, and through other motifs and doctrines based on it. These, in turn, were collected in commentaries on the book in the last two centuries of this period.

7. Through speculations concerning the *shekhinah* and other theological-mystical subjects found in the late Midrashic literature of the Gaonic period. These conceptualizations may be the result of the influence of medieval rationalism in its earliest phases.

8. Through the transformations of some philosophical ideas into mystical symbols when they were adopted by Jewish culture. For example, Scholem felt that the influence of Rabbi Judah ha-Levi on Jewish mysticism was more significant than usually assumed. Ha-Levi, besides being an original philosopher, also presented in his works traditional material which he derived from earlier sources.

II

It is very difficult to distinguish between those mystical works included in the *Hekhalot* literature which originated from Eretz Israel in ancient times, between the third and fifth centuries C.E., and those which originated from Babylonia in the Gaonic period, the sixth century and later. Even in those cases where the linguistic characteristics indicate a later origin, there is still some doubt, for while the final language and form might be the work of later editors, the basic concepts could be ancient in origin. Still, Scholem viewed several of the *Hekhalot* texts, especially those devoted to magic and written in Babylonian Aramaic, as the product of the Gaonic period in Babylonia rather than belonging to the first age of the flourishing of Jewish mysticism in Eretz Israel.

Works like *The Sword of Moses*[3] and the *Havdalah of Rabbi Akiba*[4] belong, according to Scholem, to this group of later Jewish mystical texts.

The schools of the *gaonim,* the leaders of the great academies in Babylonia, preserved the tradition of *Hekhalot* mysticism. Rav Hai Gaon, in the beginning of the eleventh century, mentioned in his writings many of the *Hekhalot* texts.[5] It is difficult to know, whether this interest was only literary, or whether there was creative, mystical activity in these schools. The work of editing and preserving many of the *Hekhalot* texts was undertaken in Babylonia in this period, but how much of the material which has reached us was traditional, and how much was the result of the creativity of these editors, we cannot ascertain. Thus, for example, the great anthology of esoteric speculation concerning the alphabet, cosmology, the heavenly realm, the angels and the divine name, known as *The Alphabet of Rabbi Akiba* or *The Letters of Rabbi Akiba,*[6] was most probably edited in Gaonic Babylonia. But what parts of this vast collection were ancient, and what were added by the editors, cannot be stated with any certainty. For instance, the work contains a brief description of the story of Enoch and his metamorphosis into the Prince of the Countenance, Metatron, along with a list of the secret names of Metatron.[7] The problem is: Did the brief version, included in the *Alphabet of Rabbi Akiba,* precede the long, detailed version in *3rd Enoch,* or vice versa? That is, did some late editor compare the abridged version and add it to an already extant anthology attributed to the ancient sage? There are several philological elements which support each of these possibilities, and a decision either way is impossible at this time.

Similarly, the *Sar Torah* text appended to *Hekhalot Rabbati (The Greater Book of Palaces)*, is most probably a work written in Eretz Israel in the Gaonic period by a group of mystics who preserved the traditions of the ancient mystics and developed them according to their own needs, relying heavily on the ancient texts of *Hekhalot Zutarti (The Smaller Book of Palaces)*, and *Ma'ayan ha-Hochmah*.[8] It is possible that the apocalyptic work *The Book of Zerubavel,* which is connected with the *Hekhalot* tradition, was written in the early Gaonic period,[9] signifying a new, messianic trend among the Jewish mystics of the period.

The conquests of Islam in the seventh century brought the Jews into contact with a new, vigorous civilization, which left an impact on works they wrote after this period. One of the earliest books which can safely be dated to the period immediately following the conquests of the Arabs is the *Pirkey de-Rabbi Eliezer (Chapters of Rabbi Eliezer),* a collection of Talmudic and Midrashic homilies adapted into a narrative description of the events told in the books of Genesis and Exodus,[10] and attributed to the ancient sage Rabbi Eliezer ben Hyrkanus. Two subjects dealt with in this book had a meaningful impact on later, European, Jewish mysticism. One was the description of the creation, in the third and fourth chapters of the book, which follows *Hekhalot* cosmology and cosmogony; the other was the story of the events leading to the sins of Adam and Eve in the Garden of Eden in the thirteenth chapter. This story contains the earliest appearance of Samael as the satanic power, who took the shape of the snake and did his evil work through him.[11] In earlier *Hek-*

halot mysticism Samael is described only as the evil representative of the Roman Empire in the divine worlds.

The early Jewish communities in Europe, like some in
Babylonia, continued to follow the traditions of *Hekhalot*
mysticism. This is evident from several sources. The arch-
bishop of Lyon, Agobard, in an anti-Jewish polemical work
written sometime between 822 and 828, tells in surprising
detail what his Jewish opponents believed. His description
reflects accurately the text of the *Shiur Komah,* which, so it
seems, was very much an influence on some Jewish circles in
early medieval France.[12] A Jewish chronicle written in Italy
in the eleventh century, but reflecting older traditions, describes the rabbis and poets of eighth-century southern Italy
as studying and following the esoteric secrets of the *Hekhalot*
works.[13] This activity is also attested by the religious hymns
written by the early European poets of Italy.

A tenth-century work of cosmogony and cosmology, Rabbi
Shabatai Donolo's commentary on the verse "let us make a
man in our likeness" and his commentary on the *Sefer Yezirah*
also testify to the vitality of the *Hekhalot* mysticism in the
early awakenings of Jewish culture in medieval Europe. Donolo, who was a physician and who also left several important
works in the field of medicine, tried to formulate in his commentaries a coherent cosmological system based on the descriptions of the creation and of the nature of the world as
given in the *Hekhalot* mystical texts. While he was not a
creative mystical thinker, his works reflect the importance of
the ancient mystical texts to the Jewish communities in Europe, and in return had an impact on later Jewish European
mystics and cosmologists. Especially influential was his for-

mulation of the relationship between the macrocosmos and the microcosmos, between Man and Creation, based on the ancient traditions.

III

One of the most perplexing problems concerning the development of Jewish mystical speculations in the Gaonic period is the one concerned with the meaning of the concept *shekhinah* in some texts of this period. There is little doubt that this term, often used in Talmudic and Midrashic literature, meant for the ancient sages nothing but another appellation of God himself.[14] It did have some specific connotations, denoting that aspect of God which was closest to the temple in Jerusalem and to the Jewish people in its sufferings and exile, but there was no distinction between it and the Godhead. By the Middle Ages, Jewish philosophers, Ashkenazi Hasidim, and kabbalists all agreed that the *shekhinah* was a distinct, separate power, which should not be confused with the Godhead itself. When did this idea originate?

Scholem devoted several essays to this problem, holding that its solution was to be located in a section of the *Midrash on Proverbs*. In this Midrashic source the homilist repeats an old Talmudic story about the fate of King Solomon after his death, a story found in many versions in classical rabbinic literature. The version of the *Midrash on Proverbs* is, however, different. According to it, "the shekhinah prostrated herself in front of God" and asked for mercy for Solomon.[15] There can be no mistaking that the *shekhinah* was regarded by the homilist who introduced this novel element into the familiar story as a divine power separated from God himself and acting on her own.

It is very difficult to ascertain when this version of the homily was written. The entire *Midrash on Proverbs* is most probably a late composition which was then edited in Europe in the ninth or tenth century.[16] This, however, does not necessarily mean that the concept of the *shekhinah* as it appears in this section is as late as that. The editor of the Midrash undoubtedly used material from several literary periods. Scholem was certain that this concept of the *shekhinah* was independent of the philosophical developments concerning the meaning of the *shekhinah* which began to appear early in the tenth century.[17] Sometime in the Gaonic period Jewish mystics introduced an element of division in their concept of the divine world, probably by following and developing *Hekhalot* traditions. Thus they created one of the most powerful and profound symbols of Jewish medieval mysticism.

The early Jewish philosophers in Babylonia and in Europe who studied this concept and used it also contributed, unknowingly, to the richness of this symbol in the works of later Jewish mystics. Rav Saadia Gaon, like other rationalists in the tenth century (some of them belonging to the Karaitic sect, which opposed Saadia and rabbinic tradition and relied directly on the Bible), found in the concept of the *shekhinah* an answer to their difficulties with the anthropomorphic verses in the Bible and Talmud. They used this symbol to attribute all anthropomorphic descriptions of God not to the Godhead itself but to a lowly, created power, an archangel, which the Bible called *kavod* or "divine glory," and the rabbis called *shekhinah*.[18]

To achieve the goal of cleansing the sacred books from any hint of anthropomorphism these philosophers had to attribute descriptions of God in the Bible and Talmud to two different principles, one divine and eternal, God himself, and one angelic and created, the *shekhinah*. The distinction, however, survived even after their original rationalistic aims were lost. Thus, the Jewish mystics of medieval Europe proceeded in their interpretations of Biblical verses as relating to several different divine powers, creating thereby the pleroma of medieval Jewish mysticism.

This task was facilitated further by another development which occurred, most probably, in the Gaonic period: the concept of the hidden, esoteric names of God. In the important early works of the Jewish mystics in Europe in the twelfth century and onward the belief in the existence and importance of esoteric names of 12, 42, and 72 letters is presented as an old, traditional concept. Both the kabbalistic book *Bahir* and the Ashkenazi Hasidim incorporate these traditions.[19] Several traditional commentaries on these names were known, some of them attributed to sages of the Gaonic period such as Rav Hai Gaon.[20] The name of 12 letters is usually interpreted as a three-fold repetition of the four letters of the holy Tetragrammaton; the name of 42 letters, *AVGITAZ KRAS-ATAN* etc., which consists of seven groups of six letters each, has not been satisfactorily explained, and the European mystics did not have a consistent tradition concerning its origin.[21] The name of 72 letters is formed out of the combination of three verses in Exodus (14:19–21), each of which contains exactly 72 letters, so that the name consists really of groups of three letters each.[22] There are very few hints to indicate that these names could have been known in antiquity, and it is most probable that this tradition developed only later. Unlike many other names in the mystical tradition, these were not used primarily for magical purposes, though examples, though rare, can also be found. It seems that they had a deeper, mystical and theological significance, denoting the inner structure of the divine world and giving the mystic who knows them access to the most hidden secrets of the Godhead. The commentaries on these names was undoubtedly one of the most salient manifestations of ongoing Jewish creativity in the realm of mystical speculation in the Gaonic period.

IV

The commentaries on *Sefer Yezirah* are a direct source from the early Middle Ages. They were used by the medieval mystics and preserved unbroken the chain of esoteric traditions in Jewish thought. The first kabbalistic work by a kabbalist whose name we know is the commentary on *Sefer Yezirah* by Rabbi Isaac Sagi Nahor, written in southern France in the early thirteenth century. It reflects the tradition of commentaries on this ancient text begun centuries earlier.

The most influential among these works was Rav Saadia Gaon's commentary, which was first written in Arabic but later translated into Hebrew by an unknown eleventh-century scholar who minimized the rationalistic and scientific elements in the work while giving it a poetic, exalted style which endeared it to the mystics. Saadia, in his attempt to explain the cosmogony and cosmology of the ancient text, introduced into Jewish esoterical thinking several terms, which, stripped of their rationalistic origin and intent, served later as profound mystical symbols. Similarly, Shabatai Donolo's commentary, though written by a physician and a scientist, became a profound text of esoteric traditions for the Ashkenazi Hasidim and other medieval mystics.

Rabbi Judah ha-Levi included an almost complete commentary on the *Sefer Yezirah* in the fourth part of his major theological work, the *Kuzari*. This commentary became one of the most important treasuries of symbols and concepts for later Jewish mystics. Scholem even found an answer to one of the more perplexing problems concerning kabbalistic terminology.[23] Ha-Levi almost certainly preserved in the *Kuzari* (as well as in some of his poems and hymns) some old traditions, which were passed in this way to the medieval mystics. (Scholem also studied the impact of another poet-philosopher on Jewish mystical symbolism, Rabbi Solomon ben Gabirol, though his influence was probably less manifest than that of Ha-Levi.)[24]

The commentary on the *Sefer Yezirah* employed to the greatest extent by medieval mystics one written by Rabbi Judah ben Barzilai of Barcelona. This great halachist collected every piece of esoteric text or tradition that he could find, and assembled all of them into his commentary. His commentary is thus more of an anthology than an original work. This vast treasury of ancient mysticism and esotericism was collected no more than two generations before the emergence of the kabbalah.[25] It served as one of the most meaningful links between the ancient mystical traditions and the new eruption of mystical creativity in the Jewish communities of Europe in the twelfth and thirteenth centuries.

The long centuries that separate the peak of creativity of *Hekhalot* mysticism and the emergence of the new schools of mystics in Europe still hold many secrets. But Scholem's detailed studies have demonstrated a hidden continuity in the mystical dimension of Jewish culture even in this period.

NOTES

1. The most recent and detailed survey of this period written by Scholem is to be found in *Kabbalah* (Jerusalem: Keter, 1974), pp. 30–42.

2. See Gershom Scholem, *Reshit ha-Qabbalah* (Jerusalem: Schocken, 1948), pp. 36–40, 195–238; G. Scholem, *Ursprung und Anfänge der Kabbala* (Berlin: Walter de Gruyter, 1962), pp. 15–42.

3. See ch. 2, n. 37.

4. See ch. 2, n. 38.

5. See M. Levin, *Otzar ha-Geonim* (Jerusalem: The Hebrew University Press, 1931), vol. 4, "Tractate Hagigah," pp. 13–15.

6. The text has been published several times. See S. Wertheimer, ed., *Battei Midrashot* (Jerusalem: Ketav ve-Sefer, 1968), vol. 2, pp. 343–418. Wertheimer published two rescensions of the text. See ch. 2, n. 5.

7. Wertheimer, op. cit., pp. 351–53. This section was also included in the Hebrew book of Enoch; see Hugo Odeberg, *3 Enoch or the Hebrew Book of Enoch* (Cambridge: Cambridge University Press, 1928), pp. 71–74 (Hebrew text) and his commentary, pp. 172–79. Concerning the names of Metatron in this section and the possible antiquity of some of the traditions included in this passage, see J. Dan, "The Seventy Names of Metatron," *Proceedings of the Eighth World Congress of Jewish Studies* (Jerusalem, 1982), vol. 3, pp. 19–23.

8. See Ithamar Gruenwald's remark concerning this text in *Apocalyptic*

and Merkabah Mysticism (Leiden: E. J. Brill, 1980), pp. 169–73. It is remarkable that while all earlier speculations concerning the "Sar Torah" are connected in some way with traditions attributed to Moses on Mt. Sinai, this text relies on a revelation of the Shekhinah to the builders of the Second Temple at the time of Zerubavel, thus disregarding Moses and the ancient prophets.

9. See J. Even-Shmuel's edition in *Midreshei Ge'ulah* (Jerusalem: Mosad Bialik, 1954), pp. 55–88. The editor believed, like all previous scholars, that this work was written in the Byzantine period, a short time before the onslought of the Arabs in the early seventh century. The relationship between this work and the Hekhalot has not been studied yet. The divine power which reveals the secrets of the messianic age to Zerubavel in this text is called in some versions Metatron, and in others Michael. Scholem discussed in detail the impact of this work on later Jewish mysticism; see G. Scholem, *Sabbatai Sevi—The Mystical Messiah 1626–1676,* translated by R. J. Zwi Werblowsky (Princeton, Princeton University Press, 1973), pp. 8–15, 737–38.

10. See G. Friedlander, *Pirke de Rabbi Eliezer* (New York: Hermon Press, 1970). Cf. J. Dan, *The Hebrew Story in the Middle Ages* [Hebrew] (Jerusalem: Keter, 1974), pp. 134–36.

11. See G. Scholem, *Kabbalah,* pp. 386–88; J. Dan, "Samael, Lilith and the Concept of Evil in Early Kabbalah," *Association for Jewish Studies Review,* 5 (1979), pp. 17–40.

12. This text is included in P. Migne, ed., *Patrologia Latina,* vol. 104, col. 86–97.

13. See B. Klar, ed., *Megilat Aḥima'atz* (Jerusalem, 1944), p. 13. Cf. J. Dan, *The Esoteric Theology of the Ashkenazi Hasidim* [Hebrew] (Jerusalem: Mosad Bialik, 1968), pp. 19–20.

14. Recent discussions of the problem are to be found in: Arnold Goldberg, *Untersuchungen über die Vorstellung von der Schekhinah in der Frühen Rabbinsichen Literatur* (Berlin: W. de Gruyter, 1969); E. E. Urbach, *Ḥazal: Pirqei 'Emunot ve-De'ot* (Jerusalem: Magnes, 1975), pp. 29–52. [English translation: *The Sages: Their Concepts and Beliefs,* translated by I. Abrahams (Jerusalem: Magnes, 1975), pp. 35–65.]

15. S. Buber, ed., *Midrash Mishle* (Jerusalem, 1965), 47a.

16. Concerning the date of this midrash, see *Encyclopedia Judaica* (Berlin, 1932), s.v. "midrash."

17. See Scholem's discussion in *Reshit ha-Qabbalah,* pp. 33–36 and

passim, *Ursprung und Anfänge der Kabbalah,* pp. 77–84 and passim, and see his major study of the development and history of the concept of shekhinah, "Zur Entwicklungsgeschichte der kabbalistischen Konzeption der Schechinah," *Eranos Jahrbuch,* 21 (1952), pp. 45–107 [Hebrew translation by J. Ben Shlomo in *Pirqei Yesod be-havanat ha-Qabbalah u-semaleha* (Jerusalem: Mosad Bialik, 1976), pp. 259–307].

18. Saadia Gaon, *Emunot ve-De ot,* translated by Judah ibn Tibbon (Leipzig, 1859), pp. 85–86; *The Books of Beliefs and Opinions,* translated from the Arabic and Hebrew by S. Rosenblatt (New Haven: Yale University Press, 1948), pp. 125–27.

19. See R. Margaliot, ed., *Sefer Bahir* (Jerusalem: Mosad ha-Rav Kook, 1951), sec. 107–112, pp. 47–50. [Cf. G. Scholem, *Das Buch Bahir* (Darmstadt: Wissenschaftliche Buchgesellschaft, 1970), par. 76–81, pp. 77–84.] The most important Ashkenazi Hasidic work on the subject is R. Eleazar of Worms's *Sefer ha-Shem (The Book of the Holy Name),* extant in several manuscripts (Munich 81, British Museum 737), which is a treasury of traditions collected by the author as well as of his and his circle's own speculations. A group of commentaries on the holy names is included in R. Eleazar's *Sefer ha-Ḥokhmah (The Book of Wisdom).*

20. See. J. Dan, *The Esoteric Knowledge of the Ashkenazi Hasidim,* pp. 124–25.

21. Concerning these and other holy names, see Joshua Trachtenberg, *Jewish Magic and Superstition* (Philadelphia: Jewish Publication Society, 1939), pp. 90–100.

22. The Holy Name is created by writing the three verses in long lines, one below the other, with the second verse being written from end to beginning, and each group of letters being read vertically. [Cf. Rashi, *T.B. Sukkah* 45a, s.v. *"Ani ve-hu."*]

23. See Scholem's discussion of this name in *Reshit ha-Qabbalah,* pp. 83–84; *Ursprung und Anfänge der Kabbala,* p. 86 and p. 164.

24. See G. Scholem, "Traces of Gabirol in the Kabbalah" (Hebrew), *Me asef Sofrei Eretz Yisra el* (Tel Aviv, 1940), pp. 160–78. The paper deals especially with the possible influence of Gabirol on the thirteenth-century kabbalistic school which Scholem named "the lyyun circle."

25. See R. Judah ben Barzailai, *Commentar zum Sepher Jezira,* edited by S. J. Halberstam with additional notes by D. Kaufmann (Jerusalem: Maqor, 1970).

CHAPTER 4

THE ASHKENAZI HASIDIC
MOVEMENT

I

ONE OF THE most important contributions of Gershom Scholem to the study of Jewish culture in the Middle Ages in central Europe was his integral inclusion of the Ashkenazi Hasidic movement in the history of Jewish mysticism and pietism. Scholem was the first to study this movement as a whole, including in one and the same analysis a discussion of the movement's ethics as well as its mysticism, two elements which all previous scholars had treated separately. Scholem revealed the mystical element in the pietistic and ethical works of this movement and demonstrated the integral unity between these two factors. He then went on and analyzed the relationship of the whole body of literature produced by the Ashkenazi Hasidim to the more general outlines of development of Jewish culture in medieval Europe.

Ashkenazi Hasidism (Jewish pietism in Germany) was the most important religious movement among the Jews of Germany in the Middle Ages, flourishing between 1170 and 1240.

Its central school was that of the Kalonymus family located in the cities along the Rhine, mainly Mainz, Spier, and Worms. The three generations of teachers were those of Rabbi Samuel ben Kalonymus, known as the "Hasid, Saint and Prophet," his son Rabbi Judah the Pious (died in 1217), the great teacher of the movement, and his disciple and relative, Rabbi Eleazar ben Judah of Worms (died about 1230). There were also other schools, circles, and groups of mystics and writers of esoteric theology in Germany at the same period.

Ashkenazi Hasidism is best known for its ethical system, presented in *Sefer Hasidim (The Book of the Pious)*, written mainly by Rabbi Judah the Pious, which had an enormous impact on the history of Jewish ethical thought and practice. Besides their ethical works, however, the Ashkenazi Hasidim also created an extensive esoteric theology, which includes several mystical trends and which was united with kabbalistic mysticism at the end of the thirteenth century. The history of the Ashkenazi Hasidic movement and its mystical and esoteric literature demonstrates the continuity of esoteric speculation in Judaism throughout the ages.[1] Unlike the kabbalah, which relied on sources unknown to us, and whose earliest appearance is shrouded in mystery, the Ashkenazi Hasidic movement openly described its sources. The movement both claimed and substantiated its origins in the remote past, connecting itself with ancient times in Eretz Israel and Babylonia. While Ashkenazi Hasidism is clearly a medieval phenomenon, deeply rooted in the historical reality of central Europe in the twelfth century, its leaders derived their inspiration from many earlier layers of Jewish mystical and esoteric literature and traditions.

93

A demonstration of the combination of legend and historical fact in the traditions of this movement is the story of the mystic and magician, Rabbi Aaron ben Samuel of Baghdad. A great writer of Ashkenazi Hasidic esoteric literature, Rabbi Eleazar ben Judah ben Kalonymus of Worms recorded in his commentary on the prayers the history of the secrets concerning the structure and mystical meaning of the daily prayers. His description includes a list of previous generations of scholars in medieval Germany from whom he received his esoteric knowledge.[2]

This list states that the medieval German Jewish mystics received their traditions from southern Italy, from where the Kalonymus family emigrated to Mainz in the ninth century.[3] The Jewish center in southern Italy received its esoteric information, according to Rabbi Eleazar's statement, when a mysterious messenger arrived from Babylonia, Rabbi Aaron of Baghdad,[4] bringing with him the true meaning of the Jewish prayers and other secrets.[5] According to Rabbi Eleazar, Aaron came to Italy "because of a certain affair," which he leaves unspecified. This "affair," however, happens to be described in detail in another source, the family history found in the Ahimaaz Scroll, a literary work written in southern Italy in the eleventh century.[6] According to this account, Rabbi Aaron was the son of the gaon, the head of the academy. He was expelled from his country because of an inappropriate use of his magical knowledge. When his donkey was devoured by a lion, in his anger, Rabbi Aaron made the lion work in the donkey's place by magical means. As the king of the animals should not be treated in this way, Rabbi Aaron was sent into exile and went to southern Italy. There he communicated his esoteric knowledge to the sages of the

Kalonymus family. A few generations later some members of this family were invited by the emperor to reside in Mainz. Thus the great center in Ashkenaz was founded, in which the Ashkenazi Hasidic movement, generations later, began to develop.[7]

While the details of Rabbi Aaron's career may be legendary, there is no reason to doubt that there is a historical basis to the main point, namely, that there were contacts between the Jewish sages in Italy and the great center in Babylonia in the eighth century, and that some of the traditions, mainly those concerned with the "esoteric meaning of the prayers," were indeed received by Europe's scholars from Eastern sources via an oral tradition.

Scholem included a chapter on the Ashkenazi Hasidic movement in *Major Trends in Jewish Mysticism*.[8] He saw in this movement one of the major expressions of Jewish mystical and esoteric creativity, but he never actually described it as "mystical" in the technical sense. Moreover, he differentiated between the historical role of this movement and subsequent mystical movements which relied on the works of the Ashkenazi Hasidim. He recognized that although this movement was closely interwoven with the historical fabric of Jewish mysticism, this does not necessarily mean that its speculations were mystical, nor that its sages and teachers were mystics.

II

The *Hekhalot* and *Merkabah* mystical literature served as a basis for all Jewish European mystical schools, from the book

Bahir in the late twelfth century to modern Hasidism of the eighteenth century. While our knowledge concerning the transmission of *Hekhalot* mysticism from the East to Europe is incomplete, there is no doubt about the way that this mysticism spread in Europe from the twelfth century onward. Even today, the most important manuscripts containing the works of the *Hekhalot* mystics are preserved in manuscripts which were copied and edited by the Ashkenazi Hasidim. The works of these Hasidim themselves are full of quotations and paraphrases of *Hekhalot* works.[9] They also mentioned, and made use of, several works of Eastern Jewish mysticism which are lost to us, and the few quotations included in the Ashkenazi Hasidic works are all that we know about them. Sometimes only the title is known.[10] There can be no doubt that the spiritual world of the Ashkenazi Hasidim was based on the *Hekhalot* mystics. Among the Ashkenazi Hasidim the most popular literature was commentaries on the *Sefer Yezirah;*[11] their works include commentaries on the *Shiur Komah*[12] and various parts of *Hekhalot* literature, especially the hymns.[13] When Rabbi Eleazar of Worms set out to describe the various sections of the celestial and divine worlds in his esoteric *Sodei Razaya (The Secrets of the Prayers),* he reproduced several parts of the *Hekhalot* literature; others were presented in paraphrased and re-edited versions.

Not only the texts of the *Hekhalot* literature served as a basis for Ashkenazi Hasidic speculations; their central ideas remained the main inspiration of the Ashkenazi Hasidim spiritual world. The creation, according to their detailed works on the subject, was based on the letters of the Hebrew alphabet, as the Ashkenazi Hasidim understood this teaching as presented in the *Sefer Yezirah*.[14] The idea, which may be inherent in the *Sefer Yezirah* itself, that the mystic studying this work can follow the Creator to some extent and use the same methods to create something himself—e.g., a *golem*, a homunculus—was known to the Ashkenazi Hasidim. They also prepared manuals for carrying out such projects, and it is possible that these speculations did not remain merely on the theoretical level. When Scholem described the history and development of the idea of the *golem*, his main source was the writings of the various Ashkenazi Hasidic sects.[15] Several stories, some of them old and some of them of later origin, connect the sages of the Ashkenazi Hasidic movement with the creation of just such a creature.[16]

When Rabbi Eleazar commented on *Sefer Yezirah* he gave detailed instructions, possibly tried out by his circle on how actually to perform the process of creation. Does the same rule apply to his descriptions of the seven heavens, the throne of glory, the hosts of angels, the divine glory itself? Did the Ashkenazi Hasidim treat the traditions of the ascension to the divine world only as a theory, to be understood and transmitted, or also as instructions for the contemporary mystic in the ways of religious worship of a very high degree, to be followed by the elect, namely by the sages of Ashkenazi Hasidism?

The works of the Ashkenazi Hasidim do not state clearly that the traditions of ancient Jewish mysticism they preserved and commented on are to be followed in practice. There are no clear instructions concerning the actual performance of mystical ascensions, nor do we find any records of personal experiences of this sort. Yet, in several places, the tone of the presentation suggests that mystical ascensions were not a purely academic, theoretical subject in their eyes. That some of the persons mentioned in Ashkenazi Hasidic traditions are described as prophets,[17] and that there was a practice of receiving halachic information from heaven in these circles[18] seems to indicate that the Ashkenazi Hasidim might have had an element of actual mystical experience in their spiritual world. The frequency and depth of these experiences cannot be determined from the sources we have today. There is no doubt that the impact of the various sects of the Ashkenazi Hasidim was based not on the achievement of personal mystical visions, but on the detailed knowledge and erudition they showed in the preservation and presentation of the ancient materials of the *Hekhalot* mystics.

III

"The Secrets of the Prayers" seems to have been one of the main concerns of Ashkenazi Hasidic esoteric lore. In their explorations in this field they may have approached mystical practice. Rabbi Eleazar of Worms wrote an extensive commentary on the prayerbook, which was his "magnum opus" and may have been written and rewritten several times by the author himself.[19] This commentary is the earliest full commentary on the daily Jewish prayerbook to reach us. We do have, however, many quotations, preserved in several Ashkenazi Hasidic sources, from a previous commentary on the prayers written by Rabbi Eleazar's teacher, Rabbi Judah ben Samuel ben Kalonymus the Pious, the leader and greatest sage of Ashkenazi Hasidism.[20] This lost work might have been the earliest commentary on the prayers written in Hebrew.

That the Ashkenazi Hasidim were the first to expound on the prayers indicates that they saw in the Jewish daily prayerbook hidden strata of meaning and religious avenues unknown or unmentioned by their predecessors. This possibility is strengthened when we check the actual contents of their commentaries.

Rabbi Eleazar's commentary on every section of the prayerbook is divided into three parts. One is the detailed explanation of the words themselves in an almost literal fashion, connecting them with the biblical verses that used the same words, sometimes hinting at rabbinic passages which include the same term or the same idea. This part is really a literal commentary of a quite elementary nature.

The second part of the commentary deals with what Rabbi Eleazar calls the "secret," which in this context means the theological background of the terms used in the prayers. The divine glory, the various angelic powers, the nature of Man and his soul, and many other subjects are dealt with in detail in this part of the commentary. Rabbi Eleazar regarded the "secret" hidden in the prayers as denoting the theosophy and philosophy of the Ashkenazi Hasidic theology. He concluded that the ancient prayers, composed by the sages of antiquity, already included all the ideas accepted by the teachers of his medieval movement.

The third part of the commentary presents a system which analyzes the numerical structure of each prayer, and even of each sentence or word within a prayer. The numerical structure takes into account the number of words, the number of letters, the number of specific words (like divine names), the number of specific letters, the number of final letters, etc. He also uses the numerical value of individual letters, words, or even complete sentences, indicating a deep sense of mathematical awareness and a world view which sees numerical constructions in everything. The figures he discovered in the prayers themselves are compared and harmonized with corresponding numbers found in other parts of Jewish sacred literature, mainly the Bible itself, but also in the Talmud and Midrash traditions. According to Rabbi Eleazar, there is a basic harmony between the numbers found in the analysis of the prayers and those hidden in the structure of biblical verses and chapters. His main endeavor in his commentary is to discover and present the deep unity between the prayers and the biblical sources, which can be revealed only by such numerical analysis.[21]

The same harmony is also found between numbers in the text of the prayers and numbers apparent in creation and history and in the cosmos as a whole. Chronological dates, numbers of years, numbers of miles between heaven and earth, and other such figures share the basic harmony found in the sacred compositions. There is no doubt that this commentary reflects a well-developed world view, which sees existence as a whole as governed by the relations inherent between numbers and the characters of the Hebrew alphabet. The origin of this system is undoubtedly to be found in the ancient *Sefer Yezirah.*

The quotations we have from Rabbi Judah the Pious's commentary on the prayers seem to indicate that he dealt exclusively with numerical harmony. It seems that Rabbi Judah wrote his voluminous work to prove how those who introduce changes into the text of the prayers for various reasons based on the actual content, or literal meaning, of the prayers, are incorrect.[22] Rabbi Judah insisted that since the main source of the sanctity of a prayer is the numerical harmony reflected in it, then the smallest change in a single word or even a single letter can destroy this harmony completely. He attacked certain rabbis, described as those of "France and the Islands" (meaning, probably, the British Isles), who introduced such changes, and listed the mathematical basis for his opposition.

The concentration of the Ashkenazi Hasidim on the exposition of the hidden meaning of the prayers was motivated by their insistence that the texts of the prayers as they had received them from their elders were the only true ones, and even the minutest change could not be tolerated. They also believed that numerological analysis of the prayers reveals the hidden divine design underlining the structure of the whole universe, and is harmoniously connected with other parts of sacred literature as well as the secrets of the creation and of history. Rabbi Eleazar also demonstrated in his commentary that the interpretation of the prayers proved the validity of Ashkenazi Hasidic theology. While these reasons certainly suffice to explain the Ashkenazi Hasidic interest in the prayers, their structure, their literal, philosophical, and esoteric meanings, there is still a question of whether or not there was also a mystical dimension to their interest.

After reading the detailed expositions by the Ashkenazi Hasidim of "The Secrets of the Prayers," one may ask whether these secrets have anything to do with the everyday practice of prayer. Should one—or at least the elect, the sages of Ashkenazi Hasidism themselves—use this knowledge when actually praying? Is there a difference between a prayer said without the knowledge of these secrets and one said when the devout Jew concentrates on the knowledge of these esoteric things? Does the numerical harmony exposed by the commentators serve a religious purpose?

Answers to these questions are decisive when we try to analyze the mystical element in Ashkenazi Hasidic thought. If indeed the expositions of "The Secrets of the Prayers" were not intended for polemical and theological reasons only, but also constituted a system of "intentions" (*kavvanot*) in prayer, then the mystical character of the whole movement becomes much more pronounced. Unfortunately, we do not have sufficient material in the works of these sages to decide with certainty that they really had such a system of intentions. Indeed, Scholem was justified in presenting the mystical character of the Ashkenazi Hasidic movement in a most qualified manner.

IV

Scholem emphasized the eclectic character of the Ashkenazi Hasidic movement's theology and its heavy reliance on the works of the early Jewish philosophers. The Ashkenazi Hasidim did not come into contact with Jewish philosophy as such, that is, with works written in a formal philosophical manner, influenced by Arabic philosophy and ultimately by

the Greek philosophers. The Ashkenazi Hasidim, most probably were not familiar with even one such work, because none
was available at that time in Hebrew. Arabic, which was
used by most Jewish philosophers up to the end of the twelfth
century, was unknown to them.[23] It also seems that they did
not have any direct access to Latin philosophy because of their
deep negative attitude to the Latin language which was, unlike Arabic, not the language of countries and peoples but
the language of the Church.[24] The only philosophical sources
they could use were those either written in Hebrew or translated into Hebrew.

The most important text was the "paraphrase" of Rav Saadia Gaon's two philosophical works *Beliefs and Ideas* and the
Commentary on Sefer Yezira. They did not have the accurate
translation of the first made by Rabbi Judah ibn Tibbon late
in the twelfth century, and the *Commentary on Sefer Yezira* was
not translated in a philosophical manner at all. They received
an earlier, probably eleventh-century translation of both works,
probably made by an anonymous Jew in the Byzantine empire.[25] This work, called usually the "paraphrase" of Saadia,
contains no philosophical terminology; it is written in a poetic style, as if the content of these two works were not the
result of logical deliberation but of mystical revelation. The
style of the "paraphrase" is very close to that of some of the
sacred poets who wrote in Eretz Israel before the Islamic conquests. It is no wonder, therefore, that the Ashkenazi Hasidim described Rav Saadia as a master of esoteric knowledge,
and not as the founder of Jewish rationalistic philosophy. The
poetic style of the "paraphrase" had great impact on the contents and style of Ashkenazi Hasidic theology.

One of their earliest theological works, the *Shir ha-Yihhud (A Hymn for Divine Unity),* which Scholem believed could have been written by Rabbi Judah the Pious himself,[26] clearly reflects both the ideas and the style of this "paraphrase."

Among the other important sources of the theology of the Ashkenazi Hasidim were the works of Rabbi Abraham ibn Ezra, the philosopher and commentator on the Bible, who wrote in Hebrew so that Jews in Christian countries could read him, and also traveled in Europe and the East, where his personality left a mark together with his philosophy. Rabbi Judah the Pious wrote a commentary on a chapter of Rabbi Abraham ibn Ezra's brief theological and ethical treatise, *Yesod Mora (The Foundation of the Fear of God).*[27] Indeed, ibn Ezra's discussions of the structure of the human soul served as the basis for Rabbi Eleazar of Worms' treatment of the subject in his book on psychology, *Hochmat ha-Nefesh (The Wisdom of Natural Perfection).*[28] Even descriptions of the creation of a *golem* were attributed by one of the Ashkenazi Hasidic sects to ibn Ezra and his disciples.[29]

Another important influence on Ashkenazi Hasidic theology were the works of an early twelfth-century Hebrew philosopher in Spain, Rabbi Abraham bar Hijja. Scholem dedicated several essays to his impact (which was all very important in connection with the book *Bahir* and the early kabbalah) on the Ashkenazi Hasidic theology, especially its conception of the five "worlds" *(olamot).*[30] It seems that bar Hijja adopted a neo-Platonic attitude, telling of five spiritual worlds which he adapted to Hebrew terminology and world view. This fascinated some of the Ashkenazi Hasidic writers, who inserted this into their description of the celestial realms.

The Ashkenazi Hasidim do not seem to have had any clear knowledge of the works of Rabbi Judah ha-Levi,[31] and only a minimal knowledge of the works of Maimonides. They certainly did not know anything about Maimonides' central philosophical work, *Moreh Nevuchim* (*The Guide for the Perplexed*), which caused a major controversy in European Jewry after the Hebrew translation by Rabbi Samuel ibn Tibbon became known, especially in the years 1232–1235. Rabbi Eleazar of Worms may have heard about the structure of Maimonides' great legal work, *Mishneh Torah,* because like Maimonides he dealt with ethics in the beginning of his own legal work, the *Roqueaḥ.*

An Ashkenazi opponent of Jewish philosophy, Rabbi Moses Taku, who also attacked the works of Rabbi Judah the Pious, wrote a polemical work called *Ktav Tamim (A Book on Simple Faith)* probably in the second or third decades of the thirteenth century. Although he attacked several sections in Maimonides' *Mishneh Torah,* even he was ignorant of the *Moreh Nevuchim.*[32]

Scholem described Rabbi Moses Taku as one of the two great reactionaries of the Jewish Middle Ages.[33] Taku's polemics are directed mainly against the theories presented by Saadia Gaon concerning divine revelation and immanence, but he also included the Ashkenazi Hasidim in his attack because he believed, with good justification, that they followed the works and ideas of Saadia. Taku insisted that one should never deviate from the literal meaning of the scriptures when they describe divine phenomena, even if these descriptions can be interpreted as thoroughly anthropomorphic. All speculations concerning the nature of the divine realms are forbidden, and dealing with such ideas is sinful and leads directly to heresy. Taku's criticism is the only historical polemical work which we have which attacks Ashkenazi Hasidism together with Jewish philosophy, especially the works of Rav Saadia Gaon, which he regarded as heretical and which he compared in their common threat to that of Christianity. While Taku undoubtedly opposed the philosophical influence on Ashkenazi Hasidism, his basic world view is not very far from that of his opponents, who did not expound Jewish philosophy in the technical sense. Rather, they developed their theology by assembling scattered, unorganized, and unsystematic ideas derived from the very few Hebrew philosophical works which could be obtained in the middle of the twelfth century.

V

The influence of the philosophers on Ashkenazi Hasidic theology is most apparent in its thorough and lengthy analysis of the phenomenon of divine revelation. This problem interested the Ashkenazi Hasidim for two reasons. First, they wanted to cleanse the scriptural verses of anthropomorphic expressions, which usually appear in the context of biblical accounts of divine revelations, like those to Moses on Mount Sinai and in Exodus 33, to Isaiah in the Temple in Jerusalem (chapter 6), or Ezekiel's vision of the chariot on the river Kvar. Second, they had an intense religious interest in the structure of the divine realm, hoping that a knowledge of the structure would let them come into contact with that realm during religious worship and ritual, and especially during prayer.

The main contribution of the Ashkenazi Hasidim in this area was a reformulation of the idea of divine glory, which had a clear mystical character in the works of *Hekhalot* mysticism, but which the philosophical discussion of the early Middle Ages in Babylonia and Europe had almost completely erased, only to see it resurrected to some extent by the works of the Ashkenazi Hasidim. While the *shekhinah* and the divine glory *(kavod)* were terms denoting divine powers in the texts of the early Jewish mystics of antiquity, medieval philosophy tried to deprive them of their status as divine attributes and described them instead as created, angelic powers. In this the Jewish philosophers, especially Saadia, followed the practice of the translators of the Bible to Aramaic, i.e., they replaced clear anthropomorphic references to God in the biblical accounts of revelations by the use of the term *kavod* or *yeqar,* denoting that this term refers to something which is below or beside God himself.

Rav Saadia (and some Karaites in the tenth century) systematized the intuitive work of the translators of the Bible into Aramaic by formulating the idea that a certain great angel revealed the divine power to the prophets. God created the angel specifically to fulfill the task of revelation to the prophets and serve as a sign and witness to the divine origin and veracity of the prophecy. According to Saadia, this angelic power is called by the Bible *kavod,* and by the Talmudic sages the *shekhinah.* Both terms refer to the same created entity. All anthropomorphic descriptions which could not be explained as metaphors or parables should be understood as describing this special angel. Saadia's views, with some variations, were accepted by many Jewish rationalists.[34]

The Ashkenazi Hasidim respected Saadia very much as an early gaon and the possessor of many esoteric traditions, but they did not accept his views concerning the *kavod* and revelation. They made use of a passage, not completely clear in itself, in ibn Ezra's commentary on Exodus 33, which seems to include the idea that the divine glory, the *kavod*, has two aspects, or "faces," one turned toward God himself, which cannot be seen by humans, and a second, the lower, which is the one revealed to the prophets and all those who achieve an exalted religious status. It seems that ibn Ezra described an emanated divine glory (as opposed to Saadia's created one), which is an integral part of the divine realm. Rabbi Judah the Pious, Rabbi Eleazar of Worms, and other Ashkenazi Hasidic writers developed this symbol to describe the divine glory revealed to the prophets as an emanated divine entity. They thus introduced into Jewish medieval thought the idea that the divine realm is a divided one, including several strata of divine powers emanating one from another.[35]

The Ashkenazi Hasidim were primarily interested in the study of divine glory to remove anthropomorphic elements, since they believed that the revelation of a lowly divine power does not affect the complete transcendence of the Godhead itself. But they also succeeded in retaining the divine character of the phenomenon of prophecy, which, in the works of the philosophers, tended to become either a psychological phenomenon occurring within the heart of the prophet, or the revelation of an angelic, created power, which deprived prophecy of its sanctity.

The Ashkenazi Hasidim raised a major question undreamt of by the philosophers: If there is a divine power, emanated from the Godhead, which is revealed in part to the prophets, why can it not perform other divine functions? The divine glory need not be restricted only to the task of revelation. If it is really divine, it can serve and appear in other religious contexts; for example, when guidance of the created world is needed, or to be the power that accepts the prayers of the worshippers.

Ashkenazi Hasidism was not one monolithic group in which a system was formulated and then adhered to by all. There were various sects and groups, some of them unconnected to and unaware of the existence of others. The central group or circle, that of Rabbi Judah the Pious and Rabbi Eleazar of Worms, was also not united in every respect, and some differences of opinion and attitude can be discerned even between them.[36] The differences among the various Ashkenazi Hasidic circles and groups are the greatest concerning the nature and tasks of the divine glory. They were united in the belief in the existence of this secondary divine power and its being a part of the divine realm itself (thus opposing Saadia's views), but the actual descriptions of the *kavod* differ considerably.

The author of the *Sefer ha-Ḥayim (The Book of Life),* for instance, describes a system of ten *kvodot,* "divine glories," each emanating from the one above it, in a way that brings it close to the picture of the divine realm drawn by the kabbalists. He did not, however, give a detailed account of the nature and tasks of each of these powers.[37]

More complicated is the system developed by the circle

which used the pseudepigraphic works attributed to Joseph ben Uzziel.[38] Scholem sensed a deep affinity in their system to that of some early kabbalistic sources, as well as some mystical elements hidden within the theosophic speculations. They went one step further than the system developed by Rabbi Judah the Pious and Rabbi Eleazar (probably independently, and they may have preceded the central group). According to them, the *kavod* itself, while being an emanated power, is too exalted to be the power revealed to the prophets. That task is relegated to another emanated power below the divine glory, called *ha-keruv ha-meyuhad,* "the special cherub," a name probably based on Saadia's description of the angel whose task it is to provide revelation to the prophets. This cherub sits on the throne of glory while the *shekhinah* is above it. It is called God's *gedulah* (greatness) and it is the power described in the *Shiur Komah* texts which measure the limbs of the Creator. He is stationed in the eastern side of the divine realm, while the *shekhinah* traditionally is in the west. The power above the cherub is also called the *kedushah,* or "divine holiness," and it has no characteristics that will enable it to be perceived by human beings. The main task of this *kedushah-kavod* is to accept the prayers of human beings.[39] Indeed, one of the most detailed descriptions of this hierarchy is found in a short treatise presented as an answer to the question, toward whom should one pray—where man should direct his prayers. The author insists that prayers should never be directed toward a revealed power, only toward the hidden divine holiness and glory above the special cherub.[40]

It seems that Rabbi Judah the Pious and Rabbi Eleazar of Worms regarded divine glory and divine revelation as esoteric, and therefore did not discuss them in treatises intended for wide circulation. They wrote several works of the *sodot ha-yihhud,* "secrets of the divine unity," type,[41] with the goal of fighting anthropomorphic conceptions. In these brief works they did not emphasize the many tasks of the divine glory, and only hinted at its purpose concerning the prayers. But in their more esoteric works, which were given only to selected disciples after a specific ritual, they revealed some of their more radical ideas.

The Ashkenazi Hasidic *kavod* theories had a considerable impact on the symbolism of the later kabbalists, though there is no basis for believing that it was this influence which brought about the formulation of the kabbalistic system of the ten *sefirot.* The works of the Ashkenazi Hasidim do not contain the mythical element which so profoundly shaped the ideas of the kabbalists, nor do we find any significant element of gnostic influence in their works. In the very few places in this literature where there is the possibility of an Eastern, gnostic or at least mythological element, it is clear that the Ashkenazi Hasidim only copied the ancient sources, but made no use of their terminology and imagery when formulating their own ideas.[42] The importance of the various Ashkenazi Hasidic theories concerning the divine glory is that they prove that the drive toward a more complicated, structured, and variegated picture of the divine realm was not exclusive to the kabbalists, but a basic characteristic of twelfth-century Jewish thought.

VI

The most influential works of the Ashkenazi Hasidim on subsequent Jewish thought were their ethical books.[43] The most important among these was the *Sefer Hasidim* (*The Book of the Pious*), written mainly by Rabbi Judah the Pious in the first years of the thirteenth century. Rabbi Eleazar of Worms also wrote several ethical treatises, as did other writers who belonged to, or were influenced by, the Ashkenazi Hasidic movement. (Scholem was the first scholar to combine a discussion of Ashkenazi Hasidic esoteric theology with a study of their ethical teachings in an effort to show the underlying themes that led to the creation of both systems.)[44]

Ashkenazi Hasidic ethics insist on traditional values, rejecting all innovation as such and believing that all truth was revealed to the forefathers of the Hasidim, yet they also developed radically new approaches and attitudes which departed from accepted norms quite drastically. The Hasidim did not see this as paradoxical, however. They believed that every idea presented in their works had a foundation in tradition, and that close reading of the scriptures and of Talmudic ethical sections led without deviation to their ethical values.

Scholem believed there were close connections between the ethical norms described by the Ashkenazi Hasidim and the influence of the surrounding non-Jewish culture. He felt that their system of repentance (discussed below) reflected a Christian influence.[45] He even found certain ancient ideas, like that of the *ataraxia* of the Stoics, in their works.[46] There is no doubt that the Ashkenazi Hasidim were greatly influenced by the surrounding society, an influence clearly revealed in their beliefs concerning magic, sorcery, demonology, and folklore; they even used Germanic names for many such phenomena.[47] The larger problem of specific non-Jewish sources for specific ethical ideas and practices is, however, not yet completely settled.[48]

Ashkenazi Hasidic ethics, as expressed by Rabbi Judah the Pious and Rabbi Eleazar of Worms, define ethical behavior as the striving to achieve what is beyond the minimal norms of the *halachah*. Their attitudes clearly reflect the world of Europe during the Crusades, when every generation brought forth a new wave of the crusading movement, and each of these waves started with massacres and persecutions of the Jewish communities of central Europe. Believing that these cruel historical circumstances were the results of divine decrees, they derived from them moral strength and made them the cornerstones of their moral teachings.

The highest ideal of these generations of German Jews was the "sanctification of the name," *kiddush ha-shem*, i.e., martyrdom, which meant the supreme victory of the pietist over the crusading persecutors. If a Jew died for the sanctity of God, refusing to save his life by conversion to Christianity, he attained the highest possible religious achievement and earned a high place in paradise.[49] Ashkenazi Hasidic ethics aimed to prepare German Jews for this ordeal by developing a martyrological attitude toward life as a whole, and insisting that *kiddush ha-shem* was the preferred resolution of man's earthly life and religious efforts.[50]

The feeling of persecution should direct every deed of a Jew's religious practice. He should always view every attempt of his evil inclinations not to perform even the minutest daily details of ritual in the most complete and perfect way, as an example of a *kiddush ha-shem* situation. He should always see himself as tried by God as to whether he can overcome the

demands of the material body and sacrifice his desires to the
religious martyrological ideal. Thus religious life was viewed
as a constant struggle in a situation when persecution was
only a supreme culmination of everyday strife. Ashkenazi
Hasidic ethics are, therefore, extreme and demanding, as well
as spiritualistic in character. The material world, the persecutions by the gentiles, the material body, and the evil inclinations within one's heart are all part of the great trial that
God uses to test adherence of the righteous to His commandments.

The same feeling of persecution is expressed in the *Sefer
Hasidim* even with regard to the status of the righteous within
Jewish society.[51] The Ashkenazi Hasidim defined the term
"hasid" as derived from "white,"[52] explaining that a "hasid"
is a person who can remain unmoved when criticized and
denounced by his neighbors and friends. This Scholem interpreted as reflecting the attitude of *ataraxia,* the complete negation of all feelings and responses to events in the surrounding world, a counterpart to the Hebrew term *hishtavut* which
conveys a similar meaning in Hebrew philosophical texts.[53]

The detailed descriptions found in the *Sefer Hasidim* of the
difficulties endured by the pietists from the contemporary society surrounding them might be the result of a basic martyrological attitude of the Ashkenazi Hasidim; it can hardly
be based on historical fact. The Kalonymus family, to which
most of the Ashkenazi Hasidim of the central group belonged, was the most prominent in German Jewry, and one
can hardly believe that people like Rabbi Judah the Pious or
Rabbi Eleazar were ridiculed and denounced by the society
they lived in. The problem of the historical meaning of the

descriptions of the social standing and social activities of the groups of the Hasidim is still open to various interpretations.

The attitude of martyrdom is to be found in the Ashkenazi Hasidim system of penitence, presented in the *Sefer Hasidim* and in several works of Rabbi Eleazar of Worms.[54] This system emphasized an element not found in previous Jewish discussions of repentance, either in the ancient Talmudic and Midrashic sources or the ethical works of the medieval philosophers: *sigufim,* self-inflicted pain and suffering. According to this system, the penitent had to assume enough pain and suffering to outweigh the pleasure he had derived from his sin (the "sin" usually indicated was explicitly or inexplicitly a sexual one). This he could do either by following the biblical punishment for that crime, or by devising self-tortures equivalent to his sinful pleasures. Usually these tortures were just long periods of fasting from sunrise to sunset, but sometimes more picturesque tortures are mentioned. It must be stressed that these Hasidim discuss this self-inflicted suffering only in the context of penitence and not as a required way of life for the righteous in general. They generally practiced abstinence, not *sigufim.*[55]

Was there a mystical drive behind their extreme ethical demands, their self-negation and their spiritual denial of the demands of the flesh? It is very difficult to answer this question. There is no doubt that the idea of the proximity of the *shekhinah,* a distinct emanated power from the Godhead which is not as transcendent and hidden as He is, had an effect on the way of life described by the ethical teachings of this movement. The *shekhinah* or the *kavod* can be present only in places and situations of complete purity and sanctity, unlike the immanent Godhead, which is present equally everywhere, regardless of the circumstances. Because of its exalted stature and transcendence, the Godhead cannot be affected by any specific detail of earthly existence; like sunlight, dirt does not leave any impression on it. But the revealed divine glory can be affected by evil and sin, and therefore can appear only where purity of body and heart can be achieved. Sometimes the act of *kiddush ha-shem* is perceived as containing an element of union with the divine glory, and there is no doubt that a righteous life, according to Ashkenazi Hasidism, leads the pious to the proximity of the *shekhinah,* sometimes during life itself though more usually after death, when the righteous receive their rewards around the throne of glory in paradise.[56] While there might be some mystical element in this attitude, it is a minor and subdued one. The Ashkenazi Hasidim did not develop a literature describing their personal religious and spiritual achievements, which might have enabled us to discern the mystical element in it.

VII

In all his works concerning the early development of Jewish mysticism in medieval Europe, Scholem repeatedly emphasized the impact of Ashkenazi Hasidic ideas and traditions. They preserved for the European mystics not only the mystical literature of the *Hekhalot* and *Merkabah,* but also much of the esoteric traditions concerning the secret names of God and their interpretations. They developed, from traditional sources, the esoteric systems of using the letters of the Hebrew alphabet and numerical values and computations to a degree never found earlier, but often found later in the works of medieval mystics. They opened the paths of a non-philosophical use of philosophical terminology, turning it into theosophic symbolism. They established schools and centers of esoteric lore which spread their influence among circles of mystics in southern Europe. Their disciples, real or imaginary, relied on them when they developed kabbalistic systems in the second half of the thirteenth century. Some kabbalists even insisted that the kabbalah itself was received from the Ashkenazi Hasidim who preserved it after receiving it from the sages in the East.[57]

A school of German-Jewish kabbalists developed in central Europe late in the thirteenth century, and flourished for several generations. Most of the kabbalists who belonged to this school absorbed the teachings of the Ashkenazi Hasidic esoteric theology, and combined it with the new kabbalistic symbolism developed by the Jewish mystics in Spain and Provence. Among them were the direct descendents of Rabbi Judah the Pious himself.[58]

However, some great kabbalistic writers of the fourteenth and fifteenth centuries, like Rabbi Menachem Ziuni, a commentator on the Bible who wrote several mystical works, or the editor of the great kabbalistic treasury *Yalkut Reuveni*, made use of the works of Rabbi Judah the Pious, Rabbi Eleazar of Worms, and other Ashkenazi Hasidic sources, believing that the esoteric theology found in them was identical with the kabbalah itself. For later generations, therefore, Ashkenazi Hasidic teachings were completely fused with the kabbalah to create a new whole. Yet it should be emphasized that relatively speaking this was a minor source of influence, which could not compete with the great mystical works of the Spanish kabbalists.

Some of the ideas and symbols of the Ashkenazi Hasidim made their way into the mainstream of kabbalistic thought, usually by means of their inclusion in the *Zohar*. One of these was the system of the four *kelipot,* the four shells which surround the holy chariot, found in Ashkenazi Hasidic commentaries on Ezekiel's chariot, which might have been based on ancient sources.[59] From this the *Zohar* developed the symbolism of the "external" powers, the powers of evil, which surround the divine realm. A school of Jewish mystics in Spain in the second half of the thirteenth century, headed by Rabbi Jacob and Rabbi Isaac, relied heavily on material received from the Ashkenazi Hasidim, and they described themselves as disciples of Rabbi Eleazar of Worms's school.[60] Their teachings were absorbed by later Spanish kabbalists, and thus still more ideas of Ashkenazi Hasidic origin penetrated into the world of the kabbalists.

Though this influence of Ashkenazi Hasidic thought on later kabbalistic ideas was meaningful, there can be no doubt that it is relatively insignificant when compared to the impact of Ashkenazi Hasidic ethics. During the fourteenth and fifteenth centuries the *Sefer Hasidim* and works that followed it were the almost exclusive source of ethical instruction to the Jewry of central Europe. When great Jewish centers began to be built in eastern Europe by Jewish emigrants from the West, the teachings of the Ashkenazi Hasidim spread into these new centers. Even in the great center of Jewish thought in the sixteenth century, Safed, where the central figures were refugees from the Spanish expulsion in 1492, the teachings of the Ashkenazi Hasidim were revived, reinterpreted and combined with the emergent ethical system of the kabbalah.[61] Ashkenazi Hasidim was the first movement which combined esoteric and mystical speculations with practical ethical teachings; it showed for the first time that such speculations and achievement of the highest possible religious and ethical standards go hand in hand. Other movements in the sixteenth century and later followed, knowingly or, more often unknowingly, this example, thus shaping Jewish life, in thought and deed together, according to their mystical drives and profound symbols.

NOTES

1. The main discussions of Scholem on Ashkenazi Hasidim are: *Major Trends in Jewish Mysticism*, 3rd rev. ed. (New York: Schocken, 1954) [henceforth cited as *Major Trends*], pp. 80–118; *Kabbalah* (Jerusalem: Keter, 1974), pp. 35–40; *Ursprung und Anfänge der Kabbala* (Berlin: Walter de Gruyter, 1962), index, s.v. "*Chassidim, deutsche.*" It is interesting to note that in Scholem's letter to Bialik, written soon after his arrival in Jerusalem (1925), he wrote a list of mystical texts that needed to be published in scholarly editions. At the top of his list he put *Sefer ha-Ḥayim (The Book of Life)*, an esoteric work he connected with the Ashkenazi Hasidim. See Gershom Scholem, *Devarim Be-Go* (Tel Aviv: Am Oved, 1976), vol. 1, p. 65.

2. See J. Dan, *The Esoteric Theology of the Ashkenazi Hasidim* [Hebrew] (Jerusalem: Mosad Bialik, 1968) [henceforth cited as *The Esoteric Theology*], pp. 14–20. Rabbi Aaron of Baghdad was the subject of an interesting controversy between Scholem and Israel Weinstock. The latter claimed to have discovered the key to identify the works of R. Aaron using the system of *gematria*, i.e., computations of the numerical value of Hebrew letters. Weinstock argued that Aaron identified himself with the angelic

name Adiriron, and ascribed to him every appearance of this name or its numerical value. Scholem responded to Weinstock in great detail, analyzing the manuscript he used (British Museum 752), and ultimately disproving his thesis. Scholem could not refrain from noting that the numerical value of Adiriron is exactly that of the name Weinstock! See I. Weinstock, "Discovered Legacy of Mystic Writings left by Abu Aaron of Baghdad" (Hebrew), *Tarbiz,* 32 (1963), pp. 153–59, and Scholem's response, "Has a Legacy been discovered of Mystic Writings left by Abu Aaron of Baghdad?" (Hebrew), ibid., pp. 262–66. Cf. also Weinstock's rejoinder, "Otzar ha-Sodot shel'Abu 'Aharon: dimyon 'o metzi'ut?", *Sinai,* 54 (1964), pp. 226–59.

3. A. Grossman recently published a new study of the historical problems involved with the story of the immigration of the Kalonymus family from Italy to Germany which cast some doubt about the accuracy of the traditions quoted by Rabbi Eleazar. See A. Grossman, "The Migration of the Kalonimos Family from Italy to Germany" (Hebrew), *Zion,* 40 (1975), pp. 154–85. The history of this family requires further study before a clear historical picture will emerge.

4. See J. Dan, *The Esoteric Theology,* pp. 15–20. Cf. I. Weinstock's study of the chronology of R. Aaron's arrival in Italy, *Hekhal Shlomo Annual* (1964), pp. 2–25.

5. See G. Scholem, *Major Trends,* pp. 41, 84, and 355, n. 2.

6. The story is included in "The Chronicle of Ahumaʿaz. See B. Klar, ed., *Megilat Ahumaʿaz,* (Jerusalem, 1944), pp. 13–26. Cf. J. Dan, "The Beginnings of Jewish Mysticism in Europe," in C. Roth, ed., *The World History of the Jewish People, Second Series: Medieval Period, Vol. II: The Dark Ages* (Tel Aviv, 1966), pp. 282–90.

7. See A. Grossman, op. cit., pp. 174–83. Grossman concluded that it was chronologically impossible for any emperor by the name of Karl (Charles) to have been involved in this immigration. He suspected that Rabbi Eleazar was carried away by the legends of Charles the Great, and therefore the whole story is legendary. The difficulty with this view is that we do not find in Ashkenazi Hasidic literature any reference to Charles the Great and there is no reason to believe that his legends were known to them.

8. G. Scholem, *Major Trends,* pp. 80–118.

9. An example of the attitude of the Ashkenazi Hasidim to the Hekhalot hymns is discussed in J. Dan, "The Ashkenazi Hasidic Commen-

taries on ha-ʾAderet veha-ʾEmunah" (Hebrew), *Tarbiẓ,* 50 (1981), pp. 369–404. Cf. J. Dan, *Studies in Ashkenazi Hasidic Literature* [Hebrew] (Ramat Gan, 1975), pp. 52–57.

10. One of the most important examples is that of the book *Raza Rabbah (The Great Secret),* some quotations of which Scholem discovered in the works of an Ashkenazi descendant of the Rabbi Judah the Pious and published as an appendix to *Reshit ha-Qabbalah* (Jerusalem: Schocken, 1948), pp. 195–238. Another example pointed out by Scholem is the *Sefer ha-Kavod she-masar ha-Malakh le-RabbiʿAkiva, (The Book of Divine Glory given by the Angel to Rabbi Akiva).* See ibid., pp. 65, 205; and cf. J. Dan, *The Esoteric Theology,* p. 56, n. 21 and p. 206.

11. Rabbi Eleazar's commentary was printed in Przemishel, 1883 [reprinted in Brooklyn, 1978]. Another commentary on *Sefer Yeẓirah* stemming from the Hasidei Ashkenaz was that of Rabbi Judah the Pious, now lost, which was known to Abraham Abulafia, a kabbalist of the second half of the thirteenth century.

12. An Ashkenazi Hasidic theological work, *Sefer ha-Navon (The Book of the Wise),* contains a commentary on the *Shiur Komah.* See J. Dan, *Studies in Ashkenazi Hasidic Literature,* pp. 112–33.

13. See J. Dan, "The Ashkenazi Hasidic Commentaries on ha-ʾAderet veha-ʾEmunah," *Tarbiẓ,* 50 (1981), pp. 396–404.

14. Rabbi Eleazar wrote a book on the process of creation, which constituted the first treatise in his large collection of esoteric works, *Sodei Razaya (The Secrets of Secrets).* The book was organized in the form of a commentary on the 22 letters of the Hebrew alphabet. A part of the book was printed in the anthology, *Sefer Raziel* (Amsterdam, 1701), beginning on fol. 7a.

15. For references, see above, ch. 2, n. 85. See also G. Scholem, *Kabbalah,* pp. 351–55.

16. A story about Rabbi Samuel the Pious and his created servant is found in the hagiographic cycle of stories on the Ashkenazi Hasidim which served as a basis for the hagiographical part of the early collection of stories in Yiddish, the *Maʿaseh Buch.* See *Ma aseh Book: Book of Jewish Tales and Legends,* translated by M. Gaster, new ed., (Philadelphia: Jewish Publication Society, 1981), p. 335. The Yiddish version of the story omitted the reference to the golem which was preserved in the Hebrew source. See G. Scholem, *On the Kabbalah and Its Symbolism,* translated by Ralph Manheim (New York: Schocken, 1965), p. 198.

17. Scholem discussed this phenomenon in *Major Trends*, pp. 102, 11–113.

18. See G. Scholem, *Major Trends*, p. 102. A version of the "Questions and Answers from Heaven" was attributed to Eleazar of Worms. Scholem paid particular attention to the Ashkenazi Hasidic tradition concerning a special ritual to be followed before a rabbi could transmit the secret of the Holy Name to the disciple. The ritual is described in the first part of Eleazar's *Sefer ha-Shem*, extant in several manuscripts, e.g. Munich 81 and British Museum 737. See G. Scholem, *On the Kabbalah and Its Symbolism*, p. 136, and cf. J. Dan, *The Esoteric Theology*, pp. 74–76.

19. The three most important manuscripts of this central work differ considerably from each other, differences which may have resulted from the author's own editing. They are: Ms. Oxford Bodleian Lib., Neubauer Catalogue no. 1204; Ms. Paris 772; and Ms. Vienna 108. See J. Dan, *The Esoteric Theology*, p. 65.

20. On this work, see J. Dan, "The Emergence of Mystical Prayer," in J. Dan and F. Talmage, eds., *Studies in Jewish Mysticism* (Cambridge: Association for Jewish Studies, 1982) pp. 87–93.

21. See ibid., pp. 91–92.

22. Cf. G. Scholem, *Major Trends*, pp. 100–02.

23. The first translations of philosophical works by Judah ibn Tibbon were not known to the Ashkenazi Hasidim in the beginning of the thirteenth century. The first Ashkenazi Hasid who used this material (along with other sources from Spain) seems to have been Eleazar's disciple, Abraham ben Azriel of Bohemia, who wrote the voluminous commentary on the piyyutim entitled 'Arugat ha-Boshem. The work was published in four volumes by E. E. Urbach (Jerusalem: Mekize Nirdamim, 1939–64), with a detailed introduction in vol. 4. See my review of this work in *Studies in Ashkenazi Hasidic Literature*, pp. 58–71.

24. See I. Baer, "The Social and Religious Background of the *Sefer Ḥasidim*" (Hebrew), *Zion*, (1938), pp. 1–50. Baer concluded that the Ashkenazi Hasidim were familiar with Latin and were acquainted with theological works of their Christian neighbors. The only further support for this possibility was supplied by G. Vajda in his study of the works of Elhanan ben Yaqar of London. See Vajda, "De quelques infiltrations chrétiennes dans l'oeuvre d'un auteur anglo-juif du XIIIe siècle," *Archives d'Histoire Doctrinale et Littéraire du Moyen Âge* (1961), pp. 15–34. Vajda

presented examples which attested to the fact that Elhanan, who wrote his commentary on *Sefer Yezirah* after 1230, was familiar with some sections of Christian theological works. We do not, however, have any proof that Judah the Pious or Eleazar of Worms knew any Latin or that they were using Latin theological works in any way.

25. See Scholem's comment on the paraphrase in *Kabbalah*, p. 38.

26. Scholem commented on this work in *Major Trends*, p. 374, n. 90. Cf. G. Scholem, *Reshit ha-Qabbalah*, pp. 211, 224–25. See J. Dan, "Introduction," *Shir ha-Yihud: The Hymn of Divine Unity, Thiengen 1560* (Jerusalem: The Jewish National and University Library Press, 1981), pp. 7–22.

27. This section from R. Judah's esoteric work was published in J. Dan, *Studies in Ashkenazi Hasidic Literature*, pp. 152–60.

28. See *Hokhmat ha-Nefesh* (Lvov, 1876), f. 7a–b, following ibn Ezra's commentary to Exodus 22:22.

29. See G. Scholem, "The Idea of the Golem," *On the Kabbalah and Its Symbolism*, p. 190. This story is included in an Ashkenazi Hasidic commentary on *Sefer Yezirah* attributed to Saadia Gaon but written by the circle of mystics who followed the tradition of Jonathan ben Uzziel; see below, n.38.

30. See G. Scholem, "Reste neuplatonischer Speculation bei den deutschen Chassidim," *Monatsschrift für Geschichte und Wissenschaft des Judentums*, 75 (1931), pp. 172–91.

31. Judah the Pious did not know the *Kuzari* itself. However, he heard a story, probably originating from a false description of the book, about an Arab king in Spain who was converted to Judaism and used this story as a format for a theological work in which several Jewish scholars argue with that king. See J. Dan, *Studies in Ashkenazi Hasidic Literature*, pp. 26–33.

32. The only part of this work that is extant was published by A. Kircheim on *Otzar Nehmad* (Vienna, 1980), vol. 3, pp. 54–99.

33. For Scholem's comments on Moses Taku, see his study "New Contributions to the Biography of R. Joseph Ashkenazi of Safed" (Hebrew), *Tarbiz*, 28 (1959), pp. 59–89, 201–35.

34. Concerning this problem, see above, ch. 3, pp. 85–86.

35. The doctrine of kavod was discussed by Scholem, *Major Trends*, pp. 11–16; see J. Dan, *The Esoteric Theology*, pp. 104–68.

36. See I. Marcus, *Piety and Society* (Leiden: E. J. Brill, 1980), pp.

109–29. Marcus pointed out deep differences between Eleazar of Worms and his teacher, Judah the Pious, with respect to their attitude toward ethical problems.

37. See *Sefer ha-Hayim* (Jerusalem, 1977), pp. 4–5.

38. The literature and traditions of this unique circle of mystics were described by me in *Studies in Ashkenazi Hasidic Literature*, pp. 89–111.

39. See G. Scholem, *Major Trends*, pp. 113–14.

40. See J. Dan, "The Emergence of Mystical Prayer," pp. 94–101.

41. For a list of the main treatises written by members of this group, see J. Dan, *Studies in Ashkenazi Hasidic Literature*, pp. 72–88.

42. The problem of the appearance of some symbols in the works of Eleazar of Worms which closely resemble kabbalistic terminology was discussed by Scholem in *Reshit ha-Qabbalah*, p. 37, n. 1, and p. 60, n. 3. Cf. G. Scholem, *Ursprung und Anfänge der Kabbala*, pp. 162–66. See also J. Dan, *The Esoteric Theology*, pp. 118–29, where I tried to show that these terms appear in a text attributed to Rav Hai Gaon which was received by Eleazar as an ancient tradition.

43. Scholem discussed *Sefer Hasidim* and its teachings in *Major Trends*, pp. 88–106. The edition of the book he used was published by J. Wistinetzki and J. Freimann (Frankfurt am Main: Wahrmann, 1924). An inferior edition was later published by R. Margaliot (Jerusalem: Mosad ha-Rav Kook, 1957). The latter was based on the traditional printed edition of Bologna, 1538, and contains little more than half the material contained in the Parma manuscript used by Wistinetzki and Freimann. For a survey of previous scholarship on the subject, see I. Marcus, *Piety and Society*, pp. 2–10; see my review of this work in *Tarbiz*, 51 (1982), pp. 319–25.

44. A. Epstein, for instance, who called his studies of Ashkenazi Hasidim "The Ashkenazi Kabbalah," completely separated their theology from their ethics. See A. Epstein, *Qadmoniyot ha-Yehudim*, edited by A. M. Haberman (Jerusalem, 1957), pp. 226–50.

45. In this Scholem agreed with Baer who in his detailed study, "The Social and Religious History of *Sefer Hasidim*" (see above, n. 24), pointed out similarities between Ashkenazi Hasidic ethics and contemporary attitudes in Christianity; see G. Scholem, *Major Trends*, pp. 83–86.

46. See G. Scholem, *Major Trends*, pp. 96–97, and see below, n. 48.

47. On Ashkenazi Hasidic demonology, see M. Guedemann, *Geschichte des Erzichungswesens und der Kultur der Juden in Frankreich und Deutschland*

(Vienna, 1880), vol. 1, ch. 7; J. Trachtenberg, *Jewish Magic and Superstition* (Philadelphia: Jewish Publication Society, 1939). See also J. Dan, *The Esoteric Theology,* pp. 184–202, and *Studies in Ashkenazi Hasidic Literature,* pp. 9–25, 34–43.

48. It should be pointed out that while Baer and Scholem were certain that Ashkenazi Hasidic ethics was deeply influenced, in several instances, by the surrounding Christian culture, studies in the last twenty years by I. Marcus, H. Soloveitchik, and me have failed in their attempts to substantiate this claim with specific examples of influence. The subject should be viewed as still uncertain and awaiting further study.

49. On the attitude of Ashkenazi Jewry to *kiddush ha-shem,* see I. Baer, op. cit., pp. 3–6, and cf. his study of the 1096 persecutions in *Asaf Jubilee Volume* (Jerusalem, 1953), pp. 126–40.

50. I. Tishby stressed this aspect of Ashkenazi Hasidic ethics. See J. Dan, *Hebrew Ethical and Homiletical Literature* [Hebrew] (Jerusalem, 1975), pp. 143–44.

51. These and other key elements in Ashkenazi Hasidic ethics were studied in great depth by H. Soloveitchik, "Three Themes in the *Sefer Hasidim,*" *Association for Jewish Studies Review,* 1 (1976), pp. 311–57.

52. The exegesis is based on an interpretation of the fact that the stork in Aramaic is called *hivarita,* i.e., "white," whereas in Hebrew it is called *hasidah,* i.e., "pious," thus equating "white" with "pious" and concluding that a pietist is one who lets his face be "whitened," that is, insulted, in public. See Wistinetzki and Freimann, eds., *Sefer Hasidim,* sec. 975, pp. 240–41.

53. See G. Scholem, *Major Trends,* pp. 96–97. Tishby raised the objection that *Sefer Hasidim* cannot really be regarded as supporting ataraxia insomuch as it gives great importance to the honor of the pious in paradise. See J. Dan, *Hebrew Ethical and Homiletical Literature,* p. 142.

54. On the Ashkenazi Hasidic literature concerning repentance, see I. Marcus, "*Hasidei Ashkenaz* Private Penitentials: An Introduction and Descriptive Catalogue of their Manuscripts and Early Editions," in J. Dan and F. Talmage, eds., *Studies in Jewish Mysticism,* pp. 57–83.

55. See G. Scholem, *Major Trends,* pp. 104–05.

56. A description of the righteous in paradise sitting around the Shekhinah was given by R. Eleazar in *Hokhmat ha-Nefesh* (Lvov, 1876), f. 1 a–c.

57. This tradition probably originated in the circle of R. Jacob and

R. Isaac, sons of R. Jacob ha-Cohen. See G. Scholem, *Ursprung und An-fänge der Kabbala,* pp. 85–88.

58. A survey of works written in this manner, a combination of Ash-kenazi Hasidism and kabbalah, can be found in J. Dan, *The Esoteric The-ology,* pp. 251–62.

59. This subject, which is part of the tradition describing the divine world in the form of a nut and its shells, was discussed by A. Altmann, "Eleazar of Worms' *Ḥokhmat ha-ʾEgoz," Journal of Jewish Studies,* 11 (1960), pp. 101–13, and by me in *The Esoteric Theology,* pp. 207–10; *"Ḥokhmat ha-ʾEgoz,* its Origins and Development," *Journal of Jewish Studies,* 17 (1966), pp. 73–82, and in "On the History of the Text of *Ḥokhmat ha-ʾEgoz"* (Hebrew), *Alei Sefer,* 5 (1978), pp. 49–53.

60. Examples of such an influence are presented in J. Dan, "Samael, Lilith and the Concept of Evil in Early Kabbalah," *Association for Jewish Studies Review,* 5 (1980), pp. 17–40.

61. See J. Dan, *Hebrew Ethical and Homiletical Literature,* pp. 202–30.

CHAPTER 5

THE ENIGMATIC BOOK
BAHIR

I

MONG THE RIDDLES that Jewish mysticism presented him with, none bothered Gershom Scholem more
than the enigma of the book *Bahir,* the first book of the
kabbalah, which became known in southern France at the end
of the twelfth century. Scholem wrote his Ph.D. thesis at the
University at Munich on this book, preparing a German
translation of the work and a commentary which included an
anlysis of the sources and kabbalistic works that used sections
from it.[1] Scholem, however, was very far from satisfied with
the work he had done in his early twenties on this subject.
He later reopened the whole problem of the emergence of the
kabbalah in medieval Europe and wrote his first detailed description of the nature of the book *Bahir* and its place in the
history of Jewish mysticism. A lengthy paper was published
in 1945,[2] summing up the results of this examination. That
paper was the basis of a small book published in 1948 entitled *The Beginnings of the Kabbalah.*[3] The book had several

important appendices dealing with central problems of the early kabbalah, concerning the works of the Iyyun circle[4] and quotations from the ancient Jewish mystical work *The Great Secret (Raza Rabba),*[5] which had an important bearing on the understanding of the book *Bahir.*

Scholem continued to work on the book *Bahir* while completing his major work on the Sabbatian movement. In 1960 Scholem began a four-year lecture series on the beginnings of the kabbalah, using the notes he had prepared for a revised and enlarged version of *The Beginnings of the Kabbalah.* (The revised work was published in Berlin in 1962.)[6] Between 1960 and 1963, four volumes of his edited lectures on the early kabbalah were published in Jerusalem.[7] The enigma of the book *Bahir* was central to all these works.

Scholem also dedicated a two-year seminar to a systematic reading of the *Bahir.*

Scholem based his 1920 translation of the *Bahir* on the Munich manuscript of the book.[8] This proved to be the oldest and one of the most reliable manuscripts of this work.[9] Much later Scholem discovered that the manuscript carried the emblem of Pico de la Mirandola, a great Italian scholar and philosopher of the late fifteenth century, who was the founder of the Christian kabbalah and probably the first non-Jew to learn Hebrew in order to read kabbalistic texts in the original.[10] With luck and intuition Scholem identified the book *Bahir* as the first work to contain kabbalistic symbolism. He thus rejected Adolf Jellinek's suggestion that the earliest work of the kabbalah was *Masechet Azilut (A Tractate on the Divine Emanations),*[11] which Scholem proved to be a much later work.[12]

II

Scholem faced an interrelated combination of chronological, literary, historical, and ideological problems concerning the *Bahir*. For example, any conclusion concerning literary style immediately influenced the ideological side; chronology and history were very closely interconnected. Still, when presenting Scholem's conclusions in this chapter we shall try to deal with them one after another, and in the final section we shall present a general picture of the book and its impact on the history of Jewish mysticism.

The book *Bahir* is written in the form of a traditional Midrash. It is divided into many sections, each of which is a complete literary and thematic unit that could be presented as a brief independent treatise, even though the units are often connected, in ideas, terminology, or literary form, to the preceding or following sections. Scholem arranged the book into 130 such sections in his translation because the manuscripts and the traditional printed versions did not contain any systematic division of the text.

In each section there is a speaker, a rabbi to whom the homiletical interpretation of a biblical verse, of which almost every section contained at least one example and often more than one, is attributed. Some of these rabbis are prominent tannaim, like Rabbi Akiba; many sections are attributed to fictional characters, like "Rabbi Amora," who is probably a generalized representative of all of the amoraim.

The first section in the book is attributed to Rabbi Nehunia ben ha-Kanah, a relatively obscure tanna who earned a prominent place in the early mystical work *Hekhalot Rabbati* as the teacher of Rabbi Ishmael.[13] He therefore was reputed to be the leader of the circle of mystics of *Hekhalot* literature. Because of this attribution, the book *Bahir* as a whole was thought to be by Rabbi Nehunia, and some kabbalists referred to it as the "Midrash of Rabbi Nehunia ben ha-Kanah."

The chronological problem, therefore, begins with the question of whether or not the *Bahir* was an ancient mystical Midrash. Scholem decided that the *Bahir* was a twelfth-century work and not an ancient Midrash, based on the works of two of the greatest Jewish writers in Spain in the first half the twelfth century, Rabbi Abraham bar Hijja, the philosopher whose neo-Platonic material was used by the Ashkenazi Hasidim,[14] and the great halachist from Barcelona, Rabbi Judah ben Barzilai, who wrote a detailed commentary on *Sefer Yezirah*.[15] Scholem discovered a close connection between a homiletical interpretation of the first chapter of Genesis in bar Hijja's book, *Hegyon ha-Nefesh (Contemplation of the Soul)*[16] and the description of the creation of matter and form in the opening paragraphs of the *Bahir*. Both understand the biblical phrase *tohu va-bohu* (Genesis 1:2, "null and void") to refer to the creation of matter and form in the Aristotelian sense of these terms. Creation necessitated the combination of matter with the spiritual element, the form. These are the true philosophical meanings of the terms *tohu* and *bohu,* according to Abraham bar Hijja.

The *Bahir* explained the creation as the result of the combination of matter and spirit, using the same homiletical elements—the traditional Midrashic connection between *tohu* and "nothing" *("davar ha-matheh bnei adam")*[17] and the medieval interpretation of *bohu* as "spirit."[18] According to the structure of bar Hijja's homily this seems to have been his original contribution. Therefore, the *Bahir* as we have it today cannot be earlier than the second half of the twelfth century.

While his comparison between bar Hijja and the *Bahir* rested on positive proofs, Scholem's analysis of the relationship between Rabbi Judah ben Barzilai and the *Bahir* rested on an argument *ex silentio*. Rabbi Judah was one of the greatest scholars of his time. He was not only interested in Talmudic exegesis, but also with the collection of ancient material pertaining to every problem he dealt with. His halachic works contain a deep knowledge of the literature of the gaonim, and his commentary on *Sefer Yezirah* is a vast anthology of ancient material and medieval sources related to the problems associated with the book. Rabbi Judah included in this work large sections from Rav Saadia Gaon's commentary on the same work, as well as many quotations from Saadia's other works (some of them unknown from any other source), which elucidated the Gaon's understanding of the problems of creation, revelation, and cosmology. Similarly, he included large sections from the *Hekhalot* mystical literature, and from early Jewish works on scientific and cosmological matters. Some of the works used by Rabbi Judah have been lost, and his quotations from them are our only remaining source. It is evident that Rabbi Judah saw his main duty as a commentator on *Sefer Yezirah* to collect all the material he could that had any bearing on mystical, cosmological, or cosmogonical problems in ancient and medieval Hebrew literature. He had the resources to be as exhaustive as possible.

Scholem thus came to the conclusion that it was unimaginable that a whole sphere of Jewish mystical, cosmogonical, and cosmological thought could be completely unknown to Rabbi Judah ben Barzilai in Barcelona.[19] He might not have been exhaustive concerning every detail, but if the basic kabbalistic terminology and the major ideas of the *Bahir* existed when he was working on his commentary on *Sefer Yezirah*, they would have been included in one way or another. This omission from such a major work seemed to Scholem to substantiate the conclusion that the *Bahir* as it is known to us could not have existed before the second half of the twelfth century.

The dating of the parts of the *Bahir* was also based on a close philological analysis of the various sections of the *Bahir*. But this could date only the analyzed sections and not the book as a whole. Scholem decided that the *Bahir* should be studied section by section, term by term, so that while the book was undoubtedly edited only a short time before it began to be used by the early kabbalists in southern Europe, its terminology and ideas could have been the product of much earlier periods. Scholem thought that some of the innovative ideas and terms used by the *Bahir* must have an early, Eastern source.

Some such sources are obvious. Some selections in the *Bahir* include terms and exegeses used in the *Sefer Yezirah;* whole sections from the ancient book of cosmogony were interwoven into the fabric of the *Bahir,* although a word or a term might be changed to alter the meaning of the sections to some extent.[20] In a similar way, the *Bahir* included many paragraphs taken from, or based on, the *Hekhalot* mystical literature, beginning with lists of names of supreme powers to the characteristic terminology of the "descenders to the chariot."[21]

Ancient mystical and cosmological Midrashim were used extensively in the *Bahir*.[22] But, Scholem insisted, the *Bahir* must have had some other Eastern sources which were not preserved in the *Hekhalot* or Midrashic literatures. Philology revealed the impact of Arabic in several cases on the homiletical interpretations of biblical verses in the *Bahir,* and the study of its ideas revealed that some gnostic sources, which did not leave any other impression on Hebrew mystical works, were known to the *Bahir* and influenced its terminology and theology.

Scholem, again, described the book *Bahir* as a medieval work of Jewish mysticism, edited in the second half of the twelfth century in the form that it became known to the early kabbalists in Europe and is known to us today. But this relied on a series of ancient sources, many of them now lost to us. These sources included the gnostic tendencies which formulated kabbalah as a gnostic mystical school of thought.

III

The gnostic character of the book *Bahir* is based on the conception of the divine tree, the *ilan*. It has ten branches, one above the other. They constitute the divine *pleroma,* which the *Bahir* calls by the Hebrew term *male* or *milo,* a very probable translation of the Greek term.[23] This concept, which cannot be found in any of the earlier Hebrew sources, is what allows us to call the book *Bahir* "kabbalistic" and claim it to be the first kabbalistic work in the history of Jewish mysticism. The system of the ten divine emanations, which the

kabbalists usually called *sefirot,* using the *Sefer Yezirah* terminology even though the meaning is completely different,[24] is
presented here for the first time. The later formulations of
this system rested, completely or in part, on the cryptic
homiletical paragraphs of the *Bahir.*

Scholem was convinced that this system of ten divine powers organized in the form of a *pleroma* symbolized by a divine
tree was not an invention of a twelfth-century Jewish mystic
in Europe. He felt that the medieval editor of the *Bahir* must
have received it from an earlier Eastern source. His view was
strengthened by his discovery of an Ashkenazi Hasidic commentary on the *Shiur Komah,* written in Germany in the thirteenth century, which includes quotations from a book called
Sefer ha-Sod ha-Gadol, or, in Aramaic, *Raza Rabba (The Great
Secret).*[25] This work, of which we have only these very late
quotations, is mentioned in lists of esoteric works that had
been written in the gaonic period. There is no doubt, therefore, that this work, which is quoted in the thirteenth-century commentary on the *Shiur Komah,* is an ancient one, originating in the East, and by chance was not used by other,
earlier writers in works which reached us.[26]

The extant quotations from the *Raza Rabba,* or *Sefer ha-Sod
ha-Gadol,* are identical or similar to some of the sections of
the book *Bahir.* The relationship is unmistakable. However,
the few quotations that we have from the *Raza Rabba* cannot
answer all our questions concerning the date of the *Bahir*
because the author of the Ashkenazi commentary on the *Shiur
Komah* was familiar with the *Bahir* itself and quoted it very
often (sometimes he even combined quotations from the *Raza
Rabba* with those from the *Bahir*). Indeed, in some cases it is

difficult to be completely sure whether the *Bahir* is being quoted or the *Raza Rabba.* This problem is especially crucial concerning the system of the ten divine emanations which constitute the divine tree. There is a possibility that the *Raza Rabba* included a reference to the divine tree, but the text itself prohibits us from stating that as an established fact. Could this quote be interpreted syntactically, it could determine whether the system of the ten emanations is known to us only from later twelfth-century sources, or if it existed within Judaism many centuries earlier.

Several references to the basic symbols of the book *Bahir,* like *keter elyon,* "the supreme crown," for the highest divine power, or the way that the *shekhinah* is described, are found in the works of Rabbi Eleazar of Worms and other Ashkenazi writers. In addition, kabbalists in the second half of the thirteenth century described the history of their tradition as being brought from Eretz Israel to Germany, and then transferred from the sages of Germany to Provence and to Spain. Gershom Scholem, with these facts in mind, proposed that the tradition of the book *Bahir* might have been transmitted to southern France via the Jewish esoteric circles in Germany. The scarcity of early Ashkenazic references to terms and quotes from the *Bahir* makes this a very difficult conclusion, but we do not have as yet a better alternative.[27]

Scholem felt that the picture of the divine tree and its ten divine branches attested to the reliance of the sources of the *Bahir* on ancient gnostic mythology and theology. He was very careful not to accept the obvious alternative: the influence of the contemporary gnosticism of twelfth-century southern France, namely the Catharist, or Albigensian, gnostic movement. While taking into account the chronological connection between this major spiritual upheaval in Christian society and the emergence of gnostic mythology in Jewish academies, Scholem still sought more evidence of connections between the Catharist movement and the *Bahir* or the early kabbalists. Though he spent much effort in an analysis of our meager knowledge of the Cathars' theology, he found no conclusive proof of a direct historical connection between them.[28] Scholem concluded that the gnostic symbols of the *pleroma* and others were not transmitted to the kabbalists from the gnostics around them, but were received from the East in works like *Raza Rabba.* They were transmitted, probably via the esoteric schools of the Ashkenazi Hasidim, to the mystics of southern Europe, who were ready to absorb them because of the great impact of the Catharist religious insurrection.

IV

The most important gnostic element in the *Bahir* is the list of the ten *ma'marot*, or *logoi*, which constitute the divine *pleroma* in the *Bahir*, which is similar in many respects to the gnostic myth of the *aeons.*[29] But Scholem, when studying the *Bahir*, emphasized another intriguing myth—the myth of the *shekhinah*.

The early kabbalists, and certainly the later ones, especially the *Zohar*, concentrated an important part of their mythical descriptions and their theological speculations on the feminine power within the divine realm, called by them *malchut* or *shekhinah*. This power was the tenth and lowest of the divine emanations, but the closest to man and to religious and visionary contact. This power is described in kabbalistic texts as the heavenly mother, as the bride and wife of the Godhead, as the divine daughter, as both the opponent of the evil powers and their first victim, and in many other ways.[30] The concept of the *shekhinah* is central to ancient Jewish theology and mysticism. In early Talmudic and Midrashic sources the *shekhinah* is described only as one of the names, or one of the aspects, of the supreme Godhead itself, and not as a separate power.[31] When it later began to be described as a separate, lower power, identified with the revealed divine glory, it still did not have any feminine characteristic. It is the kabbalah alone which first presented the concept of male-female dualism within the divine realm and thus created the mythology of love, sex, and family within the *pleroma*.

The gnostic origins of this myth are quite obvious, even though the details do not always correspond to the many aspects of the divine feminine figure in ancient gnostic mysticism. The kabbalists received it from their Eastern Judaized gnostic sources. Scholem presented the possibility that the *Bahir* was the first work to reach us that contained the main elements of this most profound symbolism.

The analysis of the role of the feminine power in the symbolism of the *Bahir* is extremely difficult because of the literary character of the book. The *Bahir* is full of parables in the classic format of the Midrashic parables, especially those which compare God to an earthly king.[32] In classical Talmudic and Midrashic literature many theological problems, discussing the relationship between God and the world, in-

clude parables beginning with *"mashal le-melech basar va-dam
. . . ."* " 'it is similar to a king of flesh and blood . . .' "
Sometimes, in these ancient parables, the figure of *knesset Yisrael,* "the congregation of the people of Israel," is mentioned
in relationship to this flesh-and-blood king; it assumes feminine attributes within the narrative of the parable. The authors—or the sources—of the *Bahir* included many parables
that followed this pattern. Several of them describe the figure
of the *matronit,* "the queen," or the *bat-melech,* "the princess,"
as a divine power, the daughter or wife of the king, which is
always the Godhead itself.

The problem of determining how much can be learned from
the narrative and details of a parable concerning the reality it
intends to convey is very pertinent in this juncture. If the
parables in the *Bahir*—which are undoubtedly most profound
and central to its innovative symbolism[33]—are to be transferred accurately to the realm of the divine powers which they
intend to describe, there can be no doubt that the *Bahir* contains a myth of a feminine divine power, very similar to some
of the gnostic descriptions of such a power. However, if we
remember that in the classical Talmudic parables of this genre
a feminine figure is often found in the narrative even though
there is nothing feminine in the real counterpart of that figure, much care and hesitation are called for before concluding
that a myth of a feminine divine power existed. Scholem was
very circumspect when discussing it. He relied heavily on
some unusual descriptions of the feminine power in the *Bahir,* such as the image of the *shekhinah* as the "daughter of
light" *(bat ha-or,* which is almost literally the same as the
gnostic *nurea),* who is in exile from the source of light, to

suggest that it is very probable that the *Bahir* is the first Jewish mystical text to describe a feminine divine power in mythological terms, thus serving as a source for later kabbalistic speculation and the enormous eruption of mythological and sexual symbolism which is one of the most prominent characteristics of the kabbalah as a whole.

V

Another theme in the book *Bahir,* which had great impact on later kabbalists, is the dualism of good and evil elements within the Godhead or its messengers.[34] Many of the paragraphs in the *Bahir* which deal with this are extremely obscure in language and symbolism. Scholem did not describe the theology of the *Bahir* as being dualistic in the full religious meaning of the term, namely that there is a mythological struggle between good and evil within the Godhead itself. It seems that in the *Bahir* evil is a divine messenger which serves a divine purpose, emanating from the divine tree like all other phenomena which constitute the celestial and earthly reality.[35] The dualism has, however, some symbolical formulations which laid the basis for the development of much more radical and profound dualism in the kabbalah of the late thirteenth century on.

The *Bahir* finds the source of all evil in the feminine aspect of existence.[36] The editor of the work included in its concluding paragraph an adapted version of the story of Satan, called here Samael (the ancient appellation for Christianity and the Roman Empire in the *Hekhalot* texts), and the original sin of Adam and Eve in Paradise, as described in the eighth-century Midrashic narrative, the *"Pirqey de-Rabbi Eliezer."*[37] This is the earliest and clearest description of an independent satanic force in Hebrew before the development of the kabbalah. It is also the source of the profound symbolism of the snake, which became central to Zoharic and later kabbalah. The *Bahir* described the evil powers in the created world as the fingers of the left hand of God,[38] serving as agents for every deed of evil needed by the divine program.

This character of the evil powers in the mythology of the *Bahir* proves that the last element of classical gnosticism to be accepted by Judaism in any way was the dualistic myth of good and evil. *Hekhalot* mysticism did not adopt it. The first appearance of the stark, gnostic dualism familiar from Marcionite, Ophitic, and Manichaean sources cannot be found in the kabbalah until the second half of the thirteenth century, and then it is expressed in ways which are very difficult, if not completely impossible, to explain as resulting from external influences. It seems that Jewish symbols and mystical drives independently produced an extremely close parallel to ancient gnostic dualism.[39]

Another concept in the book *Bahir,* which Scholem presented and discussed in all its perplexing aspects, is the belief in the transmigration of souls. According to the *Bahir* (in a section attributed to Rabbi Akiba), the souls of every new generation are those of the older, departing one.[40] This belief is stated without any qualification or hesitation, as a well-known, traditionally accepted truth. It is, however, the first positive expression of such a belief in Jewish literature.[41] Previous Jewish writers (most prominently Rav Saadia Gaon) categorically and unhesitatingly rejected that belief when they referred it, which they did very seldom. It is, therefore, most peculiar to find a Hebrew work accepting and praising an idea so vehemently denied by all previous Jewish sources.

The belief in transmigration raised a basic question concerning the circles of mystics which produced and transmitted the *Bahir*. Were they a part of any Jewish center? Did they belong to the mainstream of Jewish culture? Or were they perhaps scattered and lonely half-educated people, on the remote fringes of Jewish culture, who did not know anything about the central developments in the great academies where Jewish culture was created and developed through the ages?

Scholem discussed these questions repeatedly because he felt they were crucial to understanding the role of Jewish mysticism, as well as of its sources, within the historically unfolding fabric of Jewish culture.[42] He concluded that even though its position concerning the transmigration of souls was peculiar, it was not enough to outweigh the considerable evidence which led toward the opposite conclusion. The authors of the *Bahir* and its sources could be neither ignorant nor marginal, because they were aware of current Jewish ideas and attitudes (like bar Hijja's interpretation of the first chapter of Genesis), as well as being erudite and versed in all aspects of classical Jewish culture. The *Bahir* contains many traditional Jewish literary genres. They range from ancient interpretations of the forms of the Hebrew letters (*"Otiot de-Rabbi Akiba,"* the Midrashic compilation of the Gaonic period presented as an exegesis of the forms of the Hebrew alphabet),[43] to commentaries on the Hebrew vocalization signs and many other such elements, to commentaries on the commandments and the reasons for them (*ta'amey ha-mizvot*). The utilization, in a creative manner, of so much ancient material (like the relatively unknown Midrashim *Tadsheh* and *Konen*), and the appearance of medieval forms of terms which were used by Jewish philosophy all serve as conclusive proof that the *Bahir* is the product of a central group within Jewish culture. Even the most obscure and seemingly strange ideas in it should be regarded as constituent parts of Jewish religion of the Middle Ages.

Gershom Scholem's analysis of the Bahir *changed* to a very large extent the previously held ideas concerning the character of Jewish religious thought and religious culture both before the *Bahir* and after it. Scholem's proofs that the *Bahir* is evidence for the existence of unknown and unsuspected undercurrents within Jewish culture, which preserved and transferred ancient gnostic mythology probably for generations until they surfaced in the medieval kabbalah, change our conception of the Gaonic period. The *halakhah* was not the only aspect of Jewish culture at that time, and the material preserved in the works and responses of the gaonim should not be treated as the complete expression of all that Jews thought and felt at that time. There were many aspects to early medieval Judaism. The mysticism of the *Hekhalot* and *Merkabah* literature continued to develop, and most probably the scholars dealing with that were open to accept, preserve, and transmit other myths, symbols, and ideas. There was a mystical and mythical dimension of Judaism in the Gaonic and early medieval culture of the Jews in Europe, a more profound, rich, and radical aspect than anyone suspected before.

NOTES

1. Gershom Scholem, *Das Buch Bahir* (Leipzig: W. Drugulin, 1923). The book was printed, without the notes, in Berlin, 1923. A reprint of the 1923 Leipzig edition was published in 1933 (Berlin: Schocken) and again in 1970 (Darmstadt: Wissenschaftliche Buchgesellschaft).

2. G. Scholem, "Hathalot ha-Qabbalah," *Keneset,* 10 (1947), pp. 79–228.

3. G. Scholem *Reshit ha-Qabbalah* (Jerusalem and Tel Aviv: Schocken, 1948).

4. Concerning this thirteenth-century circle of Jewish mystics, see below ch. 6., pp. 173–74. Scholem's appendix includes a list of 32 treatises which he considered to have been written by members of this circle. See G. Scholem, *Reshit ha-Qabbalah,* pp. 255–62.

5. G. Scholem, *Reshit ha-Qabbalah,* pp. 195–238.

6. G. Scholem, *Ursprung und Anfänge der Kabbala* (Berlin: W. de Gruyter, 1962). [Hereafter cited as *Ursprung.*] The work was also published in French: *Les Origines de la Kabbale,* translated by Jean Loewenson (Paris: Aubier-Montaigne, 1966).

7. See above, ch. 1, p. 22 and n. 28 there.

8. See M. Steinschneider, *Die Hebraeischen Handschriften der K. Hof- und Staatsbibliothek in Muenchen* (Muenchen, 1875), no. 209, p. 69.

9. The date, which is clearly mentioned in the colophon of the manuscript, is 1298.

10. Concerning Pico and the beginning of the Christian kabbalah, see G. Scholem, *Kabbalah* (Jerusalem: Keter, 1974), pp. 197–99.

11. A. Jellinek published this treatise, with an introduction, in his book on early kabbalistic texts, *Answahl Kabbalistischer Mystic* (Leipzig, 1853), pp. 1–8.

12. See G. Scholem, *Ursprung,* p. 8; *Encyclopedia Judaica* (Berlin, 1929), 3: col. 801–03.

13. See above, ch. 2, p. 53–54.

14. On the relation between bar Hijja and the Ashkenazi Hasidim, see above, ch. 4, p. 104 and n. 30 there.

15. See Judah b. Barzilai, *Perush Sefer Yezirah,* edited by S. J. Halberstam (Berlin, 1885).

16. This book includes four sermons, probably delivered on Rosh Hashanah and Yom Kippur. The first of these begins with a detailed expo-

sition of creation. The book was printed with an introduction by S. Rappaport, edited and revised by A. Freimann, in 1860 (Leipzig: Druck von C. W. Vollrath). A new edition with introduction and commentary by J. Wigoder, was published in 1972 (Jerusalem: Mosad Bialik). Cf. J. Dan, *Hebrew Ethical and Homiletical Literature* [Hebrew] (Jerusalem, 1975), pp. 68–82. Bar Hijja, though a philosopher and not a mystic, devoted a major cosmological work to an astrological computation of the time in which the messiah is due to be revealed.

17. See R. Margaliot, ed., *Sefer Bahir* (Jerusalem: Mosad ha-Rav Kook, 1978), sec. 2 and 135 [G. Scholem, *Das Buch Bahir*, par. 2 and 93].

18. The homiletical interpretation is based on dividing the word *"bohu"* into two: *"bo"* and *"hu,"* i.e. "It is within it." This was regarded as a description of form within which all existence was to be found.

19. See G. Scholem, *Reshit ha-Qabbalah ve-Sefer ha-Bahir*, edited by R. Schatz (Jerusalem, 1962), p. 58; G. Scholem, *Ursprung*, pp. 40–42.

20. See, e.g., R. Margaliot, ed., *Sefer Bahir*, sec. 95 [G. Scholem, *Das Buch Bahir*, par. 64], in which a section from *Sefer Yezirah* is quoted but related to the *Bahir*'s own gnostic concept of the divine tree.

21. A list of celestial powers, following Hekhalot mysticism, is included in R. Margaliot, ed., *Sefer Bahir*, sec. 112 [G. Scholem, *Das Buch Bahir*, par. 81].

22. A striking example is the fact that the *Bahir* copied a legend concerning Samael, Adam, Eve, and the serpent from chapter thirteen of the midrashic compilation *Pirqei de-Rabbi ʾEliezer* in the concluding section, no. 200, though the editor introduced many changes in the version included in the *Bahir*.

23. Based on Deuteronomy 33:23.

24. Concerning the nature of the *sefirot* in *Sefer Yezirah*, see above, ch. 2, pp. 64–66.

25. The most important quote from *Raza Rabba*, which denotes the existence of the concept of *sefirot*, was printed by Scholem in G. Scholem, *Reshit ha-Qabbalah*, pp. 234–45.

26. One of the important considerations concerning the date of the emergence of the idea of the *pleroma* in sources of the *Sefer Bahir* is the question whether some Ashkenazi Hasidic texts contained elements of such symbolism. See above, ch. 4, pp. 116–18.

27. Scholem supported this conclusion through an analysis of several sources, some of them found in the commentary on the Bible by

R. Ephraim ben Shimshon, an Ashkenazi author whose work is found in its entirety only in manuscript (Munich 15, for example; there are two printed editions which contain only part of the commentary). See G. Scholem *Reshit ha-Qabbalah,* pp. 39–40; G. Scholem, *Ursprung,* pp. 91–93. Cf. J. Dan, *The Esoteric Theology of the Ashkenazi Hasidim* [Hebrew] (Jerusalem: Mosad Bialik, 1968), p. 117.

28. Some more recent attempts have been made to discover a connection between the early kabbalah and the Catharist movement. See, e.g., S. Shahar, "Catharism and the Beginnings of the Kabbalah in Languedoc" (Hebrew), *Tarbiz,* 40 (1971), pp. 483–507. These attempts have not uncovered any conclusive proof concerning a possible influence of the Cathars on the kabbalah, either in the *Bahir* or amongst the circle of Provençal kabbalists.

29. The sections of the *Bahir* which discuss the ten emanations, here called *ma amarot (logoi),* begin at sec. 141 [G. Scholem, par. 96]. The ten divine powers are discussed in order, but there are many interpolations which disrupt the systematic exposition.

30. For a discussion of the history of the concept of *shekhinah,* see G. Scholem, "Zur Entwicklungsgeschichte der kabbalistischen Konzeption der Schechina," *Eranos Jahrbuch,* 21 (1952), pp. 45–107 [Hebrew translation in J. Ben Shlomo, ed., *Pirqei Yesod be-havanat ha-Qabbalah u-semaleha* (Jerusalem: Mosad Bialik, 1976), pp. 259–307.

31. Concerning the concept of the *shekhinah* in talmudic and midrashic literature, see the studies cited above, ch. 3, n. 14. These studies include detailed bibliographies.

32. Some literary studies have been made on talmudic and midrashic parables. None of them, however, compares them with the use of parables in the *Bahir.*

33. Scholem discussed the nature of parables in the *Bahir* in *Ursprung,* pp. 43–58.

34. See G. Scholem, "Gut und Böse in der Kabbala," *Eranos Jahrbuch,* 30 (1961), pp. 29–67 [Hebrew translation in J. Ben Shlomo, ed., *Pirqei Yesod be-havanat ha-Qabbalah u-semaleha,* pp. 187–212].

35. One of the important problems in this context is the question whether there is in the *Bahir* an identification between matter and evil; see sec. 161–64 [G. Scholem, *Das Buch Bahir,* par. 107–10].

36. R. Margaliot, ed., *Sefer Bahir,* sec. 199 [G. Scholem, *Das Buch Bahir,* par. 140].

37. R. Margaliot, ed., *Sefer Bahir,* sec. 200 [G. Scholem, *Das Buch Bahir,* par. 141].

38. R. Margaliot, ed., *Sefer Bahir,* sec. 163 [G. Scholem, *Das Buch Bahir,* par. 109], describes the evil messengers as fingers called "evil, evil" *("ra ra").* These fingers probably represent the left hand of God.

39. On the later developments concerning the concept of evil in kabbalah, see below, ch. 7, pp. 213–17.

40. R. Margaliot, ed., *Sefer Bahir,* sec. 121 [G. Scholem, *Das Buch Bahir,* par. 86].

41. See G. Scholem, "Seelenwanderung und Sympathie der Seelen in der jüdischen Mystik," *Eranos Jahrbuch,* 24 (1955), pp. 55–118 [Hebrew translation in J. Ben Shlomo, ed., *Pirqei Yesod be-havanat ha-Qabbalah u-semaleha,* pp. 308–57]. See also G. Scholem, "A Study of the Theory of Transmigration in Kabbalah during the Thirteenth Century" (Hebrew), *Tarbiz,* 16 (1945), pp. 135–50.

42. Scholem dedicated a brief discussion to this problem in the first lecture in *Major Trends in Jewish Mysticism,* 3rd rev. ed. (New York: Schocken, 1954), and later in greater detail in "Religiöse Autorität und Mystik," *Eranos Jahrbuch,* 26 (1957), pp. 243–78. [English translation, "Religious Authority and Mysticism," *Commentary,* 38:5 (1964), pp. 31–39, and again in *On the Kabbalah and Its Symbolism,* translated by Ralph Manheim (New York: Schocken, 1965), pp. 5–31 [Hebrew translation, see J. Ben Shlomo, ed., *Pirqei Yesod be-havanat ha-Qabbalah u-semaleha,* pp. 9–35.]

43. Concerning this work, see above p. 81, n. 6.

CHAPTER 6

THE EARLY KABBALAH

I

THE HISTORIANS OF Jewish thought who preceded Gershom Scholem were perplexed by finding a way to reconcile the appearance of the first schools of the kabbalah in the late twelfth century with the fact that the period was the one in which Jewish philosophy, and especially Jewish rationalistic philosophy, reached its peak? How can a historian accept the historical fact that the first Jewish scholars who dealt in kabbalistic, mythological symbolism, were contemporaries of Maimonides, the greatest Jewish philosopher of all time, and wrote the first kabbalistic treatises at the same time that Moses ben Maimon was writing his *Guide to the Perplexed?* How could two such extremes exist in the same cultural and historical circumstances?

Heinrich Graetz was especially concerned, for he viewed the kabbalah as inherently un-Jewish and polytheistic, the opposite of everything he regarded as meaningful and important in Jewish culture. The kabbalah represented everything that Judaism should not be, while Maimonidean philosophy

was the culmination of the pure Jewish rationalistic monotheism, when the spirit of Judaism achieved at last its ut-
most purity. Naturally enough, Graetz and other Jewish rationalists in the nineteenth century had to explain the
appearance of the kabbalah; they claimed it was the reemergence of ancient paganism and a reactionary response to the
great achievements of Jewish philosophy.[1] Under these circumstances, a serious, historically impartial investigation of
the background and historical circumstances of the early circles of kabbalists in Europe was impossible.

Others, such as David Neumark in this century,[2] believed
that an element of irrationalism, mysticism, and mythology
had always been present within Judaism, and that it emerged
in the twelfth and thirteenth centuries in response to the
atmosphere created by Jewish rationalism. But both he and
Graetz could not view the kabbalah as an entity by itself.
They believed that the appearance of the kabbalah could not
be but a response to the greater, more important, and religiously perfect phenomenon of rationalistic philosophy.

Gershom Scholem did not reject the work of earlier historians completely, even though he rejected their attitude toward
the kabbalah without reservation. He believed that there was
in the early kabbalah an element of response and reaction to
Jewish philosophy; there was in the kabbalah an element of
reemergence of ancient mythological symbolism which used
and transformed philosophical terminology into mystical
symbols, as Neumark had explained.

Scholem found, in the various manuscripts that preserved
the ancient traditions of the early kabbalists, that a mystical
tradition developed in the twelfth century in the great centers

of Jewish scholarship in southern France, in Languedoc. A story that the prophet Elijah had appeared and revealed great secrets to the heads of the academies was repeated so often that it could not be considered a legend and nothing else. The kabbalists preserved some kabbalistic ideas and quotations of these early mystics, quotes that philological analysis proved could have been uttered by the early rabbis of Provence. The important point was that these traditions did not speak about a messenger from afar (like the tale of Aaron of Baghdad found in Italy and Germany),[3] nor about the revelation of an ancient book (like the *Bahir*), but about the revelation of the Holy Spirit and the prophet Elijah; that is, no foreign element seems to have been involved. The new ideas originated within these academies, by the rabbis who dealt mainly in halachah in the most traditional manner, and who served as leaders to the communities around them.

The first clear kabbalistic traditions reach us from Rabbi Abraham ben David, known by the acronym the Ravad, who was the greatest Talmudic authority in his time, the second half of the twelfth century, in southern France.[4] The quotations that later kabbalists preserved from the Ravad deal with problems like the creation, the intentions in prayers, and other subjects, using kabbalistic symbolism in an elementary form, probably not yet systematized. The Ravad is especially known for his critique of Maimonides' code of law, the *Mishneh Torah,* and his opposing remarks are traditionally printed beside the Maimonidean text. Most of these remarks deal with purely halachic matters, but a few of them express ideological differences. The most important among them is the one opposing Maimonides' declaration that belief in a God who has anthropomorphic characteristics is heresy.[5] The Ravad wrote in response to Maimonides: "some great people, greater than you, believed in this fashion."[6] (He was careful not to include himself among them.) This statement is not motivated necessarily by kabbalistic mythology; it could be just an acceptance of the fact that literal understanding of biblical and Talmudic anthropomorphism was widespread.

The earliest work of kabbalah whose author is known to us is the commentary on *Sefer Yezirah* by Rabbi Isaac Sagi Nahor ("the Blind"), who was the son of the Ravad and was accepted as the leader of the early kabbalists. He was also called "the Pious." His commentary on *Sefer Yezirah* is a mature, complicated, and profound work of kabbalah, which includes most of the basic kabbalistic symbolism concerning the process of creation. According to Rabbi Isaac and all other kabbalists, creation is first and foremost the process of the emanation of the ten divine powers or attributes, the ten *sefirot*.[7] The names and symbols which describe the *sefirot* in this work are those which became most current in later kabbalah—unlike those of the book *Bahir,* which are, to some extent, unique to that early work.

Rabbi Isaac became the leader and the teacher of the next generation of kabbalists in Provence and, especially, in the small town of Gerona in Catalonia, not far from Barcelona. It seems that the kabbalists in northern Spain, which was a Christian country, saw themselves as the disciples of Rabbi Isaac, corresponded with him, listened to his advice, and followed his directions. Parts of this correspondence were discovered and published by Scholem, who analyzed them in great detail, for this is one of the very few sources for the history of the first stage of the development of the kabbalah.[8]

In Provence first, and then Gerona, the most important ideas of the kabbalah were formulated, its systems of symbols received shape, and its struggle to serve the religious needs of the Jewish people in the Middle Ages began. From these two centers came the messages that the kabbalah had for the Jewish intellectuals of that time, and for the whole people in centuries to come.

II

The early kabbalists in Provence and in northern Spain developed their mystical traditions in an environment in which Jewish philosophy reigned supreme. The intellectual language of Aristotelian philosphy and its terminology were commonly used, and Platonic and neo-Platonic ideas were current among Jewish thinkers. While the compilers of the book *Bahir* seem to have been almost completely free of such influences, the mystics in the kabbalistic schools of Europe could not avoid, and probably did not wish, to cut themselves away from their intellectual environment.

Since the first years of the thirteenth century the works of Maimonides aroused controversy within the Jewish world, especially in Provence.[9] Criticism first arose over the attitude of Maimonides toward messianic redemption and, especially, the belief in the resurrection.[10] The controversy spread quickly, especially after the Hebrew translations of the *Guide to the Perplexed* became known, and the whole scope of Maimonidean philosophy and its implications concerning Jewish beliefs was made apparent. Between 1232 and 1235 a great controversy, which engulfed Jewish scholars from Spain, France, and Germany, raged.[11] It became one of the most important historical events in the history of Jewish thought in the Middle Ages.

In that controversy some of the most prominent kabbalists of the period took part. One of them, Rabbi Moses ben Nachman, known as Nachmanides, the great commentator on the Torah, was the leader of northern Spanish Jewry at that time, and the leader of the Gerona circle of kabbalists.[12] There is no doubt about his central place in the development of the kabbalah; his authority was so great that several kabbalistic works written by other mystics were attributed to him.[13] Nachmanides had a most active role in the controversy. At its beginning he attempted to pacify the various factions and to minimize the differences. Soon, however, he came under attack by the rationalists, and had to join the opponents of Maimonides.[14]

Scholem emphasized that the role of the kabbalah as such, and not only that of individual kabbalists who had other roles as well, in the controversy over the rationalistic philosophy of Maimonides should be thoroughly investigated. He felt strongly that the early kabbalists saw themselves as to some extent responsible for preventing Jewish rationalism from reaching the uppermost position intellectually and achieving a dominant place in Jewish culture.[15]

While the involvement of the kabbalists in the controversy over Jewish rationalistic philosophy helps us understand the social and historical attitude of these mystics, their attitude toward philosophy as such, and their use of philosophical ideas and terminology in the formulation of their mystical symbolism, has a bearing on the very content of their teachings.

A kabbalist who wrote toward the end of that century, Rabbi Moses of Burgos, said concerning the relationship between Jewish philosophy and kabbalah: "our feet stand where their heads are," meaning that the mystics begin where the philosophers end their deliberations.[16] This dictum suggests that there is nothing wrong with philosophy itself; the problem is that the philosophers do not go far enough, or that they stop too soon. Kabbalists like Rabbi Moses of Burgos saw themselves as building a theology in nonphilosophical ways but for which philosophy might serve as a start or a basis.

It seems that while Rabbi Moses' dictum is a relatively late one, the attitude it reveals was familiar to the early kabbalists in Provence and Spain. Sections in the works of early kabbalists like Rabbi Azriel of Gerona could be read as philosophical treatises, especially as far as terminology was concerned. The very distinctive language of the Tibbonite translations of the major works of Jewish philosophy had enormous impact on kabbalistic literature, and the symbolism of the translations is often formulated in the same manner as the kabbalistic works.

It is not only kabbalistic language and terminology which reveals the impact of Jewish philosophy. The mystical symbols themselves reflect this impact, though it is important to note the differences as well as the similarities. In contrast to the book *Bahir,* the works of the kabbalists of Gerona may seem like a rejection of, or withdrawal from, the mythological and gnostic formulations of the book *Bahir,* and the construction of a "philosophical" mysticism.[17] Scholem showed in great detail in his study of the works of Rabbi Isaac the Blind, and particularly of the works of the Gerona circle, that the kabbalists indeed philosophized some of the ideas and symbols that they received in their mystical tradition, but they also introduced deep mystical layers into the rationalistic terminology used by them.

The most important field in which the mysticism and the philosophy of this period collided while using similar terminology was that of the character of the *sefirot,* the ten divine attributes in the kabbalistic system, and their hidden, sublime source in the Godhead, called by them *en sof,* "no end." The concept of *en sof* was regarded by the kabbalists as a divine realm beyond all description, which could not even be given a symbol based on any scriptural term, for it was not directly mentioned in the Bible. The appellation "no end" was regarded as an accidental term, which had no specific significance; it could as well have been called "no beginning" or "no color" or by any other negative. It was not a symbol nor a description of a characteristic; just a convenient word to refer to something which was far beyond any reference in human language.[18]

This *en sof* is the supreme Godhead, the source of all existence, the beginning of the divine realm, the eternal divine power which was not changed by the creation and will never change; the source of the divine influence over the world, but which has no connection with the world and is not influenced by it in any way. A mystic may strive to uplift his soul to the divine hierarchy from one stage to another, but he can never form any mystical contact with the *en sof,* which cannot be touched by anything out of Himself. He is not counted among the divine powers, and no mythological terminology, as found in the *Bahir,* can ever apply to Him; indeed, it does not seem that the concept of *en sof* was known to the compilers of the book *Bahir.*

The picture of the Godhead conveyed by *en sof* is reminiscent, to a very large extent, of the philosophical description of the Aristotelian primal cause, the "unmoved mover," the "thought which only thinks itself," and all the other terms used to describe the source of everything and the supreme divinity in medieval Aristotelian thought. There can be little doubt that the kabbalists in Europe used the philosophical concept in order to describe and characterize their supreme divine power.

To a lesser extent, the same could be said about the ten *sefirot* which emanate from the *en sof* according to these mystics. The concept "emanation" itself is an idea received by the mystics from philosophy, especially from neo-Platonic philosophy, which had a most profound impact on Jewish mysticism, as it had on Christian mysticism of late antiquity and the Middle Ages. The vision of the Godhead as an enormous source of light, spreading around Him diminishing circles of light each outside the other, is as central to the mystics as it was to the neo-Platonic philosophers.

The Jewish mystics in Provence and Gerona accepted this basic neo-Platonic picture, but introduced into it other elements, especially the element of dynamism. While the philosophers usually described a permanent, fixed structure of the descending steps from the hidden Godhead to the earthly realm, the mystics saw movement and change in the same

155

descent. The various emanated powers in the mystical structure could undergo processes of rising or falling, of diminishing and enlargement. They formed intense relationships between them of a mythological nature, and thereby a much more profound and variegated symbolism was created.

The structure of the ten *sefirot* themselves is also reminiscent of a philosophical system—the divine attributes. Some of the *sefirot* are called by the kabbalists by names which include ethical connotations, like Justice, Mercy, and Compassion, as we also find in the terminology of some philosophers, who defined the ethical maxims not as characteristics of the Godhead itself but as attributes of divine action in the lower realms.[19] There is a close connection between these two systems, and there can hardly be any doubt that the formulation of the system of the ten *sefirot* and their relationship to their source, the *en sof* in the process of emanation all carry the signs of the great impact of Jewish philosophical formulations on the works of the early kabbalists.

It should be remembered, however, that while the way the *sefirot* are described by the kabbalists in Europe was influenced by philosophical terminology, the system of the *sefirot* is not dependent on that terminology. The *sefirot* as a system of symbols preceded this influence, as witnessed by their description in the book *Bahir.*

It would be a mistake then, as Scholem often stressed, to imagine that because the early kabbalah assumed a philosophical garb, and because some of its symbols revealed the impact of Jewish philosophy, the kabbalah was only a reaction to Jewish philosophy, and not an opposing alternative to it. The kabbalah probably existed in some way before the mystics came into contact with the terminology of the philosophers. Although in Provence and Spain in the first half of the thirteenth century it assumed some characteristics of the culture of that time and place, it was not dependent on them. In the coming generations the kabbalah would revert to mythological symbolism, which was very far from the systems adopted for it by the Gerona kabbalists.

III

According to Scholem, a "symbol" in the context of the kabbalah is a term or a description that nothing further can be said about in human language. It is the maximum linguistic approximation to something which is actually and permanently beyond full expression by language. Symbols are terms used not to express what we know, but to indicate that we know little about the substance behind the symbol.[20]

The term "emanation" is a good example of the nature of the kabbalistic symbol. In Hebrew it is called *azilut,* and it is a medieval Hebrew term which evolved, most probably, under the impact of Jewish philosophy; Scholem found its first appearance in Hebrew in a poem by Rabbi Judah ha-Levi.[21] Later it was extensively used by the Tibbonites in their translations of the masterpieces of Jewish philosophy into Hebrew, translations which were made for the sake of the Jewish scholars in Provence who were not familiar with the Arabic originals and who wanted to take part in the new rationalistic movement. The mystics used the term in the earliest treatises of European Jewish mysticism—it is found

even in the works of Ashkenazi mystics.[22] A biblical conno-
tation was coupled with it to justify its use in Hebrew contexts.[23] It is probable that some mystics were unaware that
it was a medieval term, introduced into Hebrew to translate
a non-Hebrew concept. By the time the kabbalists of Gerona
used it, it was a commonplace term in both mysticism and
philosophy in Hebrew.

But the problem is: Does the term mean the same thing
when used in a philosophical work and a mystical one? Or,
in other words, what is the difference between a kabbalistic
symbol and a philosophical term? According to Scholem, the
difference lies in the fact that the philosopher uses the term
to mean exactly what it says; he strives for accuracy and un-
ambiguity, trying to formulate his system as clearly as possible, because his philosophical training requires that he prove
logically all his conclusions, which cannot be done unless
complete accuracy is achieved. For the philosopher, the terms
he uses are vehicles for exact communication between him
and the reader.

The mystic cannot use the term in the same way, because
he deals with contents which are beyond logic, beyond language, beyond human experience; he deals with mysticism,
a positive term which really conveys the unknown and the
unknowable. Accuracy and clarity are out of the question;
complete communication is absolutely impossible. If it were
possible, the contents would not be "mystical" any more and
could not convey truths which are far beyond human logic,
which is the philosopher's vehicle. The mystic cannot com-
municate the truth which is in his heart and his vision. But
he does write books, even quite lengthy ones. He does try to

form some kind of communication with his fellow mystics, if not with his fellow men. He does that via symbolism.

The mystic uses the term "emanation" as a symbol, declaring, "The subject I am describing is beyond language, beyond human understanding and expression; yet the closest human word to the completely mysterious truth describing the relationship between two other such symbols—this *sefirah* and that *sefirah*—is the word 'emanation.' " No bigger mistake can be made than to understand that the relationship between the two *sefirot* is "really" one of emanation. If it were so, nothing would distinguish between the mystic and the philosopher. Yet the mystic begins where the philosopher's logic is exhausted.

The symbols cannot convey contents, that is, ideas, pictures or feelings in a complete form. They can only give the vaguest hint at the truth which is beyond them.[24] But these truths—the mystical ones hinted at by symbols—are so great, so profound, and represent such a high religious attainment, that even in this vague and remote form they are much more worthwhile, religiously and spiritually, according to the mystic, than the accurate, clear, but mundane and earthbound truths, of the philosopher. When the mystic, therefore, uses the term *azilut* he does not and cannot obey the philosophical chain of reasoning, of logical examination and proof. He just gives a hint, which cannot be scrutinized nor criticized. He knows that this term is the closest possible approximation found in human language to a divine truth which, in any other way, is completely beyond human reach.

This is the source of the great freedom that mysticism allows its believers. They can never be taken to account, their

ideas analyzed and accepted or rejected. The mystic can always claim, when criticized, that he "never meant it this
way," with pure heart and clear conscience, because he really
never meant the symbol to be taken literally, as if it really
represented divine truth. That truth is completely beyond
communication, and no one can expect the mystic to write it
and convey it to the logical human mind. Therefore he can
say whatever he feels, being certain that terms like "heresy"
do not apply to him, for he has experienced divine truth and
tried to convey it, however incompletely, by using human
words as symbols.

This is also the source of the deep gulf that separates mystics from nonmystics in a religious community. The mystic
believes that God cannot express anything which is untrue,
and the truth cannot be expressed in human language. Thus
the words of divine revelation incorporated in the holy writ,
be it the Bible, the Gospels or the Koran, cannot be understood literally because then they would be conveying only
partial truth or even completely false messages. Their divine
source proves that they are set in symbolic language, and in
order to be understood they have to be read as such. The
mystics could not reconcile themselves to the nonmystic's reliance on the literal meaning, while the nonmystics could
hardly understand how the mystics discovered such unimaginable interpretations to seemingly simple biblical verses.

A case in point is the kabbalistic interpretation of the first
chapter of the book of Genesis, the story of the creation. As
this chapter presented the beginning of everything, the early
kabbalists could not read it just as the story of the creation
of heaven, earth, fauna, and flora. The first event in cosmic

history is the emanation of the ten *sefirot* from the hidden Godhead, the *en sof*. These verses should be read, therefore, as the description of this process of emanation, although the source of the emanated divine attributes cannot be mentioned even in the symbolic language of the Bible. Rabbi Isaac the Blind and his followers, therefore, understood the first verse of the Bible as telling how the *sefirot* emerged from the *en sof*.[25] "In the beginning God created heaven and earth" was read as "With the divine wisdom {*reshit*, 'beginning,' is a reference to this power, the second *sefirah*}, the Godhead, [unmentioned in the verse or anywhere in biblical symbolism], created the Divine Intelligence [*binah*, the third *sefirah*, also called *elohim*, 'God'] and the divine magnificence [*tiferet*, the sixth *sefirah*, which is the central power in the structure of the divine world, and often represents the other five around it, also called 'heaven'], and the divine kingdom [*malchut*, the *shekhinah*, the tenth *sefirah*, also called 'earth']." Thus this first verse tells of the emanation of the ten *sefirot* in a very brief form, not mentioning the hidden emanator, the *en sof*. Of course, this way of reading is completely foreign and unacceptable to anyone who cannot adopt his mind and feelings to the symbolical reading of the holy scriptures. For the mystic, however, reading the story of the creation as if a divine power toiled and brought forth the physical world is unacceptable and at least mundane if not completely sacrilegious. For the mystics, the holy scriptures are a divine dictionary of symbols. It is not the mystic who has to search through the whole human language to find the appropriate symbol which will express, in the maximal way possible, the hidden divine truths; God himself did it when he revealed his secrets in human language to Moses on Mount Sinai, to the prophets, and to the writers who wrote under the influence of the Holy Spirit.

Not the scriptures alone serve the mystic as a treasury of symbols. Creation as a whole, which was made by God, reflects inner divine truths in a symbolic way. Morning and evening, light and darkness, are nothing but earthly symbols of hidden divine processes, which can be understood by the mystic who is aware of their symbolic significance. The same is true about Man, his creation in "God's image" really means that his body and soul reflect in their structure hidden divine truths in a symbolic manner. The study of human psychology, therefore, like the study of physics or cosmology, is really the study of the divine symbolism which was used by the Creator when he transformed divine structures into forms in the physical world. Human history, the relationships between nations, natural upheavals and catastrophes, insofar as they are directed by God, are also symbolic reflections of mystical truth. Thus the mystic denies the veracity of all that is learned by the senses or the mind, all that is literal and apparent. He believes that all apparent phenomena are symbolical reflections of an unknown and unknowable divine truth, of which the earthly manifestations are remote symbols, understood only by those who reject the literal and the logical. "Where their heads are, there our feet stand," where the literal and physical understanding of nature, man, history, and the scriptures ends, there begins the symbolical understanding of the underlying secrets of the divine world.

Scholem always emphasized the difference between symbolism and allegory. Allegory, according to him, means two corresponding layers of truth, one revealed and the other hidden, but the revealed layer can be accurately used to reveal the hidden one. For instance, the presentation above of the kabbalistic interpretation of the first verse of Genesis was really allegorical: the verse says "earth" but means to say "the *shekhinah*," and all one has to do is to translate from one set of words to another. But for the mystic, "*shekhinah*" is not a word corresponding to "earth;" it is a symbol which can be understood by the human mind only as a hint to something which is far beyond it. When one "translates" "earth" to "*shekhinah*" one does not explain or clarify anything; rather, one obscures and mystifies the verse, for nobody knows, or can ever know in a logical fashion, what the *shekhinah* really is. We can know many, even hundreds, of different symbols which refer to various aspects of this divine power and its characteristics and functions, but we can never know the *shekhinah* as it really is. Symbolism is the maximum we can know, and this maximum is extremely minimal.

In an allegory, the connection between one layer of meaning and the other one is artificial. On an allegorical level, the choice of "earth" to represent "*shekhinah*" is completely arbitrary because there is no underlying, inherent connection between the two. In mystical symbolism, the connection between the symbol, although it expresses only a very small part of its content and meaning, and the symbolized power is real and essential. "Earth" and "*shekhinah*" equally represent the hidden divine essence in a remote way, and they are part of that mysterious and hidden entity which is beyond man's reach. This has been frequently described as the relationship between the revealed and hidden parts of an iceberg.

The revealed part, the symbol, is really a part of the iceberg, but anyone mistaking it for the iceberg itself will be making a very great, indeed, a titanic mistake.

The study of kabbalistic works is therefore the study of the symbols the Jewish mystics used when they described the divine world in their intricate system of symbolism. Scholem did not see himself as studying the divine world of the kabbalists as it "really" was, and therefore the question "Are there really ten *sefirot?*" was for him completely irrelevant.[26] He dealt with the symbols, their emergence and development, and especially with their historical impact, and not with the underlying content, which, according to kabbalists, cannot be approached by sensual and logical means anyway. This understanding of the nature of the kabbalistic symbol is necessary also to understand the kabbalist's standing within the framework of Jewish orthodoxy.[27] Throughout history, the kabbalists were, with the notorious exception of the Sabbatian movement, preserving, traditional, and orthodox. They helped Judaism to survive in the hostile environment of the European Middle Ages and Eastern Europe of modern times.

One may rightfully ask how a movement which describes ten divine powers, and hence is clearly polytheistic, can be an orthodox power within a monotheistic religious group. The answer, of course, is the nature of symbolism. In the literal and physical world "ten" means much more than one, and therefore the clash between monotheism and polytheism. But when symbolism is introduced, why assume that in the mystical hidden realm "ten" is "more" than "one"? Such a claim can be put forward only by someone who pretends to know how much really is ten and how much is one; but as

the mystic cannot express the mystical content of these symbols, it is possible to claim that within the divine realm "ten"
is the true essence of "one," and that there is no contradiction
between them, one being a specific aspect of the other. This
is probably why, throughout history, there has been so little
theological criticism of the kabbalah among Jewish intellectuals (except for a few bursts in thirteenth-century Spain and
in Italy during and after the Renaissance period).

It is doubtful whether many of the Jewish nonmystics
throughout the ages understood the intricacies of kabbalistic
symbolism concerning the *sefirot* and the Godhead, or accepted the kabbalistic way of interpreting scriptural verses.
But another aspect of kabbalistic symbolism had a profound
impact on Jewish religious thought and practice, and demonstrated the orthodox and constructive character of the kabbalah. This is the kabbalistic attitude toward the practical
commandments of the Jewish religion, the deeds required of
every Jew in his ethical behavior, his social and religious life—
the *mitsvot*.

The Middle Ages found Judaism confused concerning the
multitude of *mitsvot* that the Jew has to perform as commanded by the Torah, the Talmud, and the rabbinic interpretations of the ancient requirements. The culture of the
Middle Ages, under the combined impact of Christian spiritualization of religious life, and neo-Platonic philosophy, which
described matter and spirit as two opposing poles never to be
reconciled, tended to identify religious life and getting closer
to God as a process of increasing spiritualization. One's level
of religious attainment was measured by one's purity of spiritual life and by one's distance from matter and everything

connected with the physical world. Judaism had to reconcile this otherworldly attitude with a religious practice which seemed to concentrate almost exclusively on the practical, physical performance of material deeds. Jewish religious law seemed to decide one's level of religious attainment solely on one's physical and bodily behavior, and not on any spiritual element.

All the Jewish theologies and ethical systems of the Middle Ages had to answer the question: How can Judaism claim to be a superior religion when its demands are addressed almost exclusively to the physical? Each system devised its own way to spiritualize religious life.[28] Some, like Rabbi Bahya ibn Paqudah in eleventh-century Spain,[29] did it by devising a whole system of spiritual commandments, which they claimed were much superior to the physical ones, founded on the demands of the Torah. Most philosophers chose to give spiritual meaning to physical deeds, thus demonstrating the belief in the unity of God and devotion to him; some even gave allegorical meanings to the *mitsvot*. Most Jewish philosophers tried to interpret in a rational manner the reasons for the commandments *(ta'amey ha-mitsvot)*, emphasizing the social and religious spiritual needs for them.[30]

The Ashkenazi Hasidim chose a more radical answer, but also a more conservative one. It is not the physical deed that has a religious meaning, but the spiritual effort involved in carrying it out.[31] They did not see the *mitsvot* as supplementing human life and happiness, but rather as a trial put before Man by God to test his devotion to Him and his rejection of all worldly temptations and even his attachment to his own body. *"Kiddush ha-shem,"* the supreme sacrifice of life for the sake of God's glory, was the purpose for all the *mitsvot*. Each commandment requires the sacrifice of a portion of Man's human desires for the sake of heaven. God does not judge a man according to the number of the commandments he has performed, but by the hardships, suffering, and sacrifices that he underwent in order to perform them. A commandment performed easily is worth much less than the same one performed while overcoming many difficulties. On the one hand, this system insists on the spiritual significance of religious practice, giving no intrinsic value to the mere physical performance. But on the other hand, this system does not allow a "spiritual religion" which neglects the actual commandments and concentrates instead on spiritual values, as most of the philosophical systems seemed to allow. If the actual performance of a commandment is the proof of one's successful negation of the physical world, and every failure in carrying it out proves that one has yielded to worldly temptations, then the only criterion of religious achievement remains the performance of the *mitsvot*. No spiritual substitute is possible; physical success is the only way for spiritual achievement.

The kabbalists chose a completely different answer. Historically speaking, it proved to be the most successful. It was adopted by all orthodox Jewish movements in early modern times, and survives today among the most orthodox Jewish groups.

The kabbalists interpreted the commandments as symbols. Every human deed has a counterpart in the divine world. Each human good deed contributes something to the process to which it is connected in the divine world, and each bad deed is detrimental to that divine process. As it is impossible to know the actual mystical content of these processes, all man knows are the symbols. The content of the *mitsvot,* therefore, is purely spiritual; they involve divine powers and their dynamic life within the divine realm. The physical commandments, however, represent the earthly symbolic counterpart to these divine and completely hidden purposes.[32] The building of a *sukkah,* a "tabernacle," certainly does not seem to be a spiritual deed, though its traditional meaning is the remembrance of the redemption from Egypt; one may claim that one has better ways to remember that event than spending a week in autumn in a loose hut in the yard. According to the kabbalists, the *sukkah* really symbolized something connected with the union between the sixth *sefirah, tiferet,* which is the male element in the divine realm, and the *shekhinah,* the female element. The form of the tabernacle is modeled, according to them, after the bridal canopy under which these divine powers are united. Mystical symbolism hints at the spiritual divine processes with which the commandments are connected; the understanding of these processes is impossible, because the mystical truth beyond the symbols is unknown and unknowable. Therefore, in order to participate in the mystical union in the divine realm a mystic can only adhere to the symbol and perform it as strictly as possible with maximum attention to the minutest detail. Not knowing its significance, one can never be sure whether a given detail is a crucial or secondary element in that mystical process. Thus, while physical deeds themselves may seems to lose their intrinsic importance, the religious message remains clear and unambiguous: Only by strict adherence to every physical element in the practical commandments of Jewish tradition can one achieve contact with the spiritual, divine content hiding behind them. The content, being mystical, can never be understood or approached in an intellectual manner, but only through the detailed observance of the commandments as such. Symbolism in this way created a unity between the spiritual and the physical, and strengthened the orthodox element in medieval Judaism.

The adherence to basic orthodoxy contributed to the fact that the kabbalah was almost never criticized in the Middle Ages, whereas Jewish philosophy came under most heavy attack. While the kabbalah was undoubtedly more radical in its ways of thought and concepts, as far as deeds were concerned it was above reproach. Indeed, it formulated a new system of *ta'amey ha-mitsvot* ("reasons for the commandments"), which gave new spiritual reasons for their observance. Judaism tended to leave alone any thinker who did not interfere with the practical behavior of Jews, although it attacked vehemently anyone attempting to change one of its practices. It may be said that while in Christian history heretics receive more attention than sinners, in Judaism they were little recognized; it was very easy to become a sinner. The kabbalists were neither: their symbolism protected them from heresy because they could claim that their expressions should never be taken literally; they were saved from sin by seeing the commandments as a set of symbols given to them by God in order to enable the mystics to come close to Him and to participate in and influence the inner dynamism of the divine realm.

IV

The early kabbalists in Spain and Provence concentrated their efforts on the development of kabbalistic symbolism concerning the secret of the creation and the divine process which governed it and the following stages of the development of the world. They did not dream as yet that their symbols would one day transform Judaism and that mass movements would emerge, preaching kabbalistic ideas to all Jews. It seems that from the beginning their orientation was toward small, closed circles and groups dealing with esoteric ideas for their own sake, practicing communion with God alone. They did not demand that the community as a whole follow them. Their insistent concentration on the "secret of the creation" *(sod ma'aseh bereshit)* resulted from the way they understood the process of mystical communion with God.

Rabbi Isaac the Blind, in his commentary on *Sefer Yezirah,* and the other early kabbalists who analyzed in great detail the process by which the first divine attributes emanated from the Godhead and assumed their personalistic character, were not only interested in an academic inquiry concerning the roots of all existence and the emergence of the world as we know it. They saw the process of emanation as the one which led down from the complete unity—a spiritual unity, which existed when all begin, when the different divine powers were still united within the Godhead—to the enormous plurality of the physical world, where nothing is identical with the other and nothing can be united with anything else. The soul of the mystic wishes to deny this plurality, to turn away from it, and to be part of the true divine unity. This unity is a situation of the past, and therefore the past has to be sought and understood, and a way to return to it has to be found. For these kabbalists the *sod ma'aseh bereshit* was a divine ladder, leading down from the early unity within the Godhead to the plurality of the created world.[33]

If the symbolism of the divine ladder could be unveiled before the eyes of the mystic, the mysteries involved in it would become embedded in his innermost soul, there would be a chance that the mystic could then try to use the ladder of descent in which the divine powers emanated stage by stage as a ladder to ascend and uplift his soul toward the sublime unity which always lies above, and before him (in the chronological sense because the earlier the time the closer he is to the complete original unity). "The secret of creation" is thus the means by which the mystic discusses the symbolism which represents not only the origin of the world, but also the target toward which the mystic tries to advance—an advance which is a retreat toward the past.[34]

This mysticism of a retreat toward the unity with the Godhead which was in the beginning of all, and diminished during history, is not a national or community endeavor. It means that the mystic turns his back on contemporary history and has no interest in current affairs and in the advancement toward a better future. This is an individual path; there is nothing to preach to the masses, no message of salvation or redemption. This explains the surprising neglect of the messianic element in early kabbalistic works, from the *Bahir* through the kabbalists in Provence and Gerona. They repeated the traditional formula of messianic belief, but did not add anything to it and did not connect it with kabbalistic symbolism. The symbolism of redemption was, for them, the story of the process of emanation in the beginning of all, the *sod ma'aseh bereshit.*

The early kabbalistic circles in medieval Europe were not interested in the world around them. As individuals, however, they could be leaders of communities and of academies and do their best to protect and enhance the interests of their fellow Jews. Thus, the Ravad at the end of the twelfth century and Nachmanides in the thirteenth century, were important leaders. Yet no element of leadership is apparent in their kabbalistic works. As mystics, they closed themselves in small groups, produced their obscure symbolism which could not be understood by anyone not initiated in one of these circles, and dealt with their individual kind of redemption and mystical unity which was completely separated from historical events around them.[35]

Their works do not reveal much interest in the more popular and practical side of religion. The problems of the commandments are not central in the *Bahir;* several of them are interpreted in it in a symbolical, mystical manner, but no clear message can be discerned.[36] Rabbi Isaac the Blind and the kabbalistic works of the Gerona circle followed the same line; not much is found in them concerning everyday life, ethical behavior, and reasons for the ritualistic commandments, even though the basic attitude toward them as symbols of divine processes is clearly present. Only in the next generation, in the second half of the thirteenth century, did kabbalists begin to write specific works on these subjects.

Scholem showed that the concentration of the early kabbalists in closed esoteric circles was not achieved without opposition and internal strife. He discovered a letter by Rabbi

Isaac the Blind to the kabbalists in Gerona, a letter written in the manner of a Rabbi chastizing his disciples.[37] In it he complained that in Gerona people were talking about the kabbalah and its secrets "in the streets and in the market-places," and that the symbols of the kabbalah were becoming public property. Rabbi Isaac admonished the recipients of the letter, saying that such wide knowledge of the secrets of the kabbalah must lead to misunderstanding and controversy, for these secrets cannot be correctly understood by the wide public. He opposed even the writing of kabbalistic books, and warned his disciples that if they believed that they could write books and keep them secret they were mistaken, for "there is no cupboard which can hide a book already written."

It seems that Rabbi Isaac the Blind directed his criticism especially against Rabbi Ezra and Rabbi Azriel, the founders of the kabbalistic center in Gerona, each of whom wrote several kabbalistic treatises, some of them of book length.[38] The younger kabbalists there did not write treatises in the manner of their predecessors, let alone books, and their mystical teachings were incorporated in other works. The members of the kabbalistic center in Gerona seemed to accept the demand of Rabbi Isaac not to talk openly about the kabbalah and not to write kabbalistic works, thus strengthening the esoteric character of the early kabbalistic circles.

A demonstration of the esoteric character of the early Jewish mystics in medieval Europe is found in the works of a circle of mystics whom Scholem called "the Iyyun circle" after a central work of this school, *Sefer ha-Iyyun (The Book of Contemplation)*. Scholem ascribed 32 treatises to this group, all of them brief works of a few pages each.[39] Some of these, including the *Sefer ha-Iyyun* and the works closest to it in their terminology and symbolism, do not use the usual kabbalistic system of ten *sefirot;* it seems that it was unknown to them. Instead, they use a symbolism of 13 divine *midot,* "attributes."[40] They seem to rely very heavily on neo-Platonic ideas and terminology.[41] Color symbolism is also very prominent in these works, as are mathematical and lingustic elements that follow the *Sefer Yezirah* but demonstrate a special tradition concerning its symbolical interpretation. All these treatises are either anonymous, or attributed to ancient writers, tannaim or gaonim, some to the ancient *Hekhalot* mystics with whom they seem to have had close spiritual ties, and some are attributed to completely fictional figures. There is nothing in these works which could be used to establish either the exact date or location of their composition. Scholem suggested that the members of the circle probably lived in southern France in the beginning of the thirteenth century. The vocabulary they used seems to support this suggestion. The almost exclusive subject of these works is the "secret of the creation," and their mysticism undoubtedly was connected with the symbolism representing that process. To this day, they remain esoteric and mysterious, an anonymous group of works created by an enthusiastic group of Jewish mystics who left their ideas to posterity in the literature of the kabbalah, but their personalities completely hidden and unknown.

V

From its earliest beginnings, Jewish mystics were especially interested in the nature of prayer. *Hekhalot* mysticism concentrates to a very large extent on the *kedushah,* the third benediction among the 18, in which the verse from Isaiah 6:4 is recited, and an identification is created between the public praying in the synagogue and the angels praising God around his throne of glory.[42] The *Hekhalot* hymns are very close to the *kedushah,* and they suggest that the mystical experience in the eyes of the ancient Jewish mystics in Eretz Israel and Babylonia was connected with prayer. The book *Bahir* discusses in relative detail the *kedushah* and the benediction of the priests,[43] hinting at the profound symbolism concerning the divine world hidden within these prayers.

Some of the earliest traditions that we have from the first kabbalists deal with the secret of the intention in prayers. The Ravad himself divided the intention of the 18 benedictions between "the creator" (*yotzer bereshit,* the term used in the *Shiur Komah* for God), and the "prime cause" (*ilat ha-ilot,* the Hebrew term which translated the Aristotelian concept). His reasoning is not completely clear.[44] It seems that he directed the part of his prayer which praises God toward the highest possible place in the Godhead, while addressing the other part, which deals with earthly requests, to a lower divine power, possibly the third *sefirah, binah.* Rabbi Jacob ha-Nazir, a contemporary of Rabbi Isaac the Blind, gave a detailed set of instructions concerning the exact *sefirot* to be aimed at during the reciting of the *shema* and the division of the 18 benedictions among the divine powers. He also insisted that there is a difference in the intentions according to the time of the prayer: in daytime prayers were directed toward the sixth power, *tiferet,* and at night, toward the third, *binah.*

Rabbi Azriel of Gerona was the first kabbalist to dedicate

a whole book to the subject of prayer. He described the symbolism behind almost every word in the prayers and the part
of the divine realm to which they relate. In his commentary
on the Talmudic *aggadot* Rabbi Azriel included a very profound commentary on the word *amen*.[45] He proved that the
various words in Hebrew which derive from that root include, in a symbolical manner, all aspects of the divine world.
Therefore all the *sefirot* are incorporated and united within the
amen; this is why the Talmud said that "One who says the
amen after the benediction is greater than the one who says
the benediction itself."[46]

Many other early kabbalists dealt with the problem of the
intention of prayers, including Rabbi Asher ben David, the
nephew of Rabbi Isaac the Blind, who was sent by Rabbi
Isaac to Gerona to instruct the kabbalists there in the teachings of the school of kabbalists in Provence. Another writer
on the subject from Gerona was Rabbi Jacob ben Sheshet, a
relatively prolific writer, who dedicated an ethical work, *Faith
and Reason (ha-Emunah veha-Bitahon)* to several subjects dealing with the spiritual observance of the Jewish traditional
commandments and norms, including the prayers.[47] This work
became popular, and undoubtedly was instrumental in the
spreading of kabbalistc ideas among nonmystics. Rabbi Jacob, however, did not write this work as a purely kabbalistic
one; most of it is comprised of Talmudic and Midrashic sayings, homiletically interpreted by the author in a manner
intended to instruct his contemporaries in traditional Jewish
ethics. His kabbalistic views are expressed in a subdued manner, but they are still quite obvious to the trained reader.

All this activity concerning prayer did not go unnoticed

outside the circles of the kabbalists, for the subject concerned every Jew. The subject of the correct ways to pray, including spiritual intentions, was also a major subject in *halachic* works. Many books of religious law dedicated their first chapters to the prayers.

The kabbalists attracted not only interest but also some criticism. In a collection of documents by Rabbi Meir ben Shimeon of Narbonne, which the author called *Milhemet Mitzvah,* Scholem found and published a letter by this thirteenth-century author, attacking the kabbalists for their beliefs in general, and especially for their teachings concerning the prayers.[48] He described them as polytheists, who "direct the day's prayer to one God and the night's to another God," and to different powers on various days and religious festivals. He mentioned the book *Bahir.* There is no doubt that he was aware, at least in a general way, of the teachings of the early kabbalists, and viewed them as a harmful new phenomenon. It is not surprising that he attacked the kabbalists on the subject most directly concerned with everyday religious practice, not on the theoretical or theological innovations of the kabbalists.

Rabbi Meir's description of the Jewish mystics as representing a mythological and polytheistic revival within Judaism was echoed throughout the ages, especially by nineteenth-century scholars.[49] Yet the most striking point about this letter is its loneliness. During the next two centuries, as the kabbalah became more and more known among Jewish intellectuals, we hardly find even a second opposing voice to join that of Rabbi Meir. The esoteric circles of the kabbalists, their strict orthodoxy, their observance of Jewish traditional commandments, and the prominence of great halachists among the teachers of kabbalah facilitated the acceptance of the kabbalah as one more feature or aspect of Jewish culture without arousing much controversy. It is doubtful whether all those who understood the kabbalah really believed it to be the true "secrets of the Torah" revealed to Moses on Mount Sinai. Their doubts, however, did not bring them to active opposition, because it was difficult to show what harm was done by its teachings.

VI

Scholem saw the early kabbalah in Provence and Gerona in two different, but complementary, historical perspectives. On the one hand, these late twelfth- and thirteenth-century mystics were both the product of the culture around them and among those who helped to change it. These mystics were profoundly connected to the spiritual world of the early thirteenth century and the major developments within Judaism and around it at that time. The three main spiritual drives which Scholem discerned were: the Catharist heresy, the renewed gnostic revolution within European Christianity; the impact of neo-Platonism, both on Christians and Jews; the impact of Aristotelian philosophy and the threat that extreme rationalism presented to traditional religious beliefs and practices. The kabbalists probably were influenced by the first movement and completely absorbed the second. They fiercely opposed the third and offered a profound, traditional Jewish alternative to it.

Many kabbalists wrote Jewish legal treatises, commentaries on the Bible and the Talmud, responses on halachic questions, and traditional ethical works based on Talmudic and Midrashic sayings. There was nothing revolutionary in their writings, neither in form nor in content. They did initiate new trends, but as Jewish intellectuals and social leaders, responding to the needs of the times, not as kabbalists. Most of them did not devote all their energies to mystical speculation, even though it was central to their spiritual and religious experience. The figure of the mystic who is nothing but a mystic at this period is an exception, not the rule.

These circles of mystics can be viewed, historically, in a much larger perspective. The appearance of the kabbalah in twelfth- and thirteenth-century Europe was nothing short of a major revolution. The mysticism of the *Hekhalot* and *Merkabah* literature, seemingly forgotten as a living force outside the schools of the Ashkenazi Hasidim, suddenly acquired a new vigor and became the inspiration, in a much changed form, for a new and dynamic system of symbols. Gnostic tendencies, either inherent in this literature or transmitted independently by other means, suddenly erupted within the major academies of Jewish law in southern Europe.

Scholem's presentation of the development of the kabbalah has a linear element: from early Jewish mysticism in the East to the Jewish mystics in Provence, where the book *Bahir* first appeared; then the scholars, who had visions of Elijah's appearance to them, developed the system of kabbalistic emanations on the basis of the *Bahir*. This was transmitted to the Gerona scholars, from whom the mystical system spread to other centers in Spain. Some enigmas still exist in this picture, like the extent of the participation of the Ashkenazi Hasidim in the spread of Eastern esoteric gnostic material, and the contributions of the Iyyun circle and its place in the chain of development of Jewish mysticism in Europe. According to Scholem, there is one stream that leads from *Hekhalot Zutarti* to the *Bahir,* and from it to Rabbi Isaac the Blind's commentary on the *Sefer Yezirah,* from that to the works of Rabbi Azriel of Gerona and Nachmanides, and onwards to other mystical circles until the *Zohar* incorporated all of them and developed Jewish theosophy and mythological symbolism to a new level of richness, sophistication, and historical impact.[50]

NOTES

1. See, for instance, Heinrich Graetz's description of the early kabbalistic circles in *History of the Jews* (Philadelphia: Jewish Publication Society, 1956), vol. 4, pp. 1–24.

2. Scholem began his discussion of the early kabbalah with a brief analysis of D. Neumark's thesis. See Gershom Scholem, *Reshit ha-Qabbalah* (Jerusalem and Tel Aviv: Schocken, 1948), pp. 10–11; G. Scholem, *Ursprung und Anfänge der Kabbala* (Berlin: W. de Gruyter, 1962), pp. 6–9. The most detailed discussion by Neumark of his views on the kabbalah is to be found in his *Toldot ha-pilosofiyah be-Yisra'el* (New York: The Stybel Publishing House, 1921), vol. 1, pp. 166–354.

3. See above, ch. 4, pp. 94–95.

4. A detailed biography and analysis of the Ravad's halakic and theological views are presented in I. Twersky, *Rabad of Posquières* (Cambridge: Harvard University Press, 1962). Scholem analyzed the few remnants of the Ravad's sayings which concern his mystical attitude in *Reshit ha-Qabbalah,* pp. 66–98; in R. Schatz, ed., *Ha-Qabbalah be-Provans* (Jerusalem, 1963), esp. pp. 57ff.; and in G. Scholem, *Ursprung,* pp. 181–200.

5. See Maimonides, *Mishneh Torah, Hikhot Yesodei ha-Torah* 1:3.

6. See G. Scholem, *Ursprung*, p. 1888.

7. Since he began to study kabbalah, Scholem paid particular attention to the quotations, scattered in many sources, from R. Isaac the Blind's books, and to traditions attributed to him. He published R. Isaac's "Commentary on *Sefer Yeẓirah*" as an appendix to his *Ha-Qabbalah be-Provans*, a book which is for the most part dedicated to an analysis of R. Isaac's views. He saw in R. Isaac the founder of systematic kabbalah, and in the study of his brief and cryptic sentences one of the most important tasks of the historian of Jewish mysticism. See G. Scholem, *Reshit ha-Qabbalah*, pp. 99–126; G. Scholem, *Ursprung*, pp. 219–272. Cf. also Ephraim Gottlieb, *Studies in the Kabbala Literature*, edited by Joseph Hacker (Tel Aviv: Tel Aviv University, 1976), pp. 60–62. For an important study of the manuscripts of R. Isaac's commentary on *Sefer Yeẓirah*, see Chaim Wirszubski, "Prolegomena to the Textual Study of Isaac the Blind's Commentary on *Sefer Yeẓirah*" (Hebrew), *Tarbiẓ*, 27 (1958), pp. 257–64.

8. See G. Scholem, "A New Document concerning the Early History of the Kabbalah" (Hebrew), *Sefer Bialik* (Tel Aviv, 1934), pp. 141–62. In this paper, which still today serves as a foundation for the study of the early kabbalah, Scholem published a letter by R. Isaac the Blind to some kabbalists in Gerona, and some other documents. From Scholem's analysis it becomes evident that R. Isaac was asked by the Gerona kabbalists to visit them. Although R. Isaac declined, he sent his nephew, R. Asher ben David, to assist them in kabbalistic problems as well as to instruct them in the proper behavior for the kabbalist in nonkabbalistic society. The works of R. Asher ben David were published by M. Hasidah in *Ha-Segulah* (1934), and republished by me, with some additions and a bibliography of manuscripts containing these works by R. Elior, under the title *Qabbalat R. Asher ben David* (Jerusalem: The Hebrew University, 1980).

9. Concerning the controversy, see I. Baer, *Toldot ha-Yehudim bi-Sefarad ha-Notzrit* (Tel Aviv: Am Oved, 1959), pp. 56–64, and the relevant notes on pp. 484–85. [English translation: *A History of the Jews in Christian Spain*, translated by L. Schoffman (Philadelphia: Jewish Publication Society, 1961), vol. 1, pp. 96–110, and notes on pp. 398–402.] See also Joseph Sarachek, *Faith and Reason: The Conflict Over the Rationalism of Maimonides* (Williamsport: The Bayard Press, 1935); D. J. Silver, *Maimonidean Criticism and the Maimonidean Controversy 1180–1240* (Leiden:

E. J. Brill, 1965). See my review of this book in *Tarbiz*, 35 (1966), pp. 295–300.

10. The first opponent of Maimonides was R. Meir Abulafia. For a description of the man and his works, and the possibility of his kabbalistic background, see now Bernard Septimus, *Hispano-Jewish Culture in Transition: The Career and Controversies of Ramah* (Cambridge: Harvard University Press, 1982).

11. The attitude of the rabbis of Ashkenaz in this controversy was studied by E. E. Urbach, "The Participation of German and French Scholars in the Controversy about Maimonides and his Works" (Hebrew), *Zion*, 12 (1947), pp. 145–59.

12. A large portion of Scholem's *Ha-Qabbalah be-Gerona* is dedicated to an analysis of Nachmanides' kabbalistic views. See also G. Scholem, *Reshit ha-Qabbalah*, pp. 146–52, 239–54; G. Scholem, *Ursprung*, pp. 325–30, 360–65. See E. Gottlieb, "The Ramban as Kabbalist" (Hebrew), *Studies in the Kabbala Literature*, pp. 89–95.

13. Several works of the Gerona kabbalists, especially those of Jacob ben Sheshet, were attributed to Nachmanides. Cf. H. Chavel, *Kitvei ha-Ramban*, 2 vols. (Jerusalem: Mosad ha-Rav Kook, 1967). Chavel has included in these volumes works attributed to Nachmanides but which were written by other members of the Gerona circle of kabbalists. See E. Gottlieb's review of this edition in his *Studies in the Kabbala Literature*, pp. 516–35.

14. On Nachmanides' role in the controversy, see the detailed exposition by D. J. Silver, *Maimonidean Criticism and the Maimonidean Controversy*, pp. 166–75.

15. An analysis of Scholem's views concerning the role of the kabbalists in this controversy as well as a presentation of new material on the subject are to be found in J. Dan, *Jewish Mysticism and Jewish Ethics* (Seattle: University of Washington Press, forthcoming).

16. The remark of R. Moses has been preserved by the kabbalist Isaac of Acre in his *Me ʾirat ʿEinayim*, the source which Scholem cites in his study "R. Moshe mi-Burgosh, talmido shel R. Yiẓḥaq," *Tarbiz*, 3 (1932), p. 263, and ibid., 5 (1934), p. 318. See now A. Goldreich, *"Sefer Me ʾirat ʿEinayim* by R. Isaac of Acre: A Critical Edition" (Ph.D. thesis, Hebrew University, 1981), p. 56 of the text.

17. Isaiah Tishby put forth the thesis that there is in the history of kabbalah a cycle leading from philosophical formulation of mysticism back

to mythological symbolism and then a return to the former. See his "Paths of Mythologization and Systematization in the Kabbalah" (Hebrew), *Netivei 'Emunah u-Minhut* (Ramat Gan, 1964), pp. 23–29.

18. Concerning the kabbalistic doctrine of *'en-sof,* see G. Scholem, *Ursprung,* pp. 230–39; G. Scholem, *Kabbalah* (Jerusalem: Keter, 1974), pp. 88–91.

19. See G. Scholem, *Kabbalah,* pp. 92–115.

20. A brief discussion was presented by Scholem in the first lecture in G. Scholem, *Major Trends in Jewish Mysticism,* 3rd rev. ed. (New York: Schocken, 1954), pp. 25–28. Cf. David Biale, *Gershom Scholem: Kabbalah and Counter-History* (Cambridge: Harvard University Press, 1979), esp. pp. 79–112.

21. See G. Scholem, *Kabbalah,* p. 62.

22. The term appears in the works of the followers of the tradition of Jonathan ben Uzziel. See J. Dan, *Early Kabbalistic Circles,* edited by I. Aggasi [Hebrew] (Jerusalem: Akadamon, 1977), pp. 99–106.

23. Cf. J. Dan, *The Esoteric Theology of the Ashkenazi Hasidim* [Hebrew] (Jerusalem: Mosad Bialik, 1968), pp. 136–40.

24. Scholem often used the word "transparency" to describe the relationship between the symbol and the symbolized realm, i.e. the symbol makes the partition hiding the symbolized mystery somewhat more transparent, thus enabling the mystic to perceive some vague outlines of the hidden truth. See G. Scholem, *Major Trends,* pp. 26–27.

25. The interpretation of the first verse of Genesis was one of the most popular subjects in kabbalistic literature throughout the ages; there are hundreds of such exegetical commentaries. The example given above is only one amongst many, though it typifies the attitude of a whole circle. Even from the school of R. Isaac the Blind we have several treatises dealing with this subject besides his own detailed discussion in the commentary to *Sefer Yezirah.* Thus we have a brief discussion on creation by Asher ben David (see J. Dan, *Qabbalat R. Asher ben David,* pp. 52–55) and one quite similar by Joseph ben Samuel included in Jacob ben Sheshet, *Meshiv Devarim Nekhohim,* edited by G. Vajda with an introduction by E. Gottlieb (Jerusalem: Israel Academy of Sciences and Humanities, 1968), pp. 193–96. Concerning the whole subject, see E. Gottlieb, "Perushei Ma ʿaseh Bereshit be-Reshit ha-Qabbalah," *Studies in the Kabbala Literature,* pp. 62–70.

26. It is not my intention to deal in this book with the intriguing

question of whether Scholem did or did not believe in any of the ideas of kabbalah, nor with the question whether he himself was mystically inclined or not. It seems that while everyone accepts that one can devote a lifetime of study to Plato without being a Platonist, one cannot study mysticism without being to some extent a mystic oneself. The scholar in the field of mysticism is expected to give an account for his choice of field of scholarship while his colleagues in other fields are not. Scholem's attitude was most complex and profound, but—it should be stated emphatically—his personal attitude did not influence the results of his philological investigations. As the notes to this volume illustrate, almost ever problem that Scholem wrote on was studied and restudied by other scholars in the last four decades, his conclusions tested by detailed and detached scholarly investigation.

27. See Scholem's detailed discussion of this problem in *On the Kabbalah and Its Symbolism,* translated by Ralph Manheim (New York: Schocken, 1965), pp. 5–32.

28. See J. Dan, *Hebrew Ethical and Homiletical Literature* [Hebrew] (Jerusalem, 1975), pp. 47–68, and the bibliography there, pp. 281–82.

29. See G. Scholem, *Kabbalah,* p. 36.

30. The material concerning the philosophers' attitudes toward the commandments was compiled and analyzed by Isaac Heinemann in *Ta ᶜamei ha-Mitzvot be-Sifrut Yisraʾel* (Jerusalem, 1954), vol. 1.

31. Concerning the views of the Ashkenazi Hasidim on the spiritualization of the commandments, see J. Dan, *Hebrew Ethical and Homiletical Literature,* pp. 134–44.

32. A monumental study of the concept of *mizvot* in the kabbalah was published by Isaiah Tishby in vol. 2 of his *Mishnat ha-Zohar* (Jerusalem: Mosad Bialik, 1961). The focus of Tishby's analyses is religious practices according to the *Zohar* as well as previous and subsequent kabbalistic views. It is interesting to note that Scholem did not dedicate a special study to this problem, notwithstanding the fact that discussions of this subject are found in many of his papers and books.

33. Scholem stressed this aspect of the mysticism of the early kabbalists especially in contrast with the "messianic kabbalah" which developed from the sixteenth century on. See his "The Messianic Idea in Kabbalism," *The Messianic Idea in Judaism* (New York: Schocken, 1971), pp. 37–48.

34. Cf. A. Altmann, "The Ladder of Ascension," *Studies in Mysticism*

and Religion presented to Gershom Scholem on his Seventieth Birthday, pp. 1–32.

35. This attitude may explain the low profile that the kabbalists kept—at least as kabbalists—in the Maimonidean controversy. It should be stressed, however, that main figures in the Gerona school devoted central works to the struggle with philosophy. One of Nachmanides' sermons is an attack on the Aristotelian conception of the beginning of the world. See J. Dan, *Hebrew Ethical and Homiletical Literature,* p. 159. Another important work is Jacob ben Sheshet's *Meshiv Devarim Nekhohim* (see above, n. 25) which is a polemic directed against Samuel ibn Tibbon's treatise on creation, *Maʾamar Yiqavu ha-Mayim.* (Samuel ibn Tibbon is the celebrated translator of Maimonides' *Guide of the Perplexed* into Hebrew from Arabic.) It is not accidental that these two polemical works deal with a refutation of the philosophical conceptions of creation, the *isod ma aseh bereshit.* Similarly, the kabbalists kept a low profile as kabbalists in their ethical works, but their emphasis on traditional, talmudic-midrashic ethics is both a polemic against and a suggestion of an alternative to philosophical, rationalistic ethics, which flourished at that time.

36. A new analysis of the *Bahir's* attitude to the commandments is to be found in J. Katz, "Halakha and Kabbalah—First Contacts" (Hebrew), *I. Baer Jubilee Volume* (Jerusalem, 1979), pp. 148–72. [Now reprinted in J. Katz, *Halakha and Kabbalah* (Jerusalem: Magnes Press, 1984), pp. 9–33.]

37. See G. Scholem, "A New Document concerning the Early History of the Kabbalah," pp. 143–44.

38. A list and analysis of the works of Ezra and Azriel, as well as a clarification of their mutual relationship, was presented by I. Tishby in the introduction to his edition of the *Commentary on Talmudic Aggadoth by R. Azriel of Gerona,* 2nd ed. (Jerusalem: Meqize Nirdamim, 1983). A large part of Scholem's *Ha-Qabbalah be-Gerona* is dedicated to an analysis of these central kabbalists from the Gerona circle. See also G. Scholem, *Ursprung,* pp. 324–420.

39. Scholem's list was printed as an appendix to *Reshit ha-Qabbalah,* pp. 255–62.

40. See G. Scholem, *Kabbalah,* pp. 95–96, and cf. J. Dan, *Early Kabbalistic Circles,* pp. 1–11.

41. Scholem cited the Iyyun circle as the clearest example of the impact of European neo-Platonism on the kabbalah. See his "The Traces of

Gabirol in the Kabbalah" (Hebrew), *Me'asef Sofrei'Eretz Yisra'el* (Tel Aviv, 1940), pp. 160–78.

42. This subject has not been studied yet in all its aspects. For references to scholarship on this theme, see above, ch. 2, n. 29.

43. See R. Margaliot, ed., *Sefer Bahir* (Jerusalem: Mosad ha-Rav Kook, 1978), sec. 123–34 [G. Scholem, *Das Buch Bahir* (Leipzig: W. Drugulin, 1923), par. 87–91].

44. See G. Scholem, *Reshit ha-Qabbalah*, pp. 96–97. Cf. J. Dan, "The Emergence of Mystical Prayer," in J. Dan and F. Talmage, eds., *Studies in Jewish Mysticism* (Cambridge: Association for Jewish Studies, 1982) pp. 107–110.

45. See I. Tishby, *Commentary on Talmudic Aggadoth by R. Azriel of Gerona*, pp. 23–26.

46. *Berakhot* 45a.

47. Jacob ben Sheshet's *Ha-'Emunah veha-Bithon* is included in H. Chavel, *Kitvei ha-Ramban* (Jerusalem: Mosad ha-Rav Kook, 1967), vol. 2, pp. 353–448.

48. G. Scholem, "A New Document concerning the Early History of the Kabbalah," pp. 148–50.

49. See, for example, H. Graetz's famous polemical denigration of kabbalah in his *History of the Jews* (Philadelphia: Jewish Publication Society, 1891–98), vol. 4, pp. 10–24 and Solomon Rubin, *Heidenthum und Kabbalah* (Wien: Cermann & Altmann, 1893).

50. The linear description of the development of kabbalah is opened to several questions which, in turn, raise the possibility of a different interpretation. For instance, it is not at all evident that the early kabbalists in Provence received all their symbols from the *Bahir*. Indeed, it is surprising how independent they are in their terminology vis-à-vis the *Bahir:* most of their symbols are not based on it! If from this we may infer that the Provençal kabbalists had another source for their symbols, then it will follow that the *Bahir* was not the only ancient presentation of a symbolism containing a doctrine of ten divine attributes. Analogously, the texts deriving from the Iyyun circle do not contain terminology dependent on the *Bahir*. This too seems to denote the existence of mystical systems which used other sources and developed outside, or alongside, this "linear" historical stream. If so, some of the more mystically oriented circles of Ashkenazi Hasidim should be viewed as independent mystical schools emerging without close contact with or direct influ-

ence from the mainstream of mystical development presented by Scholem. It seems that we have today a meaningful body of historical facts which suggest that at the turn of the thirteenth century nearly half a dozen independent schools of Jewish mystics were operative in Europe. The centrality of the *Bahir*-Provence–Gerona line is a historical fact decided upon by later developments, but at the time there were many alternative routes to that line. From a historical point of view this picture raises with new force the question: Why did mysticism emerge exactly then? Why did Judaism flourish for such a long time without the symbolism of several divine emanations, and then suddenly, around the year 1200, a half a dozen schools begin to invent new mythologies to describe the Godhead? The study of this possibility, and the problems it raises, might add new insights into the nature of the relationship between Jewish religion and Jewish mysticism, as well as to the understanding of Jewish culture in the twelfth and thirteenth centuries. For a more detailed discussion of the problem of the autonomy of these various circles, see J. Dan, *Early Kabbalistic Circles*. See also J. Dan, "The Emergence of Mystical Prayer," p. 115.

CHAPTER 7

FROM GERONA TO
THE *ZOHAR*

I

THE FIRST PERIOD in the history of the kabbalah
begins with the composition of Rabbi Isaac the Blind's
commentary on *Sefer Yezirah,* in the beginning of the thirteenth century. It ends when the most important kabbalistic
work, the *Zohar,* began to be known about 1291. The first
half of this century-long period was dominated by the kabbalistic circles in Provence and Gerona; the second half, from
the middle of the thirteenth century, was dominated by three
major developments: the school of kabbalists in Castile, that
of Rabbi Jacob ha-Cohen, his sons and their disciples; the
activities of Rabbi Abraham Abulafia; and the school of the
Zohar itself, the works of Rabbi Moses de Leon and Rabbi
Joseph Gikatilla. At the beginning of this period, the kabbalists were scattered in small circles; when this period ended,
the kabbalah was a system that covered most subjects in Jewish culture and provided answers to the central religious
problems of medieval Judaism. This maturity was revealed in

the *Zohar,* which collected and developed previous systems and speculations and molded them into a new whole. Some of the ideas and symbols which developed in the post-Gerona schools of the kabbalah will be described, with some emphasis on those elements which contributed most to the formulation of the theosophical system of the *Zohar.*

During the first decade of his work in Jerusalem, Scholem explored the works of the Castile school of kabbalists, especially those of the brothers Rabbi Jacob and Rabbi Isaac, the sons of Rabbi Jacob ha-Cohen, and those of their disciple, Rabbi Moses of Burgos. He published their works in a series of articles beginning in 1927 and studied in detail their reliance on previous sources and their impact on later kabbalistic thought. [1] At the same time Scholem published his comprehensive study of the mystical concept of the different worlds in the kabbalah. [2] In his later publications Scholem referred back to his studies of these works, [3] and he used to call these mystics "the Gnostics of Castile," or "the Gnostic Brothers."

The major work of Rabbi Jacob ha-Cohen, the father and founder of this mystical circle, is called *Sefer ha-Orah (The Book of Light).* Scholem considered Rabbi Jacob to be an original mystic, who developed his system without direct contacts with other traditions and schools of the kabbalah. He apparently relied on his own mystical vision, his discoveries of numerical harmonies in the ancient texts, and on his own interpretation of the traditions of secret, holy names and divine powers described in the *Hekhalot* literature. Thus, for instance, the figure of Metatron, so prominent in *Hekhalot* mysticism, [4] which was almost absent from the book *Bahir* and the works of the early kabbalists, emerges in the *Sefer*

189

ha-Orah as a dominant power in the divine world. Rabbi Jacob did, however, probably derive some material and ideas from the esoteric works of the Ashkenazi Hasidim.

The works of Rabbi Jacob's sons, Rabbi Jacob and Rabbi Isaac, "the Cohen Brothers" of Castile, show clear contacts with the teachings of the book *Bahir* and of the kabbalists of Provence and Gerona. The system of the ten *sefirot*, absent from *Sefer ha-Orah,* is present and central to the works of the sons, who incorporated into it many elements that they received from their father. The best-known book of Rabbi Jacob ha-Cohen (the son) is his commentary on the letters of the Hebrew alphabet, following the tradition of the ancient *Letters of Rabbi Akiba*[5] but based on the system of the *sefirot.* The kabbalists of this circle showed a keen interest in every element connected with language: not only the letters, their sounds and their forms, but also the vocalization signs and the *teamim,* the musical signs added to the letters in the Bible in order to direct the way they should be sung in the synagogue. This interest is related to the concentration of the early kabbalists on the "secret of Genesis," for existence emerged by the power of these letters and the sounds associated with them, and the mystical knowledge of their secrets gives the mystic the power to repeat the process and incorporate himself with the source from which the creation evolved.

Scholem referred to this circle as "the Gnostics of Castile" mainly because of one important treatise by Rabbi Isaac ha-Cohen entitled *Al ha-Azilut ha-Semalit (A Treatise on the Emanations on the Left).*[6] This revolutionary work marked a completely new departure in the concept of evil, not only in the kabbalah itself but in the history of Jewish thought. The impact of this treatise was enormous, though indirect. While later kabbalists hardly mention Rabbi Isaac's works, and he was almost forgotten in the kabbalistic literature of the following centuries, one person was deeply influenced by the ideas of Rabbi Isaac—the author of the *Zohar,* Rabbi Moses de Leon.

Rabbi Isaac proposed that two lines of emanation emerged from the third divine attribute, the *sefirah binah,* consistently called *teshuvah,* "repentance." The first, a holy one, is situated on the right side, which is actually the seven lower *sefirot* of the previous kabbalistic schools; the second, situated on the left side, is that of the evil powers, the central one among them being Samael, and the female one, the counterpart of the holy *shekhinah,* is called Lilith. Never before in Jewish literature was there a presentation of an independent realm of evil divine powers. While the names Samael and Lilith are old ones in Hebrew works,[7] never before were they described as a couple, the central pair in the demonic realm.[8]

Parallelism is very prominent in Rabbi Isaac's thought. Everything evolved, according to him, in parallel pairs, even Adam and Eve were emanated as a similar pair to Samael and Lilith.[9] In Rabbi Isaac's world view all things were divided into pairs of good and evil, which were in constant struggle with each other. The classical gnostic dualism of a mythological struggle in the divine world between good and evil powers was clearly expressed by Rabbi Isaac. It remained a constant element in kabbalistic thought, in various forms, for centuries to come.

The cosmic dimension of the struggle between the "left" and "right" powers is emphasized in Rabbi Isaac's description of the creation of the world (including the divine world of the *sefirot*). He saw it as a series of attempts by the Godhead to create, attempts negated by evil so dominant that these ancient worlds had to be destroyed.[10] This myth of the ancient, completely evil, destroyed worlds was also adopted by the author of the *Zohar* and became central to kabbalistic mythology.[11]

Another revolutionary mythology incorporated in Rabbi Isaac's *Treatise on the Emanations on the Left* is the myth of the messiah. Scholem showed that the messianic element is almost absent from the works of the early kabbalists because of their interest in the "secret of Genesis," the quest for the past rather than that of the messianic future.[12] Rabbi Isaac ha-Cohen, however, is an exception. This treatise as well as his treatise on the *teamim* include a myth of the messianic struggle against evil in apocalyptic terms.[13] The messiah will revenge the suffering of earthly and heavenly creatures at the hands of the evil powers and vanquish them with a divine sword; indeed, the messiah himself is a divine sword emanated for this purpose.[14]

There is a mysterious element in Rabbi Isaac's mythology of evil and messianic redemption in Spain around 1265. No other mystics of this period reveal such tendencies. Not even the members of his own circle, including his father and his brother, include such symbolism in their works. His disciple, Rabbi Moses of Burgos, who wrote commentaries on several of Rabbi Isaac's works, tended to minimize these mythological elements in his works. Another scholar who followed to some extent the teachings of this school, Rabbi Todros Abulafia, the author of *Otzar ha-Kavod (A Treasury of Divine*

Glory), a mystical commentary on the Talmudic legends, and other works, did not emphasize the myth of evil, even if he believed in it.[15] It seems that Rabbi Isaac ha-Cohen was completely alone in his development of a myth of evil and messianism.[16]

This circle, and especially Rabbi Isaac ha-Cohen, included in its works long, detailed stories about the way in which these great secrets reached them. Usually, these stories include a tradition of the transmitting of great mysteries from the East to the schools of the Ashkenazi Hasidim. Rabbi Isaac claimed to have met a disciple of Rabbi Eleazar of Worms in Narbonne, from whom he learned many secrets.[17] Rabbi Isaac also claimed to have in his possession ancient esoteric works, from which he quoted; these included a book called *Hekhalot Zutarti,* which he said contained the whole dualistic system he adopted in his works (the ancient mystical text which we have does not).[18] Interestingly, Rabbi Isaac quoted the most important parts of these sources in Aramaic, thus suggesting that great mysteries should be discovered in ancient sources in Aramaic; this could have had a role in explaining why the *Zohar* was written in this language.

Were all the sources quoted by Rabbi Isaac imaginary, a fictitious, mystical library (like the one the author of the *Zohar* often quoted), or did Rabbi Isaac really have in his posession books and manuscripts which were unknown to other kabbalists before and after him? When he first began to study the works of this school, Scholem felt that they did have some information from ancient sources, and that the gnostic character of their works was not the reinvention of a mythology but a direct connection with Eastern gnosticism. But although the mystics of Castile doubtless knew some of the ideas of the Ashkenazi Hasidim, which they completely transformed,[19] all their speculations are explained by the independent development of their interpretations of the Bible and the ancient texts. It is very difficult to point out the influences of unknown, hidden sources.[20]

Sefer ha-Temunah is a commentary by an unknown author on the letters of the alphabet, written in a most obscure and difficult symbolism, most of which is found only in this book.[21] Many parts of this work are not understood, but Scholem identified one idea destined to have enormous religious importance centuries later—the system of the seven *shemitot*. According to *Sefer ha-Temunah,* the Godhead did not create one world, but a succession of worlds, each following after the destruction of the previous one. Each world had its own laws, its own Torah, read and interpreted according to a system unique to it. Each world was governed by one of the *sefirot*. Our world is governed by the fifth *sefirah,* that of *din,* "severe law," as demonstrated by the strict legalism of our Torah. After the redemption this world will be destroyed, and a new one will be created. It will be governed by the next *sefirah, tiferet*. It will be characterized by divine mercy, and the world will be free of the legalism of the present interpretation of the Torah.

There is an obvious antinomian element in the symbolism of the *Sefer ha-Temunah*. It offers the hope of freedom from all religious laws. This, however, is not a dangerous kind of antinomianism because such freedom will not be achieved until the present world is destroyed and a new one created; this could hardly have an immediate historical impact. Scholem pointed out the close similarity between these ideas and the thirteenth-century Christian school of the disciples of Joachim of Fiore, who believed in three testaments, each following the other throughout history, and governed by the three parts of the Christian trinity: the Old Testament, that of the Father; the New Testament, that of the Son, which is much more spiritual and less legalistic than the previous one; and the third, the testamentum aeternum, that of the Holy Spirit, which will be completely spiritual and eternal. Some of Joachim's disciples believed that their teacher's works constituted that testament. Unlike *Sefer ha-Temunah,* this system sees the transition from one set of laws to another as a process characterizing the history of the present world. It thus has acute antinomian implications, and therefore Joachim and his disciples were persecuted by the Catholic church.

The teachings of the *Sefer ha-Temunah* at first did not have a great impact on the kabbalah, but they were rediscovered by the seventeenth-century adherents of the messianic Sabbatai Zevi.[22] He revived these ideas and used them to develop a mystical conception of the new Torah of the messianic age, the Torah developed by the messianic prophet Nathan of Gaza.

II

A completely different kabbalistic system, coupled with messianic activity, was developed by a contemporary of Rabbi Isaac ha-Cohen, Rabbi Abraham Abulafia. One of the greatest Jewish mystics of all times, his mystical system was called by Scholem "the prophetic kabbalah.[23] Scholem was the first to analyze his prolific writings as a whole, and to extract from them both the biography of this unique mystic and the outlines of his kabbalistic teachings. The term "prophetic" was used by Scholem to distinguish Abulafia from the theosophical trend in the kabbalah that emphasized the ten *sefirot*. Abulafia was well aware of this system of the Gerona kabbalists, but he opposed it completely. His mysticism relied directly on the teachings of the *Sefer Yezirah*. He concentrated on the analysis of the letters of the Hebrew alphabet, their mystical significance, and the ways to use them to achieve a mystical vision or prophecy. Abulafia is one of the very few Jewish mystics who included in their works instructions concerning the way to achieve a mystical state, both spiritual and physical, ways of contemplation, and ways of exercise by which the spirit could be freed of its physical bondage and reach contact with the divine.

Rabbi Abraham Abulafia completely rejected the idea that evil has a separate, independent existence. He thought that evil arose as a psychological element within the human heart; it was one of man's spiritual drives, which did not have any divine manifestation. In this he was close to the views of many Jewish philosophers.[24] He did not see a gulf between philosophy and kabbalah and interpreted Maimonides' *More Nevuchim* as if it were a mystical work.[25] In this he joined some other kabbalists who tried, in various ways, to reconcile between kabbalah and philosophy, the most prominent among them in the thirteenth century being Rabbi Isaac ibn Latif.[26] But above all Abulafia believed that the mystical contemplation of the secrets of *Sefer Yezirah,* the alphabet, and the numerical meanings of Hebrew letters and words, and the analysis of the divine names, contained all mystical secrets. The theosophic trend of the kabbalists of Provence and Gerona was not the right way to achieve mystical knowledge.

Abraham Abulafia was motivated by messianic drives, and he took it upon himself to hasten the coming of the messianic age. Although Abulafia's teachings were overshadowed by the *Zohar*, his mystical and messianic approach had an enormous impact on subsequent developments in the kabbalah.

Abulafia had several students, as he himself was probably the student and follower of a previous circle of mystics.[27] The most important was undoubtedly Rabbi Joseph Gikatilla, one of the best-known and yet most enigmatic kabbalists of the thirteenth century.[28] Gikatilla was a prolific writer, and a score or more of his works are known to us. His most famous work is *Sha'arey Orah (The Gates of Light)*,[29] which is a description of the ten *sefirot* given in greater detail than anyone had attempted before him. The clarity and precision of Gikatilla's style made this work extremely popular. The almost complete identity of his symbolism with that of the *Zohar* made Gikatilla's book helpful in the study of that work.

While Gikatilla was and is regarded as the clearest exponent of theosophical kabbalah and the system of the *sefirot*, the major work of his early period of creativity, *Ginat Egoz*, is based on the *Sefer Yezirah* according to Abulafia's mystical approach.[30] There is no use of the *sefirot* (and Abulafia's messianism is absent as well). It seems that Gikatilla started his mystical career as a disciple of Abulafia and followed his teachings in several of his early works, and then changed his course and became an adherent of the theosophic kabbalah.

This change probably occurred after he met another adherent of the *sefirot* kabbalah, Rabbi Moses de Leon, and they became lifetime associates and friends.[31]

It is possible that Rabbi Moses de Leon was in his youth an adherent of the mysticism expounded by Abulafia.[32] One of his earliest works, called *Or Zarua (The Shining Light)*, may be a testimony to this influence.[33] He also was interested in the philosophy of Maimonides, for he purchased his own copy of the Hebrew translation of his work.[34] There can be no doubt that Gikatilla was the kabbalist closest to de Leon when he wrote the *Zohar*. Gikatilla accepted most of the theosophical symbolism expounded in the *Zohar*, but rejected many of the mythological elements. In his books Gikatilla did not dwell on the mystical symbolism so central to the *Zohar* (a basis for which can be found in the works of Rabbi Isaac ha-Cohen); the mythology of evil and the messianic motifs in the *Zohar* did not appeal to him.

Thus we see that thirteenth-century kabbalah is an enormous treasure house of mystical trends, ideas, and systems of symbols. The common ground is the ardent quest for the mystical meaning of Judaism. Rabbi Joseph Gikatilla and Rabbi Moses de Leon were the first two kabbalists to write major treatises on the subject of *ta'amey ha-mitsvot*, the mystical meaning of the Jewish commandments. By the end of the thirteenth century, on the eve of the publication of the *Zohar*, the kabbalah nearly became an all-encompassing ideological system, proposing answers to all the major religious problems facing the Jews. In this vast body of mystical lore one could find everything from stark, gnostic mythology, like that of Rabbi Isaac ha-Cohen, to an almost philosophical and seemingly logical presentation, like that of ibn Latif, a prominent kabbalist who lived in the middle of the thirteenth century.

By the end of this period the kabbalah was presenting a complete mystical dimension to Jewish religious life and self-image. A century after Jewish rationalistic philosophy reached its peak with the publication of Maimonides' *Guide to the Perplexed,* Judaism produced a comprehensive mystical system of terms and symbols by which Jews could understand themselves, their fate, their destiny, and the demands that God put before them.

It is difficult to speculate what would have happened if Jewish intellectuals had been forced to choose between the *Guide to the Perplexed* and other philosophical works on the one hand and the works of Nachmanides and Rabbis Isaac ha-Cohen, Abulafia, Gikatilla, and de Leon on the other. But late in the thirteenth century all the kabbalistic trends and symbols were united in one work, highly inspired and of great rhetorical and literary impact, vast in its scope and unsurpassed in its daring symbolism—the *Zohar.* After that, it was not this kabbalistic system or that against rationalistic philosphy, but the *Zohar* against everything else. With the *Zohar* the kabbalah came of age. The mystics could start the long process of influencing Jewish religious observance, literary creativity, and even history.

NOTES

1. For bibliographic references, see above, ch. 1, ns. 17–18. To the sources mentioned there it should be added that several texts from this circle of kabbalists were included in Scholem's *Kitvei Yad ba-Qabbalah* (Jerusalem: The Hebrew University Press, 1930), pp. 31–32, 60–70, 208–13.

2. Gershom Scholem, "An Inquiry in the Kabbalah of R. Isaac ben Jacob ha-Kohen: The Evolution of the Doctrine of the Worlds in the Early Kabbalah" (Hebrew), *Tarbiz*, 2 (1931), pp. 415–42; 3 (1932), pp. 33–66.

3. For the most recent summary, see G. Scholem, *Kabbalah* (Jerusalem: Keter, 1974), pp. 55–66.

4. Concerning Metatron, see G. Scholem, *Kabbalah*, pp. 377–81, and see above, ch. 2, pp. 61–62, and n. 72 there.

5. See above, ch. 3, p. 81.

6. Published by Scholem in *Maddaʿei ha-Yahadut*, 2 (1927), pp. 244–64.

7. See Scholem's article on Samael in *Kabbalah*, pp. 385–88; cf. his "New Information Concerning Ashmedai and Lilith" (Hebrew), *Tarbiz*, 19 (1948), pp. 160–75. See also J. Dan, "Samael, Lilith and the Concept of Evil in Early Kabbalah," *Association for Jewish Studies Review*, 5 (1980), pp. 17–40.

8. There is one magical text, published by Scholem, which includes references to Samael and Lilith in a similar manner, and which bears resemblance to R. Isaac's terminology in other aspects as well. See G. Scholem, "Sideri de-Shimusha Rabba," *Tarbiz* 16 (1945), pp. 196–209. The problem is, however, whether this text was a source for R. Isaac or vice versa, or perhaps they shared a common third source. This is a difficult problem which we are unable to resolve at present. Suffice it to say that R. Isaac's treatise is the earliest dated source which includes a reference to Samael and Lilith in this way. Concerning R. Isaac's sources, I have suggested that he based his speculations on stories about Lilith and the "Great Demon" in the ancient text known as the pseudo-Ben Sira; see J. Dan, "Samael, Lilith and the Concept of Evil in Early Kabbalah," *Association for Jewish Studies Review*, 5 (1980), pp. 19–22.

9. According to R. Isaac, following an ancient midrash, Adam and Eve were originally one creature which included both sexes, and were later separated into male and female; in the same way, Samael and Lilith were one and then separated like a pair of twins. (On the midrashic theme of the androgynous nature of Adam, including references to the classical rabbinic sources, see L. Ginzberg, *Legends of the Jews* [Philadelphia: Jewish Publication Society, 1968], vol. 5, pp. 88–89, n. 42.)

10. The aggadic theme of God "creating worlds and destroying them" is found in *Genesis Rabbah* 9:2 (Theodor-Albeck ed., p. 68), Cf. *Ḥagigah* 13b–14a concerning the early generation which was lost.

11. For a detailed comparison between R. Isaac's presentation of the myth of the "destroyed worlds" and that of the *Zohar*, see G. Scholem, *Maddaᶜei ha-Yahadut*, 2 (1927), pp. 193–97. It is possible that R. Isaac was influenced here by a homily of R. Eleazar of Worms about early, evil worlds. See his *Ḥokhmat ha-Nefesh* (Lvov, 1876), pp. 10c–d. Cf. J. Dan, "Samael, Lilith and the Concept of Evil in Early Kabbalah," pp. 32–37.

12. Concerning the attitude of the early kabbalists toward messianism, see above, ch. 6, pp. 151–52.

13. G. Scholem, *Maddaᶜei ha-Yahadut*, 2 (1927), pp. 269–75.

14. These descriptions conclude the extant portion of Isaac's "Treatise on the Emanations on the Left."

15. For more details see Michal Oron's M.A. thesis on *Todros Abulafia* (Tel Aviv University, 1976).

16. See J. Dan, "The Emergence of Messianic Mythology in Thirteenth Century Kabbalah" in Zvi Baras, ed., *Messianism and Eschatology* [Hebrew] (Jerusalem: Magnes Press, 1983), pp. 239–52.

17. G. Scholem, *Maddaᶜei ha-Yahadut*, 2 (1927), p. 263.

18. For a description of *Hekhalot Zutarti*, see above, ch. 2, pp. 38–63.

19. Concerning these influences, see J. Dan, "Samael, Lilith and the Concept of Evil in Early Kabbalah," pp. 28–32.

20. Scholem could not decide at the time he published these studies whether R. Isaac influenced the *Zohar* or whether the sources of the *Zohar* were before R. Isaac, for he was not yet certain when the *Zohar* had been written. See below, ch. 8.

21. See G. Scholem, *Reshit ha-Qabbalah* (Jerusalem and Tel Aviv: Schocken, 1948), pp. 176–92; G. Scholem, *Ha-Qabbalah shel Sefer ha-Temunah veshel R. Avaraham Abulafiya*, edited by J. Ben Shlomo (Jerusalem: Akadamon, 1965), Cf. G. Scholem, *Urprung und Anfänge der Kabbala* (Berlin: W. de Gruyter, 1962), pp. 407–19. On the views of Joachim of Fiore, to whose work Scholem here drew parallels, see Marjorie Reeves, *Joachim of Fiore and the Prophetic Future* (London: SPCK Press, 1976) and Antonio Crocco, *Giocchino da Fiore* (Naples: Auria Press, 1960).

22. Concerning the *shemitot* theory in Sabbatianism, see below, ch. 11, pp. 286–311.

23. Scholem's first detailed discussion about Abulafia was included in G. Scholem, *Major Trends in Jewish Mysticism,* 3rd rev. ed. (New York: Schocken, 1954), pp. 119–55; cf. also G. Scholem, *Ha-Qabbalah shel Sefer ha-Temunah veshel R. Avaraham Abulafiya*. A major study of this mys-

tic was written by M. Idel, "Kitvei R. Avraham Abulafiya u-mishnato" (Ph.D. thesis, Hebrew University, 1976), 2 vols.

24. For a detailed analysis of Abulafia's meditational techniques, see M. Idel, op. cit., vol. 2. For an analysis of Abulafia's thought, and its relationship to philosophy, see M. Idel, vol. 1, pp. 86–128.

25. Abulafia's commentary, extant in many manuscripts, is called *Sitrei Torah (The Esoteric Meaning of Torah)*. See G. Scholem, *Major Trends*, pp. 378–79, n. 19. (See also M. Idel, op. cit., vol. 1, pp. 8–11.)

26. See G. Scholem, *Kabbalah*, pp. 52–53. See also S. Heller Willensky, "The Problem of the Authorship of the Book *Sha'ar ha-Shamayim* Ascribed to Abraham ibn Ezra" (Hebrew), *Tarbiz*, 32 (1963), pp. 277–95; idem., "Isaac Ibn Latif—Philosopher or Kabbalist?" *Jewish Medieval and Renaissance Studies*, edited by A. Altmann (Cambridge: Harvard University Press, 1967), pp. 185–223.

27. Concerning Abulafia's teacher, see G. Scholem, *Major Trends*, p. 127.

28. See Ephraim Gottlieb, "Berurim be-Kitvei R. Yosef Giqatila," *Studies in the Kabbala Literature*, edited by Joseph Hacker (Tel Aviv, Tel Aviv University, 1976), pp. 96–162.

29. The work has been printed many times (first edition, 1559). The most recent edition, with introduction and notes, has been published by J. Ben Shlomo (Jerusalem: Mosad Bialik, 1970).

30. First edition, 1615. See M. H. Weiler, "'Iyyunim be-terminologiyah ha-qabbalit shel R. Yosef Giqatila u-beyaḥso le ha-Rambam," *Hebrew Union College Annual*, 37 (1966), pp. 13–44 [Hebrew section].

31. For a recent study of the early nontheosophic works of Gikatilla, see S. Blickstein, "Between Philosophy and Mysticism: A Study of the Philosophical-Qabbalistic Writings of Joseph Giqatila" (Ph.D. thesis, Jewish Theological Seminary, 1983).

32. See A. Farber, "On the Sources of Rabbi Moses de Leon's Early Kabbalistic System" (Hebrew), *Studies in Jewish Mysticism Presented to Isaiah Tishby on his Seventy-fifth Birthday, Jerusalem Studies in Jewish Thought,* 3 (1983–84), pp. 67–96. Farber has argued that Moses de Leon belonged to a circle of esotericists who, although distinct from the school of Abulafia and Gikatilla, similarly focused on language mysticism.

33. See the critical edition of this work prepared by A. Altmann in *Qovez'al Yad*, 9 (1980), pp. 219–93.

34. G. Scholem, *Major Trends*, p. 194.

CHAPTER 8

THE *ZOHAR*

I

WHEN SCHOLEM began his studies of the *Zohar*, he was overwhelmed by its depth, its vast imagery, its profound symbolism, and the literary and ideological power contained in it. This reaction is natural when facing this enormous work. Scholem was familiar with the views of Graetz and other nineteenth-century scholars concerning the *Zohar*. He knew the prevailing view that the *Zohar* had been written by Rabbi Moses de Leon in northern Spain near the end of the thirteenth century. The young Scholem could not accept this view, which was usually presented coupled with vitriolic attacks against the kabbalah in general.

For instance, one of the arguments used by Scholem against the attribution of the *Zohar* to Moses de Leon was a comparison of the *Zohar* with the other Hebrew works of Rabbi Moses. The similarity of these works to the *Zohar* is unmistakable. Whole portions, sentences, expressions, and terms appearing in Rabbi Moses' Hebrew books seem to be a direct translation from the *Zohar*. But the overall view, the general characteristics, of these books when compared to the *Zohar* make it almost impossible to believe that the same man wrote all of them. The Hebrew works do not contain the same broad views, the strong, colorful images, the mythological strength, the depth, and the greatness of the *Zohar*. Scholem expressed doubt that the authors of all the works were one and the same. Scholem also doubted in 1924 that it was possible to attribute the enormous *Zohar* completely to a single individual. He tended to believe that the *Zohar* was composed of many layers (which is true), each added by another mystic or a group of mystics. Scholem, therefore, attributed the *Zohar* to many generations of Jewish mystics, while taking into account the possibility that Rabbi Moses de Leon had a part in its final formation and editing.

During the next 15 years Scholem studied the *Zohar* as a philologist, checking one detail after another, analyzing the language and grammatical construction, comparing symbols, terms, and ideas of the *Zohar* to those of earlier Jewish mystics. He came to the conclusion that Rabbi Moses de Leon was indeed the sole author of the *Zohar*. As a result, the exact date and sequence of the writing of the various works of Rabbi Moses presented grave difficulties, not all of them completely solved. Also, the influence of Rabbi Joseph Gikatilla on the *Zohar* had to be clarified. Gikatilla was a close friend and colleague of Rabbi Moses de Leon, and his works reflect deep connections with the *Zohar*. These matters need to be clarified, but the scholarly community accepted Scholem's conclusion.[1] A young scholar in kabbalah summed up the situation: "Today it is impossible to point out even one sentence of the *Zohar* which could have been written before the Middle Ages.[2]

II

The *Zohar* is not one book; it is a whole library, in which about 20 different works can be described as separate, even independent, mystical books. The body of the *Zohar* is a homiletical commentary, a Midrash, on the five books of the Pentateuch, arranged as if it were the deliberations of the school of rabbis led by Rabbi Shimeon bar Yoahi and his son, Rabbi Eleazar. Three other works, however, differ considerably in style and content from this central book, and are most important for the understanding, and for the dating, of the entire *Zohar*. One is the *Midrash ha-Ne'elam (The Esoteric Midrash);* another is a group of works entitled the *Ra'aya Mehemna (The Faithful Shepherd);* the third is the *Tikuney Zohar,* usually printed as a separate volume of 70 chapters, each beginning with a new interpretation of the first verse of the book of Genesis.

Midrash ha-Ne'elam differs from the main body of the *Zohar* in several respects. Large parts of it are written in Hebrew, and not in the Aramaic of the body of the *Zohar.* Medieval terminology, usually quite hidden beyond the *Zohar's* Aramaic images, is quite clear in the Hebrew sections. The homiletical literary mannerisms are not as developed in this work as in other parts of the *Zohar.* There is a specific interest in the *Midrash ha-Ne'elam* in the theory of the structure of the human soul. These characteristics formed the basis for the common view that this work is the most recent part of the *Zohar.* Those who believed that the *Zohar* was indeed an ancient book saw in the *Midrash ha-Ne'elam* a medieval addition to the archaic work. Scholem's investigations proved that the

Midrash ha-Ne'elam actually was the earliest part of the *Zohar*, and that it was also the first part of the *Zohar* to become known. Rabbi Moses de Leon wrote this part before the whole concept of the Zoharic literary format was finalized in his mind and the pseudepigraphic character of the book as a whole was conceived. The *Midrash ha-Ne'elam,* according to Scholem, contains valuable clues concerning the way that the idea of the *Zohar* was developed.

Scholem concluded that the *Ra'aya Mehemna* and the *Tikuney Zohar,* both written in Aramaic, were not written by Rabbi Moses de Leon, but by a kabbalist who wrote a generation later and imitated the style and structure of the *Zohar.*[3]

In the *Ra'aya Mehemna,* the central figure is Moses, and the homilies presented are described as ones discussed in heaven. In the *Tikuney Zohar* repeated reference to key verses of the creation is made. In both these works there is a different style and vocabulary, which sets them apart from all other sections of the *Zohar.* Scholem proved that these works represent the first attempt (among many) to imitate the *Zohar;* it was the beginning of a major literary genre in kabbalistic literature which produced many mystical books, from the beginning of the fourteenth century to the eighteenth.[4]

The *Zohar* can be divided into three parts: the early one, the *Midrash ha-Ne'elam,* which Rabbi Moses de Leon wrote first; the body of the *Zohar* and the other special treatises which are included in it, which contain the main mystical work of Rabbi Moses de Leon; and the *Ra'aya Mehemna* and the *Tikuney Zohar,* the two books later added to the *Zohar* by another kabbalist, the first imitator of Rabbi Moses de Leon.

The other treatises in the main part of the *Zohar* include, for instance, sections centered around a mystical figure, like the *sava (Old Man)* and *yenuka (Child)*, in which a narrative about the appearance of strange figures to the mystics around Rabbi Shimeon serves as a literary framework for a group of homilies. Other sections are commentaries on sections of the Bible or early mystical literature, such as the Song of Songs, Ezekiel's chariot, and the Zoharic version of the celestial palaces. Perhaps the most important treatises included in the *Zohar* are the *idras,* the "assemblies," which emphasize the special sanctity and the supreme esoteric character of the greatest secrets of the structure of the divine world. They are homiletically expounded in the framework of a specific narrative. The *Idra Raba (The Great Assembly)*, develops some of the themes introduced in *Sifra de-Zeniuta (The Book of Concealment)*. This, in turn, discusses in a most obscure manner questions concerning the creation and the emanation of the divine world. The *Idra Zuta (The Small Assembly)*, uses as a narrative framework the discussions between Rabbi Shimeon and his disciples when Rabbi Shimeon was dying.

III

Scholem described the *Zohar* as a mystical work with mythological and theosophic characteristics. By "theosophic," he explained, he meant a systematic exposition of the structure of the divine world.[5] The mythological elements refer to four main pictures: the sexual symbolism of the *Zohar,* the dualism of good and evil, anthropomorphism, and the theory of the impact of human beings on the fate and status of the divine powers. Scholem discussed these elements of the Zohar in several of his works,[6] but it is impossible here to present anything but the briefest outlines of the enormous scope of Zoharic thought.

The symbolism of the divine powers is formulated in the *Zohar* into a system which, if one forgets for a moment the subject he deals with, can be understood as a logical description of the structure of the divine world. Even though the *Zohar* is deeply homiletical in character and does not include any systematic exposition, such a system can be discovered and expounded, and many kabbalists, from Gikatilla to Luzzatto did exactly that.[7] The *Zohar* presents a basic conception of the emanation of the *sefirot,* their characteristics and their functions in the divine world and on earth. (This follows to a very large extent the teachings of previous kabbalists from Provence, Gerona, and Castile, to which Rabbi Moses de Leon added his own symbols and images.)

According to the concept of the emanation of the *sefirot,* the beginning of all, the focal point from which all existence, divine and earthly, emerged was the appearance of a point of "divine will" within the eternal and supreme Godhead. Unlike many previous kabbalists, who perceived the highest divine distinctive element in the "divine thought," the author of the *Zohar* described the creation as beginning with the emergence of a relatively specific element of will in the otherwise completely uniform Godhead. This will is symbolized by the highest divine *sefirah, keter,* "the divine crown." In some Zoharic sections it seems that *keter* is identical with the eternal Godhead, the *en sof,* whereas in other sections it seems that a distinction is made between them.[8] It is clear, however, that for the author of the *Zohar* the beginning of actual existence, even in the divine realm, occurred within the Godhead when the will of something specific was evoked. Thus began a line of increasingly specific divine attributes which emanated from each other in a successive manner, reminiscent of the neo-Platonic system of emanated divine lights.

The second stage of emerging divine specificity is called *hochmah,* "the divine Wisdom." After the will, there emerged the question: the will of what? The second *sefirah, hochmah,* gave the answer as a plan of everything which was to follow, both in the divine and the material realms. It was identified with the supreme, secret Torah, which incorporates the essence of everything.

These two first *sefirot* still do not denote anything actual, even within the divine world; they may be described as fleeting thoughts within the Godhead, of a will and a plan hardly more specific than the absolute abstraction of the eternal divinity. Actuality begins with the third *sefirah, binah,* or Intelligence, which the *Zohar* often describes by the symbol of the fountain. *Binah* is partly hidden within the Godhead itself, being an abstraction rather than a distinct divine power. *Binah* is partly revealed, flowing outward into the realm of the emanated, separated divine beings for all of whom she is a source and an early mother. While *hochmah* is the hidden father of all, *binah* is the partly revealed mother, in which potentiality is transformed into actuality. The process of emanation of the active divine powers begins with her. All existence also flows back to *binah* to immerse itself and rejuvenate itself in this divine womb of all the powers in the Zoharic *pleroma*.

From *binah* specification and specialization begin. Indeed, from her two divine powers emanate directly: the fourth and fifth *sefirot, hesed* and *din,* the divine powers of Mercy and of Justice. The *Zohar* follows the ancient Talmudic concept of the world as governed by two divine attributes, or *midot,* Mercy and Justice. The Talmudic sources emphasized that the world could not exist if one or the other of these two were absent.[9] Only the combination of divine Mercy and divine Justice could allow the world, and even the divine realm, to exist and prosper. These two powers are also described as the divine right and left hands, needed for the performance of the divine will in the early process of emanation and creation as well as during all subsequent phases of the world's existence. Thus, together they govern history.

These two elements, divine Justice and divine Mercy, are united in the sixth *sefirah, tiferet,* or divine Glory, characterized in the *Zohar* by the term *rahamim,* which is synonymous with Mercy, but in the *Zohar* it means a correct combination between Justice and Mercy. Mercy is the governing element and *tiferet* is the center, and the heart, of the divine realm. It stands in the center of the seven *sefirot* "of construction" below *binah* which created the world and support its existence. In *tiferet* the elements of Justice and Mercy are combined, but in ever-changing proportions, according to the divine needs. When the divine wisdom demands punishment for the sinners, for instance, Justice in *tiferet* is strengthened at the expense of the element of Mercy; when it is time to redeem and save, Mercy is increased and becomes dominant in *tiferet*. The character of the mixture of these two elements in *tiferet*, therefore, both reflects and decides the fate of creation at every moment.

This triad of the *sefirot hesed, din,* and *tiferet* is reflected in the lower triad of the seventh, eighth, and ninth *sefirot*. While Mercy and Justice are described as the right and left hands, *nezah,* Eternity, the seventh *sefirah,* and *hod,* Grandeur, the eighth, are described as the right and left legs. They correspond to Mercy and Justice, but because they are lower in the divine realm they are closer and more directly connected with the created world; they serve as the messengers who bring the results of higher decisions to the lower realms and execute the divine decrees. Among them resides the ninth *sefirah, yesod,* or Foundation, which is a lower counterpart of *tiferet,* being also a dynamic combination of Mercy and Justice. In the anthropomorphic sequence of symbols, *yesod* is the male organ, the source of fertility, from which the souls of human beings emerge, and which unites the male and female elements in the divine realm.

The tenth *sefirah,* the *shekhinah* or *malchut* (Kingdom) is a separate, independent being, the female element in the Zoharic system as well as in the works of other kabbalists. The *shekhinah,* except for its femininity, cannot be described as this or that divine element, because it includes all of them. It reflects all nine *sefirot,* just as the moon, which has no light of its own, reflects the rays of the sun. It is thus both nothing and everything; it is the lowest but includes the highest. It is the closest divine power to the created world and to human beings, and, as the bride and the wife, it is the intimate counterpart to all the divine powers, completing them and making them into a whole.

To these one more potent Zoharic symbol has to be added: the *shefa,* or divine influence, which, unlike the other symbols, is not basically biblical.[10] It symbolizes the divine 'Influence" or 'Providence." It is the continuous divine emanation from the *en sof* to each of the *sefirot,* filling them with the divine light, and enabling them to carry out their function. The Godhead, in the Zoharic system, is the only source of existence, and this source should provide continuously and eternally its sustenance to all lower emanations and creatures so that they can continue their functions. The conception of the *shefa* is obviously based on the neo-Platonic descriptions of the eternally flowing divine light, which the author of the *Zohar,* following earlier kabbalists, incorporated in his symbolism.

IV

The sexual myth, of which only the vaguest hints can be found in the *Bahir* and the early kabbalistic works (the clearest, but still a hint, is found in Rabbi Isaac ha-Cohen's works), has been developed by the author of the *Zohar* into a most detailed sexual saga of which the divine powers are the heroes. Very little of this myth can be found in the other works of Rabbi Moses de Leon, and almost nothing in the works of Rabbi Joseph Gikatilla. It seems as if only within the framework of the Aramaic homiletical narrative of the *Zohar* did Rabbi Moses de Leon find the freedom and the means to give full, unmitigated expression to his mystical vision of the divine world as the scene of an enormous sexual drama.

The sexual symbolism clearly separates the *Zohar* from thesophy and philosophy and brings it close to ancient gnosticism. The supreme aim of the world of divine emanations is to overcome separation and specificity and achieve complete unity. This unity is symbolized by the sexual union of the essence of the male figure, the sixth *sefirah, tiferet,* with its bride, the *shekhinah.* This union, by means of *yesod,* expresses the denial of the differences between the various *sefirot.* Thus the right hand and left hand and the right leg and the left leg take part in the anthropomorphic symbolism of the sexual union.

Almost every Jewish symbol acquired sexual dimensions in this saga. The Sabbath is the time of the union between the divine powers; the *sukah,* the tabernacle, represents the bridal canopy; heaven and earth represent the male and female elements, as do the seas and the sky, or even the written and the oral Torah. Every conceivable pair in the Hebrew language represents this sexual duality in the divine realm and the wish for unity between them. It is as if all existence had been divided into two sexual principles, and all occurrences in the world expressed the craving to abolish this division. The freedom that the author of the *Zohar* achieved in the use of sexual symbolism is most unusual, though it must be remembered that mysticism in Judaism was a purely male field; we do not have even one kabbalistic medieval work written by a woman.[11]

The Zoharic myth of the sexual union in the divine world was developed on the basis of another myth, that of the fierce struggle between the divine principles of good and evil as explained in Rabbi Isaac ha-Cohen's *Emanations on the Left.*[12] This was accepted by the author of the *Zohar,* who gave evil the symbol of *sitra aḥra,* "The Other Side," for the "Left" is so evil that it should not be mentioned even by name. This world of evil includes counterparts of the divine *sefirot,* and is in constant struggle with the powers of the Right side, the *sitra de-kedushah,* "The Holy Side."

The realm of the evil powers is described in the *Zohar* as below the divine *sefirot,* including all material creation. The struggle, therefore, is between Satan and the lowest part of the world of divine emanations, namely the *shekhinah.* As the *Zohar* relates, the *shekhinah,* while separated, falls into the clutches of Satan, who craves her as his own bride. The fight against evil is the fight to free the *shekhinah* from Samael. The myth thus acquires the characteristics of a story of love, desire, separation, and redemption, in the most extreme dualistic and sexual symbols.

Very little of this dualistic myth is to be found in the Hebrew works of Rabbi Moses de Leon and in the works of his contemporaries. His followers in the fourteenth century and later hesitated when treating this subject, which is central to the symbolism of the *Zohar,* and very few embraced it completely.

Where did this evil power come from? What is the theological basis of this mythological dualism? It seems that while describing the myth itself the author of the *Zohar* portrays Satan as an independent, powerful opponent of God. But elsewhere in the *Zohar* the position of Satan is given in much more moderate terms. It is as if the author were attempting to present a picture in which theological dualism was either muted or completely absent. This is perhaps because the problem of the origin of evil was not presented with full theological force in the extant works of Rabbi Isaac ha-Cohen, from which the author of the *Zohar* derived many of his mythological images. It is clear, however, that the source of evil is to be found below the third *sefirah, binah.*[13] Rabbi Isaac gives no clear reason, however, for its emergence. Earlier kabbalists, most notably Rabbi Ezra ben Shlomo of Gerona,[14] tended to see evil as the result of either human sins and misdeeds, or as an automatic, unavoidable result of the process of creation.[15]

One of the best-known Zoharic treatments of the nature of evil is the parable of the prince and the prostitute.[16] According to this parable, a king decided to try his son's faith by sending a prostitute to tempt him. Evil is like this prostitute: In order to fulfil the king's intention she must do her best to seduce the prince and make him commit a sin; but she does not represent an independent power. She is an instrument of the king designed to bring about the successful completion of the king's plans. In a similar way, God tempts Man with evil, but we must believe that evil is an instrument in His hands to carry out His mysterious designs. The dualism of good and evil in the world is not real. It only seems that evil opposes God. In reality evil is only one of God's many servants who assist and enhance the achievement of the divine purposes in creation.

In several sections the *Zohar* places evil below the third *sefirah,* in the realm of *din,* the divine Justice or Judgment. According to the description of this divine manifestation in the *Zohar,* it must contain some elements of evil, though they are justified and necessary elements of evil. That is, in order to punish the wicked, as they should be punished, the divine Justice must possess the powers which cause pain and suffering as part of the just punishment. However, these powers are closer to the divine world than to the human concept of evil. According to the Zoharic myth, evil emerged from *din* and was transformed in the lower strata of the cosmos into unjustified evil, the powers opposing divine intentions. If there is in the *Zohar* a conception of an independent evil power, it is not an eternal one, but a side effect of the process of the emanation of the powers of good. When they evolved from each other, somewhere along the way from the hidden, supreme Godhead toward the created earth, some elements which were contained in the divine Justice were separated from the divine tree, fell down and became an independent realm of evil.

The reason for evil does not arise from the dualism of good and evil, for the source of evil is within the divine realm, in some elements which became more extreme than originally intended and developed into an evil alternative to the rule of the good God in the created world. Very often the *Zohar* combines dualism and the development of an evil alternative, and hints that there is a hidden, divine purpose even in the separation of the elements of evil from the divine Justice. It is clear that the author of the *Zohar* did not intend to present a theology of equal dualism between the powers of good and those of evil. [17]

When the author of the *Zohar* describes the created world,

however, there can be no doubt that he conceived of it as being completely divided between good and evil, the forces of which are engaged in a struggle against each other. When no theological reservations are needed, the *Zohar* gives a colorful presentation of the powers of evil and their actions. Rabbi Isaac ha-Cohen was the first to identify worldly suffering and ailments as the result of the actions of the "emanations on the left," like leprosy and hydrophobia.[18] The *Zohar* went much further, dividing all the phenomena of the created world between the powers of good and evil. All suffering and temptation, all pain and danger which afflict Man are the result of the actions of the *sitra ahra* (the other side). The world is full of demons of many kinds (which, in previous Jewish discussions were not regarded as representatives of a principle of evil, for instance by the Ashkenazi Hasidim),[19] who are engaged in serving the devil and making all the world subservient to him. Snakes and wild beasts, witches and warlocks fill the cosmos and serve Satanic purposes.[20]

The *Zohar* tried to avoid theological dualism in the full sense of the term. However, it presented Jewish mysticism with a mythological dualism which was to exert great influence on its later development.

V

The most important contribution of the Zoharic mythology to Jewish mysticism and Jewish thought is the picture of Man's role in this vast, continually developing drama. Man is not just a bystander, or a recipient of the results of the events. Man is both the cause and the outcome of many of the changes within the Godhead.

The divine *shefa,* the continuous outflow of divine light from the supreme Godhead toward the divine *sefirot* and the created world, is the power which gives all existence its sustenance and its ability to exist. If the *shefa* were to stop descending the ladder of the emanated divine manifestations, all existence, material and divine, would immediately cease.

While the *shefa* descends constantly, its flow is not completely regular and even. When the flow of the *shefa* is diminished, the character of the divine realm changes. The highest *sefirot,* the three supreme ones, never lack divine sustenance; even when its flow is diminished, they get their full share. But the lower divine powers do not receive all the sustenance that they need. When this happens, the element of *hesed* becomes weaker, for the essence of the *shefa,* like that of the Godhead itself, is unmitigated mercy. When Mercy becomes weaker, the power of *din,* the divine Justice or Judgment, increases in the same proportion. The lower *sefirot, tiferet* and *yesod,* which are a fusion of the elements of Justice and Mercy, become disproportionally full of Justice and lack Mercy. As they are the powers which govern and guide creation, divine Mercy is absent from the created world and unlimited Justice reigns supreme. The increase of Justice, in turn, also means the increase of evil, for Justice is the source of lower evil. When Mercy is scarce or absent, the autonomous evil powers also increase, and, paradoxically, that divine Justice, rather than divine Mercy, rules the world, opens the gates for the powers of evil to become stronger and dominate creation. It is quite clear that the author of the *Zohar* held the same basic attitude of the Aristotelian philosophers toward evil, seeing it not as a real substance but as an absence: evil is the absence of good as darkness is the absence of light.

When the strength of the evil powers grows, their impact on the lowest divine power, the *shekhinah,* increases, to the point that they might capture and dominate this female element in the divine realm. The *shekhinah* is identified with the divine power which constantly watches over the people of Israel and is closest to them. When the *shekhinah* itself is captured by evil, the people of Israel are dominated by the Satanic powers in the created world, represented by the evil governments of the non-Jewish states.

In the same manner, an increase in the flow of the *shefa* means the strengthening of the element of Mercy throughout the divine world, and consequently on earth as well. Then *tiferet* and *yesod* are full of Mercy, Justice is diminished, the source of evil dries up, the Satanic powers become weakened, and therefore human evil is diminished while human righteousness becomes dominant.

The changing outflow of the *shefa* regulates the ethical and spiritual status of the divine attributes, and the fate of humanity on earth. Even the sexual symbolism of the Zoharic mythology is regulated by the same changes. When evil dominates the *shekhinah,* she is separated from her husband, *tiferet,* and therefore the mystical union between them is impossible. When evil is weakened by the increased flow of Mercy, the *shekhinah* is stronger; she can repel the attacks of the Satanic seducers, and she approaches the divine realm and sexual union is possible. The whole mythology of the *Zohar* is dependent on the rate of the flow of the divine *shefa*.

The question is: What regulates the flow of the *shefa?* What causes it either to increase, and strengthen good in the divine and created realms, or to decrease and thus allow evil to become dominant? If the answer to this question were that mysterious processes within the supreme Godhead that cannot be understood regulate the flow, then we would have in the *Zohar* a myth completely dependent on the whims of the Godhead, leaving mankind without any possibility of influencing its fate. But this is not the case. The reasons which regulate the rate of the flow of the *shefa* are presented in the *Zohar* clearly and unambiguously; the fate of all existence is in the hands of every righteous person.

The *shefa,* according to the *Zohar,* increases as a direct result of people's observance of God's commands, the ethical and ritualistic demands of the Torah. When Jews observe the Sabbath as they should, taking care to follow every detail of the intricate *mitsvot* connected with the Sabbath, the flow of the *shefa* increases, the *shekhinah* is purified from the evil elements that cling to it in the other days of the week, and sexual union between the *shekhinah* and her bridegroom, *tiferet,* is achieved. When Jews recite the prayers in the synagogue in the proper way, accompanied by the correct intentions (which need not be mystical), their prayers reach the upper parts of the divine world and cause the *shefa* to descend in renewed strength; the *shekhinah* then becomes stronger and unity between her and the male power in the divine worlds can occur. This is the secret, mystical meaning of the prayer *shema Yisrael:* "May our God be one," that is, united into one to overcome the forced separation between the male and female elements in the *pleroma* and to overcome evil and make the divine world truly one. When the *shema* is said in the synagogues in the right way, this union is achieved.

The same is true, according to the *Zohar*, about every *mitsvah,* or ethical precept. All good deeds result in the increase of the flow of the *shefa,* while all sins immediately result in its diminishing.

The *Zohar*'s myth of sexual symbolism and the struggle of the powers of evil against the powers of good is, therefore, a part of a larger myth, in which the actions of men influence and even regulate the strength of the divine powers among themselves and in relation to the powers of evil. When Man evokes the need for punishment by wrongdoing, he immediately causes the whole complexion of the divine world to shift from Mercy to Justice, bringing about a separation of the divine male and female and strengthening the devil in the lower regions of the cosmos. When, however, Man behaves righteously, unity and harmony are created in the divine world and the divine presence on earth is increased.

History, as understood in the *Zohar,* is brought about by such changes in the complexion of the divine world. The most dramatic historical event, the diaspora of the people of Israel among the gentiles, is the result of the ascendency of Justice in the face of wrongdoing. The punishment caused the *shekhinah* to be exiled with its people and subjugated to the evil powers who dominate the earth.[21] Similarly, the redemption, on which the *Zohar* dwells in greath length, will be the result of the increase in the flow of the *shefa,* the renewed unity between the *shekhinah* and her bridegroom.

The restitution of the divine powers to their original place will result also in the restitution of the people of Israel to their homeland and the rebuilding of Jerusalem and the Temple.[22] The epic myth of the divine powers is really the epic of the people of Israel, their sins and their repentance, which regulate the rhythm of both divine and earthly history.[23]

VI

It is quite understandable that Rabbi Moses de Leon could not publish this most daring mythology unless his ideas and symbols were obscured to outsiders under the double cover of a different language, Aramaic, and of pseudepigraphy. The problem of the pseudepigraphical nature of the *Zohar* interested Scholem a great deal.[24] Earlier scholars who accepted Rabbi Moses de Leon as the author of the *Zohar* described him as a forger who, for reasons of profit alone, attributed his work to an earlier sage to increase its popularity and price. However, the *Zohar* is by no means either the first or the last pseudepigraphical work in Jewish mysticism. All the *Hekhalot* literature is attributed to Rabbi Akiba and Rabbi Ishmael. Circles of Jewish mystics, like the one that wrote the "Special Cherub" mystical works,[25] or the Iyyun Circle, published dozens of pseudepigraphical treatises. The book *Bahir* was attributed to ancient sages, and in later periods books like the *Sefer ha-Kanah* and many others were attributed to ancient tannaim and gaonim.

The *Zohar*, however, was different. First, no other kabbalistic work acquired its sanctity and prestige; if the *Zohar*'s author was ethically in the wrong, the whole kabbalah became suspect. Opponents of the kabbalah in nineteenth-century Judaism happily embraced this accusation. Second, the *Zohar* is the only major kabbalistic work written in the pseudepigraphic manner whose author is actually known to us. Other similar works, though their pseudepigraphic character is undisputed, still remain anonymous.

Rabbi Isaac of Acre, a kabbalist, traveled to Spain in the early years of the fourteenth century to investigate the *Zohar*. A portion of his diary survives.[26] In it he describes a conversation he had with Rabbi Moses de Leon's wife and daughter after Rabbi Moses' death. According to his report, the widow was offered a large amount of money and the prospect of a good marriage in return for revealing the original manuscript of the *Zohar,* from which Rabbi Moses claimed to have copied the chapters of the *Zohar* he had published. The widow and the daughter testified, according to this report, that Rabbi Moses did not have any such manuscript, and when asked why he claimed to be copying things which he was really inventing, they replied that he had once said: "Who will be interested if this was known to be my work?" This answer was taken to mean that Rabbi Moses de Leon's only motives for pseudepigraphy were ambition and greed.

We do not have the last part of the diary, so it is not known whether Rabbi Isaac of Acre, a great kabbalist himself, was convinced of Rabbi Moses's authorship of the book or not. It seems that the kabbalists of Spain in the early fourteenth century treated the *Zohar* with some suspicion. When quoting it they did not mention the source at all or attributed the quote to a different work. It is quite possible that they accepted the antiquity of the traditions contained in the book, but were uncomfortable about the circumstances of their revelation.

The claim of the Jewish mystics is that the esoteric secrets which they describe in their works are not new. They were given to Moses on Mount Sinai, although they were known to the biblical patriarchs. The revelation on Mount Sinai is the source of all truth, and this truth is hidden within the revealed Torah in an esoteric, symbolical way. To the mystics, it is a contradiction to describe something new as being true. If it is true, it undoubtedly was known to Moses, Abraham, and Solomon; if it was not known to them, it cannot be true. In order that the kabbalah (literally, "tradition") can be described as revealing the truth about the divine world, it must be ancient, and its traces have to be found using the proper homiletical means to be found within the Torah itself. The kabbalah, therefore, is a tradition the veracity of which can always be checked by the study of the Torah and the Talmud. If the content of a new kabbalistic work can be proven to be identical with the deep, esoteric meaning of some verses in the Bible and some sayings of the Talmudic sages (including the *Hekhalot* mystical works which were accepted as the teachings of these sages), then it is really kabbalah, that is, ancient tradition. This is why there are relatively few kabbalistic works which present a mystical system relying only on systematic exposition or mystical revelation. Most kabbalistic works are homiletical in character to prove that nothing new is being revealed; only the inner, esoteric meaning of well-known ancient traditional texts is being presented before the reader. The mystical element in such works is not in the way the mystical truths are being revealed, but in the content itself, which was hidden and unknown to the reader until the mystically inspired author succeeded in penetrating deep into the ancient text and discovering there the mystical truth.

The kabbalist claims that his interpretation of a biblical verse represents the mystical truth concerning the divine world, and also that Abraham, Moses, and Rabbi Akiba shared this knowledge, and that it was transmitted from generation to generation in the oral tradition. The truth presented in a kabbalistic work demands to be accepted as eternal truth, both concerning the past and the future.

When a kabbalist writes a pseudepigraphical work, he, in his own eyes, is only ascribing the truth he reveals in his book to one of the ancient sages who, he deeply believes, shared it, be it Abraham or Rabbi Akiba, or Rav Hai Gaon. It is unimaginable for him that a truth which is so clear and meaningful to him could be unknown to the traditional Jewish leaders who undoubtedly knew more than he does. The difference between him and the earlier sages is only that he is actually writing down what they knew and transmitted orally to their disciples.

Zoharic pseudepigraphy should be viewed, therefore, in the context of Zoharic homiletics. In every paragraph the author of the *Zohar* finds unimaginable, mythological truth in biblical verses. He does so with a complete, sincere conviction that this is the true mystical meaning of these verses. If so, this truth could not have been revealed to him alone, bypassing every great mystic from Moses to Rav Hai. They all knew it, but none wrote it. So, when he puts this truth in the mouth of Rabbi Shimeon bar Yohai, he does not ascribe to the ancient sage something that the sage did not know or did not believe. Rabbi Shimeon did not write the *Zohar* in a cave while hiding from the Romans; the author of the *Zohar* knew that very well. But if Rabbi Shimeon had written a book in that cave it would have been the *Zohar,* for the book reveals eternal mystical truths undoubtedly known to Rabbi Shimeon. The deep conviction in the eternity of mystical truth is the source of kabbalistic pseudepigraphy, and this sincere mystical belief should serve as a background for any attempt at understanding the spiritual process which brought this magnificient literary and mystical work into existence in Spain in the late thirteenth century.

NOTES

1. See Isaiah Tishby, *Mishnat ha-Zohar,* 2 vols. (Jerusalem: Mosad Bialik, 1961, 1971). These volumes contain selected translations of the *Zohar* into Hebrew, arranged according to thematic divisions, together with commentary and preface to each chapter. The first volume contains a lengthy introduction by Tishby on subject matters pertaining to the *Zohar,* e.g. its literary character, authorship, printed editions and commentaries. This detailed study is the most exhaustive treatment of the *Zohar* to date. Besides the two chapters related to the *Zohar* in *Major Trends in Jewish Mysticism* (Gershom Scholem, 3rd rev. ed. [New York: Schocken, 1954], pp. 156–243), Scholem's most important discussions on the subject are to be found in his encyclopedia articles in the *Encyclopedia Judaica* (Jerusalem, 1972) and the *Hebrew Encyclopedia* (Jerusalem and Tel Aviv, 1977). The best and most recent research is to be found in G. Scholem, *Kabbalah* (Jerusalem: Keter, 1974), pp. 213–43.
2. Y. Liebes in a speech dedicated to the memory of Ephraim Gottlieb, published by the Institute of Jewish Studies (Jerusalem, 1974).

226

3. Scholem pointed out the special characteristics of the *Raᶜaya Meh-eimna*, and especially its social attitudes, in *Major Trends*, p. 211. See also I. Baer, "The Historical Background of the *Raᶜaya Meheimna*" (Hebrew), *Zion*, 5 (1940), pp. 1–44. His conclusions were criticized by Tishby in several sections of *Mishnat ha-Zohar*, vol. 2. Tishby also outlined the different viewpoint of the *Raᶜaya Meheimna* as compared to the body of the *Zohar* on certain issues.

4. A fifteenth-century imitation of the *Zohar* is the *Sefer ha-Qanah*. See M. Oron, "The Sefer ha-Peli'ah and the Sefer ha-Kanah: Their Kabbalistic Principles, Social and Religious Criticism and Literary Composition" [Hebrew] (Ph.D. thesis, Hebrew University, 1980). As late as the eighteenth century Moses Hayyim Luzzato wrote a "Second *Zohar*" in the language and style of the *Zohar*. See I. Tishby, *Netivei ʾEmunah u-Minhut* (Ramat Gan, 1964), p. 170.

5. Scholem explained his understanding and use of the term "theosophy" in this context in *Major Trends*, pp. 205–07.

6. Scholem's summary of the doctrines of the *Zohar* is presented in *Major Trends*, pp. 207–43. Discussions elsewhere, especially in his Eranos lectures, include relevant material. See also G. Scholem, *Kabbalah*, pp. 87–190, where his general description of kabbalistic views is based to a large extent on the *Zohar*.

7. Cordovero presented his systematic analysis of the doctrines of the *Zohar* in his magnum opus, *Pardes Rimmonim*. Luzzato's systematization is found in his *Klah Pithei Hokhmah*. See also Meir ib Gabbai, *Avodat ha-Qodesh*.

8. For a detailed analysis on the Zoharic attitude on the *ʾen-sof* and *keter*, see G. Scholem, *Kabbalah*, pp. 88–91; cf. I. Tishby, *Mishnat ha-Zohar*, vol. 1, pp. 107–11.

9. See, e.g., *Genesis Rabbah* 12:5.

10. The most frequent symbols of the *sefirot*, used in this chapter, are derived from I Chronicles 29:11; the first to employ the verse in this way was Isaac the Blind in his commentary on *Sefer Yezirah* (see G. Scholem, *Ha-Qabbalah be-Provans*, edited by R. Schatz [Jerusalem, 1963], appendix, p. 4). In the *Zohar*, each of these *sefirot* is described by dozens of symbols and the tenth *sefirah*, the *shekhinah*, by hundreds. Lists of such symbols are amongst the most popular literary genres of kabbalah; see, e.g., Gikatilla's *Shaᶜarei ʾOrah* and Cordovero, *Pardes Rimmonim*, ch. 23. It should not be understood that the symbols used here are more "correct"

than others or that the multitude of symbols is synonymous. Each symbol refers to a different aspect of the hidden divine realm.

11. Concerning the "masculine" character of the world of kabbalists, see G. Scholem, *Major Trends*, pp. 37–38.

12. Concerning R. Isaac's treatise, see above, ch. 7, pp. 191–94.

13. See G. Scholem, *Madda'ei ha-Yahadut*, 2 (1967), pp. 194, 249.

14. R. Ezra wrote a brief treatise, "The Secret of the Tree of Knowledge," on the origin of evil, analyzing the biblical story of Adam, Eve, and the serpent in the Garden of Eden. The text was published and analyzed by Scholem in "Gut und Böse in der Kabbala," *Eranos Jahrbuch*, 30 (1961), pp. 39–47 [Hebrew translation in *Pirqei Yesod be-havanat ha Qabbalah u-semaleha* (Jerusalem: Mosad Bialik, 1976), pp. 194–98].

15. Such attitudes on the origin of evil are to be found also in non-kabbalistic works of the thirteenth century such as the anonymous ethical work *Sefer ha-Yashar*. See J. Dan, *Hebrew Ethical and Homiletical Literature* [Hebrew] (Jerusalem, 1975), pp. 116–20.

16. G. Scholem, *Major Trends*, pp. 239, 406.

17. See G. Scholem, *Major Trends*, pp. 235–39; I. Tishby, *Mishnat ha-Zohar*, vol. 1, pp. 288–95.

18. See G. Scholem, *Madda'ei ha-Yahadut*, 2, p. 256.

19. Concerning the concept of evil in Ashkenazi Hasidic theology, see J. Dan, *The Esoteric Theology of the Ashkenazi Hasidim* [Hebrew] (Jerusalem: Mosad Bialik, 1968), pp. 184–202; idem., "Samael, Lilith and the Concept of Evil in Early Kabbalah," *Association for Jewish Studies Review*, 5 (1980), pp. 17–40.

20. For a discussion of the Zoharic descriptions of the powers of evil and their actions in the world, as well as of Zoharic demonology, see I. Tishby, *Mishnat ha-Zohar*, vol. 1, pp. 285–377.

21. The idea of the Shekhinah going into exile is a talmudic one (see, e.g., *Megilah* 29a) developed by the *Zohar* according to its unique symbolism. See G. Scholem, *Major Trends*, pp. 229–33, 270–76; I. Tishby, *Mishnat ha-Zohar*, vol. 1, pp. 228–31.

22. The messianic element in the *Zohar* has been studied recently by Y. Liebes, "The Messiah of the Zohar" (Hebrew), *The Messianic Idea in Jewish Thought: A Study Conference in Honour of the Eightieth Birthday of Gershom Scholem* (Jerusalem: Israel Academy of Sciences and Humanities, 1982), pp. 87–236.

23. On the anthropology of the *Zohar* and the meaning of the com-

mandments, see G. Scholem, *Major Trends,* pp. 240–43. See also I. Tishby, *Mishnat ha-Zohar,* vol. 2, which is completely dedicated to an analysis of the Zoharic passages dealing with the human soul, the commandments and their status vis-à-vis the divine world, and ethics.

24. Concerning this problem, see G. Scholem, *Major Trends,* pp. 201–04.

25. See above, ch. 4, p. 110.

26. This document was included in *Sefer Yohasin* of Abraham Zacuto (1857), p. 88. See G. Scholem, *Major Trends,* pp. 190–94; I. Tishby, *Mishnat ha-Zohar,* vol. 1, pp. 28–32 (of the introduction). Several other points, besides the testimony of the widow and daughter, are of interest in R. Isaac of Acre's report concerning his quest for the author of the *Zohar*—or for the original manuscript reported to have arrived from the land of Israel. It is very difficult to ascertain from this document what R. Isaac's conclusion was concerning the authorship of the *Zohar,* i.e., whether he was convinced that de Leon wrote the book or whether he accepted the claim of its antiquity.

CHAPTER 9

FROM THE *ZOHAR*
TO SAFED

I

THE TWO CENTURIES which separate the appearance of the *Zohar* in Spain and the establishment of the new center of the kabbalah in sixteenth-century Safed witnessed a period of intensive kabbalistic creativity, the spread of the kabbalah to Italy and Germany, the resolution of the conflict between the followers of the kabbalah and those of Jewish philosophy in favor of the mystics, and the strengthening of the kabbalah in Jewish culture. During these two centuries dozens of kabbalistic works were written, old ideas were developed and expounded, and new ones emerged, all to shape the future of Jewish mystical literature.

Scholem dedicated a significant part of his scholarly activity to the investigation of the kabbalah in this period. He wrote many papers on specific kabbalistic works of the sixteenth century on.[1]

Scholem studied the kabbalah of this period to identify specific mystical works, their authors, their date, and their background. He analyzed their mutual relationship and interdependence and characterized the original theological contribution of each.

Some examples of his work in this field are the identification of Rabbi Joseph ben Shalom Ashkenazi as the author of the important commentary on *Sefer Yezirah* which had been wrongly attributed to Rabbi Abraham ben David (the Ravad);[2] the description of his other kabbalistic work (a commentary on the Midrash on Genesis)[3] and his analysis of his theories; his identification and discussion of the works of Rabbi David ben Judah he-Hasid, one of the most important followers of the *Zohar*;[4] his identification of the works of Rabbi Shem Tob ibn Gaon[5] and of Rabbi Isaac of Acre,[6] and many others.

All these studies were based on material found almost exclusively in manuscripts. In most cases Scholem was the first to discover and read them.

II

During the fourteenth century, the kabbalah developed along two different lines. First, the growing impact of the *Zohar* led to the appearance of Hebrew mystical works relying on it, imitating it, and developing its symbolism. Second, the work of the pre-Zoharic schools of the kabbalah, especially that of Gerona, continued almost uninfluenced by the *Zohar*. During most of the fourteenth century the second trend was still dominant. The most important followers of the *Zohar* in this period were the anonymous author of the *Ra'aya Meh-*

emna and the *Tikuney ha-Zohar,* whose works, written at the very end of the thirteenth century and the beginning of the fourteenth, were included in the *Zohar* itself, and Rabbi David ben Judah he-Hasid, who was a descendant of Nachmanides, whose works include lengthy translations from the *Zohar* into Hebrew, which were then presented as new kabbalistic works.[7] It is interesting to note that in the fourteenth century it seems that the *Zohar* was more important to the kabbalah when it spread to new countries and became the basis for new centers than it was for the kabbalists in Spain itself, who continued to a very large extent the traditions of their various pre-Zoharic schools. Thus, when the kabbalah spread to Italy in the beginning of the fourteenth century, the most important spokesman for the *Zohar* was Rabbi Menachem Recanati. He wrote two major works, one a commentary on the Torah and the other an interpretation of the reasons for the commandments *(ta'amey ha-mitsvot).*[8] Both were based on the *Zohar* and strewn with quotations from that book, which are very important for the establishment of the original text of the *Zohar.* Similarly, one of the most important kabbalists in Germany, Rabbi Menachem Ziyuni, wrote a commentary on the Torah and an interesting work on mystical demonology.[9] He also used the *Zohar* extensively and combined Zoharic quotations with the teachings of the Ashkenazi Hasidic masters, especially Rabbi Eleazar of Worms. The importance of the *Zohar* in the works of the most prominent mystics in the new, emerging circles of kabbalists in these countries enhanced significantly its spread and influence.

Most kabbalists in Spain, however, should be viewed as continuing the previous schools of the kabbalah. The most important center in Spain at the end of the thirteenth century and the beginning of the fourteenth was the one Scholem called "the Rashba circle," after the name of its most important leader, Rabbi Solomon ben Abraham Adret, known by the acronym the Rashba. Rabbi Solomon was a great halachist and one of the greatest leaders of Spanish Jewry. He did not write any kabbalistic work, though his commentary on the aggadot of the Talmud includes several references to kabbalistic symbols.[10] The Rashba was regarded by the kabbalists of that period as their leader, as was Nachmanides in the middle of the thirteenth century. Among his disciples in kabbalah were Rabbi Isaac ben Todros,[11] Rabbi Bahya ben Asher of Saragossa,[12] and Rabbi Shem Tob ben Abraham ibn Gaon. A scholar from Eretz Israel seems to have joined this group named Rabbi Isaac of Acre.

Rabbi Bahya ben Asher was one of the first kabbalists to use the *Zohar,* but he did not quote it overtly because his works were intended for the wide public.[13] Another kabbalist, Rabbi Joshua ibn Shueib, later followed a similar path.[14] Both were following the Gerona tradition of Rabbi Jacob ben Sheshet and others, to write popular, ethical, and homiletical works, in which kabbalistic symbolism and theology play a hidden, subdued role. The prestige of the kabbalah grew because of its inclusion in popular culture.

Rabbi Shem Tob ibn Gaon was a halachist, who wrote an important commentary on Maimonides' legal code.[15] He came from Soria, and was familiar with the traditions of Rabbi Jacob and Rabbi Isaac, the Cohen brothers. When he was in Spain he wrote a treatise entitled *Keter Shem Tov* on the subject that most interested the kabbalists of the Rashba circle—

Nachmanides' "secrets," that is, the kabbalistic references in his commentary on the Torah. Shem Tob ibn Gaon emigrated to Jerusalem in 1315. There he wrote a completely different kind of kabbalistic work, *Badey ha-Aron,* in memory of his friend Rabbi Elhanan, who had died there.[16] He completed the work in Safed in 1325. This work reflects the influence of the Cohen brothers, and includes pseudepigraphic parts.[17] It also includes whole sections from the *Zohar,* copied verbatim, without any clear indication of the source from which they were taken. It seems that for Rabbi Shem Tob the teachings of the *Zohar* were important, but the book itself was suspect, and its name better left unmentioned.

The school of the Rashba continued the traditions of the kabbalists of Gerona in another respect. The Rashba took an important part in the renewed controversy concerning the study of philosophy, in 1305. Like Nachmanides in the previous century, the Rashba personally opposed the free study of rationalistic philosophy, but as a leader he assumed a moderate, conciliatory position.[18] In the subsequent years the attitude of the kabbalists became more and more divided over formal philosophy. On the one hand, an attempt was made to merge kabbalah and philosophy and present them as if they were two aspects of the same truth. Each would contribute its own viewpoint and terminology to the understanding of the philosophical questions. One of the most important kabbalists to follow this path was Rabbi Joseph ibn Waqar.[19] To some extent, he followed the tradition of Rabbi Isaac ibn Latif, who had been active in the previous century.[20] Ibn Waqar believed that a synthesis between the kabbalah and philosophy was possible, and it seems that some philosophers, from

Rabbi Moses Narboni[21] to Rabbi Hasdai Crescas[22] seem to
have shared this view. By the fifteenth century, however, this
movement was supported only by a few Jewish intellectuals.

On the other hand, the kabbalists wrote more works which
vehemently opposed formal philosophy and all its influences.
The best known among these was Rabbi Shem Tov ben Shem
Tov, whose *Sefer ha-Emunot (The Book of Beliefs)*, which includes many early kabbalistic traditions and quotations, represents a direct attack against Jewish philosophy.[23] During
the fourteenth and fifteenth centuries, Maimonides was claimed
as a kabbalist.[24] The name of Maimonides was too exalted
and his prestige too great to be left to the philosophers; the
Jewish mystics had to adopt him as one of their own and
reinterpret his philosophy as a special genre of kabbalistic
symbolism.

III

The fifteenth-century kabbalistic works which exerted the
greatest influence on subsequent developments in Jewish
mysticism were probably two books written by the same unknown author: *Sefer ha-Peliah* and *Sefer ha-Kanah (The Book of
{Esoteric} Wonder* and *The Book of {Rabbi Nehunia ben} ha-
Kanah.)*[25] The first is a collection of various kabbalistic traditions from earlier sources, with great emphasis on mythological symbolism and an interest in the details of the process of redemption. The second is a commentary on the reasons
for the commandments *(ta'amey ha-mitsvot)*, but in a peculiar
literary manner: The author of the *Sefer ha-Kanah* invented a

family, which was described as connected with Rabbi Nehunia ben ha-Kanah, who was regarded as the author of the
book *Bahir*.[26] The book includes several imaginative stories
of supernatural revelations which had some influence on subsequent Hebrew mystical storytelling.[27] There is little doubt
that the author of this work tried to imitate the *Zohar* in a
creative manner. Instead of following the Zoharic language
and the stories about the circle of Rabbi Shimeon bar Yohai,
he created an imaginary family of ancient mystics, and revealed his own mystical ideas through their Hebrew homilies.[28] These works were probably written in Greece[29] and
had great influence on later kabbalists up to the Hasidic
movement of the eighteenth century.

Scholem emphasized in his description of this period the
renewed strengthening of the magical element in kabbalistic
works.[30] One school of kabbalists produced works which
combined theosophic speculation with studies of secret divine
names, the meaning of the Hebrew alphabet in the tradition
of Abraham Abulafia, and clear magical formulas. The best-
known work among these is the *Brith Menuha*, published in
1648, which is a manifestation of a trend that grew considerably in the sixteenth century both in Safed and in Europe.
It seems that although the works of Abulafia were superseded
in the history of the kabbalah by the followers of the theosophical school and especially the *Zohar*, they still had an
impact. Kabbalists generations later, without any direct line
of tradition to connect them with the teachings of the "prophetic kabbalist" of the thirteenth century, found inspiration
and great insight in them.

The kabbalah became almost a popular subject when the
fifteenth century was drawing to a close. This is attested to,

for instance, by the fact that one of the most popular Hebrew ethical works of the Middle Ages was Rabbi Israel Alnaqawa's *Menorat ha-Maor*. This is based almost exclusively on quotations and paraphrases of Talmudic and Midrashic sources; it also contains quotations from the *Zohar* (as the Midrash *Yehi Or, Let There Be Light*).[31] In the early sixteenth century we find popular homilists quoting the *Zohar* freely, integrating the kabbalah completely into popular culture, and negating the admonishments of Rabbi Isaac the Blind in his letter to Gerona three centuries earlier.[32] Mysticism did not become popular in the full sense of the term, however, until the seventeenth century, under the impact of the Lurianic kabbalah from Safed, but it could not be described as appealing only to mystics. Many of the best-known and most frequently read commentaries on the Bible and collections of sermons which constituted, together with books on ethics, the popular culture of the age, were written by kabbalists and influenced, at least to some extent, by kabbalistic symbolism. If the kabbalah was not yet popular, it certainly became familiar. Its prestige was on the rise and, coupled with the rapid decline of Jewish philosophy in the fifteenth century, its position more and more central in Jewish thought.

While the kabbalah was becoming known to some extent in most Jewish communities, it was most deeply accepted and understood in Italy. Jewish intellectuals in Italy during the Renaissance period, deeply influenced by the strong neo-Platonic attitudes of their Christian neighbors, discovered similar attitudes in the kabbalah. Their increasing interest in Jewish mystical sources also reached non-Jewish intellectuals, to create the Christian kabbalah.

The problem of the emergence of the Christian kabbalah,

and especially its roots within Judaism, fascinated Scholem throughout his scholarly career, for several reasons. Here he had an opportunity to study the Jewish symbols when they were transformed into another language, another religion, and another mystical tradition; he could also follow the intrinsic force of the Jewish mystical ideas when they operated in a different culture. Another intriguing aspect was that between the Christian kabbalists and the Jewish sources there was an intervening group of people—the translators from Hebrew to Latin, who were mostly converted Jews. Scholem was particularly interested in those Jewish converts to Christianity who wrote books explaining their adherence to the new religion; he even collected a special library of their works, which he defined as "anti-Semitic books written by converts." The Jews who translated kabbalistic works to Latin to serve the religious purposes of Christian theologians and mystics fascinated him. Indeed, the appearance of the kabbalah in Latin preceded the Renaissance period by several centuries, and Scholem investigated those early beginnings.[33]

The most important kabbalist in the late fifteenth century in Italy who was deeply influenced by the Platonism of the Florentine school was Rabbi Johanan Alemano, who was a prolific writer.[34] One of his disciples, Samuel Abulfaraj, converted to Christianity and assumed the name of Flavius Mithridates. This convert wrote some sermons, one of which was delivered in front of the Pope. He suggested that Christianity could be defended against Judaism by resorting to secret Jewish works, though the material he presented was from the usual rabbinic sources.[35] But his life work was the translation of kabbalistic works into Latin, which he did systematically

238

and diligently, including works of Rabbi Judah the Pious and of Abraham Abulafia. He presented them to the prodigy of that period in Christian theology—the Count Pico della Mirandola.

Pico himself studied Hebrew, and was interested in the kabbalah together with all ancient traditions, whether magical, orphic, or anything else. In his theses he proposed to prove the veracity and antiquity of Christian truth from the kabbalah. Among his 900 theses, about 130 are based on his studies of the kabbalah. Pico, like other Christian kabbalists, completely accepted the claim of the Jewish mystics that their works reflected traditions given to Moses and to the Patriarchs and transmitted orally from generation to generation. Pico and other Christian kabbalists, especially Johannes Reuchlin, who wrote two major books on the kabbalah, also believed that by studying these sources they could discover prerabbinic truths, obscured in the Hebrew rabbinic sources, that would reflect basic Christian theology. Reuchlin was especially interested in the doctrine of the secret names of God, and presented a system according to which the true name of God was revealed only through the appearance of Christianity. In fact, Jesus' name is the full name of God, hidden from the Jews and revealed to his followers when Christianity appeared.

The Christian kabbalists spread some of the kabbalistic myths and symbols to the fertile ground of Europe during the Renaissance period. These symbols, though drastically transformed in their new cultural environment, flourished and enriched not only European thought but its literature as well.[36]

By the beginning of the sixteenth century, therefore, the

239

kabbalah spread to geographical and cultural realms far beyond the original closed circles from which it had emerged three centuries earlier.[37] The influence of rationalistic philosophy was weakening, and after the expulsion from Spain it almost disappeared. Some kabbalistic works began to be accepted throughout the Jewish intellectual world. Among these was the anonymous systematization of the kabbalah, *Sefer Ma'arechet ha-Elohut* (*The Book of the Divine Hierarchy*), to which Rabbi Judah Hayyat wrote a commentary.[38] It served as a textbook for the study of the kabbalah. Another example is a work by Rabbi Meir ibn Gabbay, entitled *Avodat ha-Kodesh* (*Holy Worship*), which presented in a coherent, systematic form the mystical meaning of Jewish ritual, especially that of the prayers, to give a mystical dimension to everyday religious rituals.

It seemed as if the kabbalah had matured into an aspect of Jewish culture. However, the expulsion of the Jews from Spain presented Judaism with new theological problems. Only the kabbalah had the answers to these problems, and thus, in the new kabbalistic center in Safed the kabbalah was transformed from a minor aspect of Jewish culture into a dynamic force helping to shape Jewish history.

NOTES

1. See especially Gershom Scholem, *Kabbalah* (Jerusalem: Keter, 1974), pp. 61–67.

2. See G. Scholem, "Chapters from the History of Kabbalistic Literature" (Hebrew), *Kiryat Sefer*, 4 (1927–28), pp. 286–302.

3. See Moshe Hallamish, "The Beginning of Rabbi Joseph Ashkenazi's

Commentary on *Genesis Rabbah*" (Hebrew), *Studies in Jewish Mysticism Presented to Isaiah Tishby on his Seventy-fifth Birthday, Jerusalem Studies in Jewish Thought*, 3 (1983–84), pp. 139–89. See also M. Hallamish, ed., *A Kabbalistic Commentary of R. Yosef ben Shalom Ashkenazi on Genesis Rabbah* (Jerusalem: Magnes Press, 1984).

4. G. Scholem, "Chapters from the History of Kabbalistic Literature," pp. 302–27.

5. G. Scholem, "Remnants of R. Shem Tob ibn Gaon's Work on the Elements of the Sefirot Theory," *Kiryat Sefer*, 8 (1931–32), pp. 397–408, 534–42; G. Scholem, *Kiryat Sefer*, 9 (1932–33), pp. 126–33. (See also, however, D. Ariel, "Shem Tob ibn Shem Tob's Kabbalistic Critique of Jewish Philosophy in the Commentary on the Sefirot: Study and Text" [Ph.D. thesis, Brandeis University, 1982], p. 15. According to Ariel, Scholem communicated orally to the author [see n. 48] that he had changed his mind about the attribution of this text: the real author was not Shem Tob ibn Gaon but rather Shem Tob ibn Shem Tob.)

6. See G. Scholem, *Kabbalah*, pp. 62–64, 119–22, 175–76, and his edition of R. Isaac of Acre's "Commentary on the *Sefer Yeẓirah*," *Kiryat Sefer*, 31 (1956), pp. 379–96. R. Isaac's major work, *Me'irat 'Einayim*, was published in 1978 and again in a critical edition by Amos Goldreich in 1981 (Ph.D. thesis, Hebrew University).

7. For R. David's most important work, see *The Book of Mirrors: Sefer Mar'ot ha-Ẓove'ot by R. David ben Yehudah he-Ḥasid*, edited by Daniel Matt (Chico, Cal.: Scholars Press, 1982).

8. On Recanati's works, see G. Scholem, *Kabbalah*, p. 62.

9. Menahem Ziyuni's "Commentary on the Torah" was one of the early works of kabbalah to be printed, while his work on demonology, *Ẓefunei Ẓiyuni*, is extant in two manuscripts in the Bodleian Library, Oxford.

10. Concerning the kabbalistic elements in the Rashba's commentary on the *aggadot*, see G. Scholem, *Kabbalah*, pp. 57, 61–62.

11. See Ephraim Gottlieb, *Studies in the Kabbala Literature*, edited by Joseph Hacker (Tel Aviv: Tel Aviv University, 1976), p. 570, and passim.

12. For a detailed study of this kabbalist, see E. Gottlieb, *Ha-Qabbalah be-Khitvei Rabbenu Baḥya ben 'Asher* (Jerusalem: Kiryat Sefer, 1970).

13. For an extensive discussion of Baḥya's use of the *Zohar*, see E. Gottlieb, *Ha-Qabbalah be-Khitvei Rabbenu Baḥya ben 'Asher*, pp. 167–93.

14. See G. Scholem, *Kabbalah*, p. 61.

15. The halakic and kabbalistic writings of Shem Tob ibn Gaon were described by S. D. Levinger in his study "Rabbi Shem Tob ben Abraham ben Ga'on" (Hebrew), *Sefunot*, 7 (1963), pp. 9–39. The paper was reprinted as an introduction to the facsimile edition of Shem Tob ibn Gaon's *Baddei Ha-'Aron u-Migdal Ḥananel*, based on MS. 840 in the National Library, Paris (Jerusalem: Orient and Occident, 1977).

16. See S. D. Levinger, "Rabbi Shem Tob ben Abraham ben Ga'on," pp. 12–15.

17. Cf. J. Dan, "The Kabbalistic Book *Baddei Ha-'Aron* and Kabbalistic Pseudepigraphy in the Thirteenth Century" (Hebrew), *Studies in Jewish Mysticism Presented to Isaiah Tishby on his Seventy-fifth Birthday, Jerusalem Studies in Jewish Thought,* 3 (1983–84), pp. 111–38. The pseudepigraphic parts include the epistle attributed to the Ashkenazi Hasidim and a response concerning the secret of "amen" attributed to Rabbi Yekutiel.

18. The controversy has not yet received full scholarly treatment and the exact role of the Rashba's circle in it has not been clarified.

19. Ibn Waqar's works have been studied by G. Vajda in his *Recherches sur la philosophie et la kabbale à pensée juive du moyen âge* (Paris, 1962), pp. 115–297.

20. See above, ch. 7, n. 26.

21. The problem is most apparent in Moses Narboni's *'Iggeret al Shiʿur Qomah*. See G. Scholem, *Kabbalah*, p. 64. (A critical edition of this text, together with an introductory study and annotated translation, was published by A. Altmann, "Moses Narboni's 'Epistle on *Shiʿur Qoma'*,'" in A. Altmann, ed., *Jewish Medieval and Renaissance Studies* [Cambridge: Harvard University Press, 1967], pp. 225–88. On the question of the harmonistic relationship between philosophy and kabbalah in Narboni's earlier works, see especially pp. 242–54.)

22. See W. Z. Harvey, "Kabbalistic Elements in Crescas' Light of the Lord" (Hebrew), *Jerusalem Studies in Jewish Thought,* 2 (1982–83), pp. 75–109.

23. See G. Scholem, *Kabbalah*, p. 65.

24. For a study of the legend of Maimonides' transformation from philosopher to kabbalist, see G. Scholem, "Me-Ḥoqer le-Mequbal," *Tarbiz,* 6 (1939), pp. 334–42.

25. Both books were printed in Koretz, which later became the center of Hasidic printing.

26. See above, ch. 5, p. 29–30.

27. See J. Dan, *The Hebrew Story in the Middle Ages* [Hebrew] (Jerusalem, 1975), p. 148.

28. For a detailed study of these two works, see Michal Oron, "The Sefer ha-Peli'ah and the Sefer ha-Kanah: Their Kabbalistic Principles, Social and Religious Criticism and Literary Composition" (Ph.D. thesis, Hebrew University, 1980).

29. The identification of Greece or areas under Greek or Byzantine influence as the place of origin of these works is based on the versions of the prayers included in them. See I. Ta-Shema, "Hekhan Nithaber Sefer Alilot Devarim?" *Alei Sefer,* 3 (1937), pp. 44–53; M. Oron, "The Sefer ha-Peli'ah and the Sefer ha-Kanah," pp. 6–15.

30. G. Scholem, *Kabbalah,* p. 65.

31. G. Scholem, op. cit., p. 66.

32. See above, ch. 6, p. 173, n. 37.

33. See the bibliography on this subject compiled by Scholem in *Kabbalah,* pp. 209–10.

34. Moshe Idel has written several studies on the life, writings, and influence of this kabbalist. See M. Idel, "The Curriculum of Yohanan Alemanno" (Hebrew), *Tarbiz,* 48 (1980), pp. 303–31; M. Idel, "The Magical and Neoplatonic Interpretations of the Kabbalah in the Renaissance" (Hebrew), *Jerusalem Studies in Jewish Thought,* 4 (1982), pp. 60–111 [English translation in B. Cooperman, ed., *Jewish Thought in the Sixteenth Century* (Cambridge: Harvard University Press, 1983), pp. 186–242].

35. See C. Wirzubski, *Plauviyus Mitridates* (Jerusalem: Magnes Press, 1963).

36. See, for example, Joseph L. Blau, *The Christian Interpretation of the Cabala in the Renaissance* (New York: Columbia University Press, 1944); F. Secret, *Le Zôhar Chez les Kabbalistes Chrétiens de la Renaissance* (1958).

37. Scholem did not devote specific studies to the kabbalah in eastern countries. It is today being studied by scholars such as M. Hallamish, M. Idel, Z. Gries, D. Maor, and others. See, for example, M. Hallamish, *Le-Toldot ha-Kabbalah be Teman (The History of Kabbalah in Yeman)* (Ramat Gan: Bar-Ilan University Press, 1984).

38. See E. Gottlieb, "The Kabbalah of R. Joseph Gikatilla and the *Ma'arekhot ha-'Elohut*" (Hebrew), E. Gottlieb, *Studies in the Kabbala Literature,* esp. pp. 289–343.

CHAPTER 10

THE SAFED SCHOOL OF
THE KABBALAH

I

THE EXPULSION OF the Jews from Spain in 1492 changed the geography as well as the ideological attitudes of world Jewish communities. Two separate centers were formed, one in eastern Europe and one in the Ottoman Empire, of which the main communities were in North Africa, Egypt, Turkey, Syria, and Eretz Israel. The hardships that the Jews exiled from Spain underwent brought home to all Jewish centers an intense sense of exile, as the largest and oldest Jewish community in Europe was destroyed overnight by one royal decree. A feeling of uncertainty engulfed even those communities which were not directly affected by the expulsion. The sufferings of the exiled were documented in historical and literary works, which were read widely in the Jewish world. This and other reasons caused the intensification of messianic expectations which had begun in the fifteenth century. Messianism, which was quite subdued in medieval Jewish culture, emerged now to become a major cultural and historical force, even a dominant one which shaped Jewish beliefs and behavior.

It was clear to Scholem that as a consequence of these historical events a dramatic change had occurred in the nature of the kabbalah itself and in its role in Jewish thought, society, and historical orientation. Scholem investigated this change in great detail, and from this point onward his studies of the kabbalah and of Jewish history merged into one. Jewish mysticism from the late fifteenth century to the nineteenth century became inextricably part of the major forces which worked within Jewish society, forces which produced some of the most vigorous and meaningful historical movements of modern Judaism.

According to Scholem, the history of Hasidism and of Sabbatianism are rooted in the Lurianic kabbalah which developed in sixteenth-century Safed. This kabbalah became the Jewish spiritual response to the historical events of the expulsion from Spain. That the kabbalah became (often in spite of the intentions of its creators), a dominant force in Jewish culture was also a result of the events connected with the expulsion. Thus, a continuous line of mystical development leads from late fifteenth-century Spain to seventeenth-century Turkey where Sabbatianism began, to the Ukraine of the eighteenth century, where Hasidism began. A complete understanding of the forces working within twentieth-century Judaism cannot be achieved without understanding Jewish messianism, its development and decline, and the emergence of Hasidism and its opponents. The spiritual processes which produced them all are rooted in the traumatic experience of the expulsion from Spain and the appearance of the new kabbalah in sixteenth-century Safed.

Among the Spanish Jews, a significant segment of the upper classes, both materially and intellectually, chose not to be exiled but accepted conversion and remained in Spain after 1492. It seemed to the generation of the exiled that the best-educated, leading part of the community in Spain was the weakest when it came to sacrificing all its worldly possessions for the sake of adherence to Judaism. These were the people who were later persecuted most cruelly by the Spanish Inquisition for continuing to be secretly faithful to Judaism. The Jews outside Spain, while they regretted the sufferings of their brothers at the hands of the Inquisition, could not forget that these Jews would not have become victims of that institution had they not (or their parents or grandparents) accepted Christianity instead of exile. The Inquisition, after all, had jurisdiction only over Christians, being an institution intended for the abolishment of heresy within the Catholic Church. There were mixed feelings among Jews concerning the martyrs of the Inquisition trials, and there were long debates concerning the process of repentance required from *marranos* who had succeeded in getting out of Spain and wanted to return to Judaism in their new homes.[1]

Judaism viewed the expulsion—and that so many Jews chose conversion over exile—as a major spiritual crisis, which necessitated a new evaluation of Jewish education and spiritual directives. Many of the rabbis of the generation of the expulsion, among them leaders of the exiled, blamed Jewish rationalistic philosophy for this crisis.[2] They compared the behavior of the leaders of Spanish Jewry to that of the leaders of Ashkenazi Jewry during the period of the Crusades, when leaders were martyred with their communities rather than yielding to conversion to Christianity. The leaders in Spain did not follow this example, according to their contemporary critics. They chose the easy way out. The fault, according to these critics, was in the spiritualization of religious life taught by Jewish philosophy. That is, what one feels and thinks is more important than what one does, if the center of Jewish religious life is within the hearts and minds of the people and not in the synagogue, the Passover seder, the kosher diet, and all other physical deeds required of a Jew by the *halak-hah*, then conversion is completely different than if the center of religion remains in the practical deeds. To love God, to contemplate his greatness and benevolence, can be done in a church as well as in a synagogue. If some ignorant Christian priests believe that by the ceremony of conversion they change the faith, the mind, and heart of a person—let them think so; it is not worth throwing away a lifetime's possessions and one's homeland. If Judaism is something one has to practice publicly and externally, then there is no middle way between exile and genuine conversion. But if Judaism is an intellectual and spiritual experience, external and pretended conversion need not interfere with the practice of it.

This, according to some leaders of the Spanish Jews in exile, was how Jewish rationalistic philosophy facilitated the conversion of so many Jews in Spain, and naturally it affected more those who did convert. The masses, the simple folk who followed the Jewish commandments because they were divine orders, could not accept this reasoning. They were expelled and suffered all the hardships of exile. But the bet-

ter-educated classes absorbed the teachings of the rationalists
and spiritualists; they preferred to stay in Spain and follow
Judaism in secret. They became *marranos*.[3]

The works of Jewish antirationalists in the early sixteenth
century, like Isaac Abravanel, and especially Rabbi Joseph
Ya'abetz, both writing in Italy immediately after the expulsion, had great impact. The sixteenth century is a period of
dramatic decline in Jewish philosophical activity. It really
marks the end of Jewish philosophy for several centuries. In
sixteenth-century Italy, for the first time, the kabbalah became a part of the basic intellectual world of Jews, even those
who had no mystical bent whatsoever. Some knowledge of
the *Zohar* became a requirement, not as a book of mysticism
but as a masterpiece of Jewish literature. Quotations from the
Zohar did not mark a writer as a mystic any more, just as a
well-read intellectual. The kabbalah did not become "popular," but it was accepted by many as an integral element of
Jewish culture and education.

While the kabbalah was undoubtedly free of the sins attributed to Jewish philosophy, and its antirationalistic character and neo-Platonic philosophy brought it close to the intellectual atmosphere of the day, it still did not provide answers
to the acute problems of the generation of the exiled. The
individualistic conception of mystical redemption presented
by the kabbalah was not radically different from the contemplation of God in an Aristotelian rationalistic system. In order to be more than a refuge for people disappointed by Jewish philosophy, the kabbalah itself had to be changed. It had
to be redirected toward the needs of Jews in this period of
crisis and upheaval. It took two generations to achieve this.

II

From the middle of the fifteenth century there occurred a change in the kabbalah in Spain, which Scholem studied closely.[4] The most important aspect of this change was the intensification of the messianic element in the kabbalah, as well as the appearance of vivid mythological descriptions and a great interest in the nature and appearance of the powers of evil.

In this period Rabbi Joseph dela Reina attempted to bring about the redemption by kabbalistic and magical means. The unusual kabbalistic work *Kaf ha-Ketoret,* which explains the Psalms as messianic poems, was written in this period, as was the *Sefer ha-Meshiv,* which attributes to God himself its mystical revelations.[5] The eschatological *Nevuat ha-Yeled (Prophecy of the Child),* was probably written, with a messianic commentary, in Italy in this period.[6] Several other similar though unrelated phenomena signified the turn of such kabbalists to intensive messianic speculation.

One of the most important writers of the first generation after the expulsion from Spain was Rabbi Abraham ben Eliezer ha-Levi. He went to Eretz Israel and wrote some of his works there. Scholem dedicated detailed studies to the analysis and publication of parts from his kabbalistic works, which dealt exclusively with messianic mythology and speculation concerning the time and nature of the forthcoming redemption.[7] Another important messianic work is the *Galya Raza (The Revealer of Secrets),* which was probably written in the second half of the sixteenth century.[8]

These works and others similar to them indicate that a

change was occurring in the attitude of many kabbalists to the messianic element in their mystical systems, but these writers were still the exception rather than the rule. The dominant stream in sixteenth-century kabbalah still was the one formulated in the fourteenth and fifteenth centuries, which drew back from the mythology of the *Zohar* and presented a mystical system which could be expressed in semirationalistic terms. The best example of this school was Rabbi Meir ibn Gabbay, the author of the *Avodat ha-Kodesh (Holy Worship)* and other works, which became very popular.[9] He described the kabbalistic attitude toward worship and the performance of the commandments with strong emphasis on the theurgic side and the impact of Man's deeds on the divine realm. Though he followed the *Zohar* closely, he minimized the elements of sexual symbolism and dualistic mythology, and the struggle between good and evil. In this he reflected the attitude of many kabbalists of the time.

Groups of kabbalists, most of them exiled from Spain, wandered east from the Iberian peninsula. Many of them settled in Turkey, then the striving center of the Ottoman Empire, but some continued to Syria and Eretz Israel. One of the most important leaders of such groups was Rabbi Joseph Taitazak.[10] Many of his disciples settled in Safed. Rabbi Joseph was a homilist, and his followers, the most important being Rabbi Moses Alsheich, founded the great center of kabbalistic homiletics and mystical ethics in Safed.

From this group also came the first inclinations of the desire to participate actively in the process of redemption. Among the halachists in Safed a great enterprise was begun—the reinstitution of the Jewish *semichah,* rabbinic ordination. According to Jewish tradition, the power to judge according to the *halakhah* was given to Moses by God, and Moses transferred it not only by teaching, but by the ceremony of ordination. This was continuous, a rabbi ordaining his disciple from generation to generation, until the chain was broken in the Middle Ages. Because of that, the rabbis since then did not have the full legal-religious power to judge their fellow Jews. Maimonides, in his great code, discussed the problem of how the *semichah* should be reinstituted in messianic times. He concluded that the messiah would not reinstitute full ordination (for he did not believe that the messiah would be greater than, or even equal to, Moses). Rather, an assembly of all the rabbis in Israel should choose one man from among themselves unanimously, who would be fully ordained and should ordain others. [11]

The halachists and kabbalists in Safed decided not to wait till the appearance of the messiah (which they believed to be imminent), to carry out Maimonides' scheme. The rabbis of Safed, under the leadership of Rabbi Jacob Berav, one of the greatest halachic authorities of the time, duly elected him to be the first ordained rabbi with the power to ordain others. [12]

There was one flaw in the scheme: Safed was not the only halachic center in Eretz Israel. There was another, greater, center—Jerusalem. In order to carry out Maimonides' scheme faithfully the rabbis of Jerusalem had to join their Safed colleagues, for all elections had to be unanimous. Rabbi Jacob Berav immediately sent a letter of ordination to the greatest halachic authority in Jerusalem and asked him and others to join them. The rabbis of Jerusalem categorically refused.

A controversy ensued, garbed completely in halachic ter-

minology and pretending to concentrate on the proper exegesis of Maimonides. The real argument, however, was whether
the rabbis should actively participate in the process of the
redemption or wait for the actual appearance of the messaiah.
This was a clash between active and passive messianic attitudes, when Safed represented the active one, supported by
kabbalistic notions. It seemed that the great Safed project
had failed when the Jerusalem rabbis refused to join, but
Rabbi Jacob Berav continued to ordain rabbis in Safed,[13] including Rabbi Moses Alsheich,[14] the great preacher, and his
disciple in the *halakah,* Rabbi Joseph Karo. The ordinations
in Safed continued for four generations; for these rabbis the
refusal of the rabbis of Jerusalem was not sufficient reason to
desist from their messianic enterprise.

Two other scholars shaped the center in Safed in the first
half and middle of the sixteenth century. Rabbi Joseph Karo
was undoubtedly the greatest halahist of the century, whose
legal code, the *Shulhan Aruch* (based on a commentary on the
halachic code the *Turim,* which in its turn was based on the
code of Maimonides), serves to this day as the most presti-
gious codification of Jewish religious law. But besides being
a sharp, commonsense lawyer, Karo was a devout kabbalist
who wrote a major work, of which only a part has survived—
The Book of the Maggid (Sefer ha-Maggid, euphemistically called
Maggid Mesharim, using the double-meaning Hebrew term,
maggid, which can be just a preacher, but also means, especially in this period, a divine power revealed to a mystic).[15]
Rabbi Joseph, like many others in this period (as Scholem
has shown),[16] believed that a divine power, the *shekhinah,*
was revealed to him in the form of the Mishnah. His ideal

was to be favored to receive the fate allotted by God to the messianic martyr Rabbi Shlomo Molcho, who was burnt at the stake by the Inquisition.[17] This work is not innovative or original, but it reflects the dominance of kabbalistic terminology and mystical attitudes in sixteenth-century Safed.

Rabbi Moses Cordovero, one of the greatest kabbalistic writers of all, was one of a group of five or six people who shaped the kabbalah for centuries.[18] His great project was to rewrite the Zoharic kabbalah in a new form, or, to be precise, in two different forms. One was a continuous, extensive commentary on every page of the *Zohar* entitled *Or Yaqar (Precious Light)*.[19] This commentary is an enormous treasury of kabbalistic ideas.

His better-known and more influential work is *Pardes Rimonim (The Promenades Orchard)*, which is a detailed presentation of the kabbalistic world. Again, this work is based on the *Zohar*. Cordovero attempted in it to present the ideas of the *Zohar* in a systematic way. Every chapter is dedicated to one subject, leading the reader step by step and elucidating in a precise language the world which the *Zohar* presented in using enthusiastic language and the homiletical method. Cordovero began with the Godhead itself. Then he discussed the divine attributes of the upper and lower *sefirot,* analyzing systematically the structure of these divine attributes, and using a wealth of material from various ancient kabbalistic sources in combination with the Zoharic descriptions. Cordovero goes on to describe the various aspects of the *merkabah* and angelic worlds and the divine order in the physical world, Man, his soul, the demonic powers, and every other subject central to the *Zohar* and the early kabbalah.

Cordovero's work can be regarded both as a systematization and a summary of the kabbalah that preceded him, and an original and profound contribution to the development of the kabbalah. He presented his work as based on the *Zohar,* and even included in the *Pardes* a dictionary of the kabbalistic symbols of the *Zohar.*[20] He was also a profound mystic who was especially interested in the Godhead and its relationship with the emanated attributes. Some describe his attitude as pantheistic, since he found the light of the Godhead itself within everything in existence.[21]

Though Cordovero was undoubtedly an original thinker and mystic, his basic attitude toward kabbalistic mythology did not differ from the prevailing one in the previous centuries after the *Zohar.* We do not find in his work a reflection of the new attitudes present in the works of some of the kabbalists who wrote after the expulsion from Spain. For instance, the messianic element does not occupy a central place in his system, nor does he follow the mythologies of evil which were reevolved in the kabbalah of the late fifteenth and the sixteenth centuries. For Cordovero, "no evil descends from heaven." The evil phenomena in the physical world are the results of developments in lower regions of the celestial world and the results of Man's sins.[22] The Zoharic myth of the "death of the kings of Edom" is interpreted by Cordovero in complete contradiction to the myth as clearly stated in the *Zohar.*[23] Cordovero did not avoid the sexual symbolism of the *Zohar,* but he did not develop it and to some extent minimized its role. Cordovero was the spokesman and the systematic formulator of the kabbalah of the pre-expulsion period, which continued to a very large extent to shape the sixteenth-century kabbalah as well. In Safed, however, many did not follow his footsteps, even though he belonged to the most exalted school of Safed kabbalists, the one which began with Rabbi Joseph Taitazak and was continued by Rabbi Moses Cordovero's great teacher, Rabbi Joseph Alkabetz.[24]

Besides the two works discussed above, Cordovero wrote a dozen or more commentaries and systematic discussions of kabbalistic problems. A small book of his had an enormous impact both in Safed and in the kabbalah of the following centuries. Entitled *Tomer Devorah (The Palm Tree of Deborah)*, this brief treatise is dedicated to the ethical consequences of kabbalistic belief.[25] Its chapters follow the order of the *sefirot*, and the author guides the reader to become united with each of the divine powers. The ethical ideas included are to some extent commonplace ones; they receive new meaning and impact by their mystical meaning. According to Cordovero, each ethical deed has a direct consequence in the divine world, and these are presented in detail in the treatise. Cordovero presents both a system of *imitatio dei,* in the full mystical meaning of the term, demanding that man imitate the behavior of the *sefirot,* and a profound theurgic system, according to which Man's deeds (and misdeeds) affect the divine powers. *Tomer Devorah* was influential in the creation of the great school of kabbalists in Safed who wrote ethical works based on the kabbalah. The most important writer was Cordovero's disciple, Rabbi Eliyahu de Vidas, the author of the basic and most influential work of ethics, *Reshit Hochmah (The Beginning of Wisdom)*. A later author of a major work on ethics was Rabbi Isaiah ha-Levi Horowitz. He incorporated *Tomer Devorah* completely in his *Shnei Luhot ha-Berit.* Other great kabbalists in Safed followed Cordovero in writing ethical treatises, among them Rabbi Hayyim Vital, the great disciple of Luria, who wrote the brief but unusual and profound ethical work *Shaarey Kedushah (The Gates of Holiness).*[26]

During his lifetime and several decades after his death Cordovero was regarded as the greatest kabbalist in Safed, and mystics from other countries, especially Italy, studied his works as the last word in the field of kabbalah. His *Pardes* was written at the request of kabbalists from Italy. But he was still alive when a new kabbalah, very different from his, emerged in Safed, the kabbalah of Rabbi Isaac Luria.[27]

III

Rabbi Isaac Luria Ashkenazi influenced the kabbalah in a dramatic and most profound way; it is even possible to describe him as a revolutionary within the kabbalah. He became the inspiration for a vast body of literature, written by his disciples and their disciples, and he is the first modern figure to be a hero of a hagiography in Hebrew literature.[28] Our knowledge of his life is very scant. Only the last two of his 38 years are documented. He came to Safed from Egypt in 1570 and revolutionized Jewish thought without ever writing one book of his own.

Luria explained the fact that he did not write his teachings in a book because he expressed himself in visions and enormous pictures. He was unable to convey them in written pages. Fortunately, his disciples succeeded in conveying some of his visions.

The best known of Luria's disciples was Rabbi Hayyim Vital Clippers. He was the author of the most important presentations of the teachings of Luria, entitled *Etz Hayyim (The Tree of Life)*, and *Sefer ha-Shearim (The Book of Gates)*, a series of monographs on the subjects that Luria dealt with, each of which is called "a gate" of that subject. This work includes a commentary on several sections of the *Zohar*, presented by Rabbi Hayyim Vital from the teachings of Luria. Though Rabbi Hayyim was very faithful to Luria, he did not present his teachings without some editing and even some censorship. When compared to the brief description of Luria's teachings recorded by another disciple, Rabbi Joseph ibn Tabul[29] it is evident that some of the more mythical teachings of Luria were deleted or minimized by Rabbi Hayyim.

Luria had no known teacher in kabbalah. His teachings therefore did not rely upon the sanctity of a chain of tradition. His disciples claimed that Luria went to heaven to participate in the deliberations of the celestial academy concerning mystical matters, heard Zoharic passages interpreted there, and revealed to his disciples what he had heard when he returned—that is, when he woke up. They believed that the prophet Elijah was his direct teacher. Luria was the first great charismatic teacher of kabbalah. He did not claim to be a prophet and did not claim to have a *maggid* dictating secrets to him. Those who believed in his personality became his disciples.[30] He was a great visionary, around whom were collected a handful of believers. His ideas captivated people who had never seen or heard him.

Luria's untimely death presented his disciples with a problem. Early death was regarded in Judaism as a divine punishment for a sin, a death of *karet*. Thus, Luria's death at the age of 38 had to be explained theologically, lest the great mystic be regarded as a common sinner. One explanation presented by Rabbi Hayyim was that Luria was punished for revealing divine secrets to his disciples. This, of course, meant that Luria indeed knew such secrets and that the new kabbalah presented by the disciples was indeed of divine origin.

Another explanation, which indicates the atmosphere in which Luria's teachings were presented, was that Luria had to die because he was the messiah son of Joseph, who, according to the ancient apocalyptic prophecy of the Book of Zerubavel and other sources, was destined to die in battle against the powers of evil before the final victory to be achieved by the messiah son of David. Rabbi Hayyim himself believed that he was destined to play the role of the messiah son of David.[31] We have a detailed diary written by Rabbi Hayyim, *Sefer ha-Hezyonot (The Book of Visions)*,[32] which he began to write before his meeting with Luria in 1570, and continued until his death four decades after Luria. In this book he assembled, from a variety of sources, proofs that he himself was going to be the redeemer of Israel. These sources include dreams (his own and others') and revelations made by Arab sorcerers and diviners. About half the book is dedicated to what Luria had told him concerning the source and mission of his messianic soul. There is no doubt that the circle around Luria was intensely messianic, even if various members formulated their messianic hopes in different forms. (They expected the redemption to occur in the year 1575, based on a phrase in Jacob's blessing to Judah.)[33]

Although Rabbi Hayyim and other members of the circle

believed in their messianic role, they did not act out any of their beliefs. Vital lived to an old age (in Damascus, where he lived the second half of his life after the center in Safed began to decline), but besides writing his secret diary he did not take upon himself any messianic or leadership role. He just wrote and rewrote the teachings he had received from Luria during those brief two years in his youth in Safed. He intended these books to be completely secret, unknown to anyone but the original circle of Luria's disciples. When Luria died, Rabbi Hayyim assembled from his fellow disciples all their written material concerning the teachings of Luria, and made them sign an agreement, the text of which has reached us in the original,[34] according to which they promised under oath never to reveal anything of Luria's teachings to any outsider, and not to study this kabbalah except in their own circle when Rabbi Hayyim was present. Rabbi Hayyim undoubtedly intended to keep Luria's revolutionary visions a complete secret from the world.

Rabbi Shlomo Shlumil of Dreznitz, who came to Safed a generation later, in the early seventeenth century, wrote several letters to Poland, telling stories about the greatness of Luria.[35]

Lurianic kabbalah spread in spite of the wishes of Luria's disciples. By the second or third decade of the seventeenth century it had become a major force in Jewish thought, replacing Cordoverian kabbalah almost completely.[36] By the middle of the seventeenth century it was the dominant Jewish theology (except for a few writers in Italy and Holland).[37] For the first time in many centuries the Jewish world was united under one theological system, one set of symbols, common terminology, and an intense mystical atmosphere. Almost all the popular works at this time were written under the influence of Lurianic mythology and symbolism.

IV

How could the ideas of an unknown pilgrim, who arrived unheralded in Safed in the previous century, who taught a small circle of students and died two years later, become such a dominant and profound force in all the scores of countries that Jews were scattered in? The three stages of the Lurianic mythology emphasized three key terms: the *tzimtzum,* the "contraction of the Godhead," the *shevirah,* the "breaking of the divine vessels," and the *tikkun,* the "correction of the broken vessels and the work toward the redemption."[38] The mythological story unfolds from the beginnings of the creation and will end with the end of the world. It is impossible to find in Jewish thought and literature a parallel to this huge myth.

According to Luria, the first act of the creation was not the positive one of the emanation of the divine powers, but a negative one, in which the Godhead withdrew from a certain part of its own existence.

Actually, Luria was answering a seemingly rationalistic question: How could creation begin when there was nowhere in which it could begin? How could the Godhead emanate anything outside of Itself when there was no "space" outside of Itself, when the Godhead was both everything and nothing, filling up all existence when there was no existence? In order for the creation to proceed, "space" had to be created, where the Godhead would not be the same as It had been (or had not been; at this stage, which even symbolism cannot describe, all opposites were united).

The process of the *tzimtzum* is the Lurianic answer. Before everything else could be emanated or created, the Godhead withdrew its divine light and contracted away from a certain space, leaving behind the withdrawing Godhead "empty" space, which Luria called the *tehiru,* meaning "empty" in Aramaic, in which the process of creation could proceed. The term *"tzimtzum"* is used in rabbinic literature to describe the contraction of the *shekhinah* into the space between the two cherubs on the holy ark in the holy of holies, in the temple in Jerusalem.[39] In the rabbinic usage, the *tzimtzum* is a divine flow into a certain place; in the Lurianic system it is contraction away from a certain space.

Into the *tehiru* then flowed the divine lights from the Godhead, in a straight line, the *kav ha-yashar,* to begin the creation of the divine world, the *sefirot.* The place in which the divine light entered the spherical empty space decided the existence of "up," and the opposite direction was now "down," for before that event no directions existed in any way. Now the flow of this divine light from the Godhead began to circle around the empty space, giving shape to the emanated *sefirot.*

The shape that the emanated divine attributes assumed was the one of Primordial Man, the *adam kadmon,* the various divine powers constituting its spiritual limbs, following in a radical gnostic way the early symbolism of Jewish mysticism which began with the *Shiur Komah* and was developed in the *Zohar* and other kabbalistic works in the Middle Ages.

261

From this point onward the Lurianic myth could have continued and unfolded in a way similar to that of the early kabbalah, having only answered the question "where" concerning the process of divine emanation. However, at this point Luria introduced his most drastic departure from previous kabbalistic descriptions of the creation as well as his most profound gnostic symbol: the *shevirah*.[40] According to Luria, this attempt of the Godhead to create the divine world by the emanation of the "straight line" of divine light into the empty space was not successful and resulted in a mythological catastrophe. The "vessels" broke, and the Godhead failed in its endeavor to complete the formation of the Primordial Man.

The concept of the "vessels" has its roots in early kabbalah, but was systematized and developed by Moses Cordovero. This symbol was intended to answer the question: How can it be that divine powers differ from each other in some way? If they are completely divine, they should be identical. Cordovero answered that the *sefirot* were the combination of two elements: divine light itself, and the "vessels" into which this light is poured which impose some difference on the essentially identical divine attributes. The content is the same among the divine powers, only the vessels differ, giving each *sefirah* its specific characteristics of justice or righteousness, masculinity or femininity, and all the other symbolic differences that the *sefirot* display.

It is easy to discern in Luria's conception the old Aristotelian distinction between matter and form; the first is identical everywhere while the form gives it its specific characteristics. The difference is, however, that in the Aristotelian

THE SAFED SCHOOL OF THE KABBALAH

system the "form" was the more divine element, while "matter" was further from spirituality. In the Cordoverian system it was the vessel, the "form," the specific, which was further from pure, perfect divinity, while the "content" was divine light itself, identical and supreme.

Luria used the Cordoverian symbolism of content and vessels to describe the catastrophe of the "breaking of the vessels." The vessels broke because they could not hold the divine lights flowing into them. When the vessels broke, the divine lights in them returned upward, toward the Godhead, and the fragments of the broken vessels fell down to constitute a special realm opposite to the Godhead. According to Luria, this process happened to the lower seven *sefirot*. The higher three, though affected by the catastrophe, were not broken.

While such a myth of a disaster within the divine realm is familiar from old gnostic mythologies, especially the Manichean ones, its appearance in this sixteenth-century Hebrew work is most surprising. Why did Luria describe the Godhead as incapable of creating vessels powerful enough to hold the divine lights which were intended to be stored in them? There can be no doubt that this complicated and radical symbolism was used by Luria to answer basic religious and mystical problems and needs.

V

The main symbol which explains the Lurianic myth of the *shevirah* is that of the *reshimu,* the "impression" or "residue" of the divine light. This concept was not clearly described in Rabbi Hayyim Vital's voluminous presentation of the Lurianic teachings; the few paragraphs of Rabbi Joseph ibn Tabul on the subject are our main source for the elucidation of this perplexing problem. According to Luria, it seems, when the *tzimtzum* occurred, not all the divine lights withdrew from the empty space. A "residue," the *reshimu,* remained behind. The metaphor used was that of a bucket of water, which when emptied remains wet; there is a residue of the water on its walls.

This residue of the divine lights was not accidental; indeed, the purpose of the whole process of the *tzimtzum* was to separate between the divine lights and this specific, and somewhat different, element within the Godhead. Here we find Luria presenting the radical view that before everything began, when only the Godhead filled up everything, the Godhead was not completely united and identical. This difference could not be observed then because nothing actually existed; yet the Godhead itself knew that there were within it some powers which, if given a chance, would assume different characteristics than the rest of the Godhead. The first aim of the *tzimtzum* was to seclude these potentially different divine lights in the empty *tehiru,* thus cleansing the Godhead of those *reshimu* elements. This aim was successfully achieved when the Godhead contracted and the *reshimu* remained behind in the empty space.

When the straight line of divine light began to create the figure of Primordial Man in the empty space, it was in order to achieve a more ambitious aim than the separation achieved by the *tzimtzum:* to correct these potential differences, to unite, for the first time, the two elements within the Godhead all at once. The *reshimu* elements served to create, together with divine lights, the vessels, and thus helped to create differentiation between the various divine attributes. In this way, the different character of these elements was used in order to achieve the common purpose of the creation of the divine emanated world. By participating in a common endeavor, the *reshimu* and the divine lights would become one.

The breaking of the vessels demonstrated the refusal of the *reshimu* elements to take part in the creative process devised by the Godhead. They rebelled against the role assigned them as contributors to the creation of the *sefirot.* The vessels broke because the *reshimu* elements did not want to uphold them, and preferred their own freedom. They fell down and created their own realm, which, when it became actual, could be called by its proper human symbol: the realm of evil.

Lurianic myth is a gnostic story of the fight between good and evil within the divine world long before Man was created. The roots of evil, separated from the Godhead by the process of the *tzimtzum,* were originally embedded in the eternal Godhead in a potential form. Lurianic dualism is therefore extremely radical, much more so than that of the *Zohar* and Rabbi Isaac ha-Cohen, for evil was not a product of the creative process. It existed eternally within the Godhead, and therefore was as divine as He was.

Most theological and mystical systems see the redemption as a return to ancient perfection. The beginning, according to them, was closest to the completely good and pure divine power. Only subsequent developments destroyed this original perfection. Thus it is the role of redemption to restore that early harmony. Luria drastically deviated from this belief. According to his mythical symbolism there was never a perfect situation. The divine world was never united and perfect in the past. Within the Godhead evil lurked in a potential form, and the attempt to correct it and abolish it from the Godhead itself resulted in the dramatic upheaval of the *shevirah,* bringing forth an independent evil realm in the lower part of the "empty space," the *tehiru.*

Lurianic myth, which seems so remote and bizarre to modern ears, is actually one of the very few theological systems which gives an answer—obviously, not a logical one—to the basic question which haunts human thought and is usually left not only unanswered but also untouched: What is the purpose of the creation? Why did God bring forth the earth, the heavens, beasts, and human beings? Luria's answer is clear. Existence is the result of an internal struggle inside the Godhead, the roots of which are eternal. Existence assumed a specific form by the process of creation. Man is not the purpose of creation, but one more battleground between good and evil. The world was created to serve as the arena of the mythical struggle between these two ancient, opposing divine powers.

It should be noted that both the process of the contraction and the process of the breaking of the vessels include in them the symbol of divine exile from a place in which God was before, thus putting the idea of exile into the essence of the divine world before the creation. There is no doubt that in this way Luria's teachings conformed to the spiritual needs of the period.

Luria's myth continues with the Godhead's second attempt at creation, this time successful, though much more moderate. It did not attempt to abolish evil in its separate kingdom in the lower part of the *tehiru*. The *sefirot* were emanated, the worlds of the angels, the Throne of Glory, the celestial bodies, the heavens were all created, and then Man himself was created in the image of the Primordial Man. Man's function was to reflect the dualism which ruled the cosmos as well as the Godhead. He included elements of good and evil together, a divine soul and a material body which struggled against each other. Man is a symbolic creature. The victories of the good in him represent victories of the good divine powers, whereas his sins represent victories of the evil powers. God entrusted the continuing struggle against evil to this symbolic creature. Its duty was to overcome the evil inside him, and in this way to bring forth the cosmic, mythic victory of good over evil. History from then onward is the story of Man's attempts to fulfill this mythological role, for which he was created.

The basic difference between this second process of emanation and the traditional kabbalistic picture of the same process is, that when it developed, the Godhead was already in exile. Actually, It had been exiled twice before Man was created. First, when It willingly contracted into Itself, a process which can be described as God's self-imposed exile from the "empty space" where creation was to proceed; second, when the vessels broke and the divine lights were driven back into the upper part of the divine world, while some divine sparks remained in the captivity of the emerging evil powers. Exile, therefore, is neither a human experience nor a Jewish one. Long before either Man or Jew existed, exile was present as a most profound experience of the Godhead itself.

VI

All cosmic and human events since the breaking of the vessels are oriented, according to the Lurianic myth, toward the *tikkun,* the correction of the initial catastrophe with which history began. The world was created as a means for achieving this aim, and Man was created for the same purpose. The divine need for the mending of the broken vessels is the supreme reason for all occurences, large and small, in worldly and human affairs.

When the *shevirah* occurred, not only the shards of the vessels, which were dominated by the *reshimu,* evil elements, fell down; with them were many sparks *(nitzotzot)* of pure divine light, which became prisoners in the realm of the evil powers in the lower half of the *tehiru.* These sparks are crucial for the process of the *tikkun,* both because they are missing in the divine, good world, which needs them for the correction of the *sefirot,* and because they give strength and sustenance to the evil powers. According to Luria, evil cannot exist by its own power. Its nature is nonexistence. It is opposed to existence. Some element of medieval philosophy, especially neo-Platonic philosophy, was retained here by the mystics of Safed. The medieval philosophers described evil as a negative essence, something which does not really exist, like darkness, which is only the absence of light; so evil is not a real substance but the absence of goodness. In the Lurianic kabbalah, evil certainly exists as a real power, but it cannot exist independently; it has to be supported and sustained by the elements of goodness. If such support is absent, evil immediately becomes nonexistent.

The fallen sparks of divine light which are imprisoned in the evil realm are the source of the power of the evil elements. From them all the opposing powers of the Godhead receive their sustenance. The strength of these evil powers is dependent on the amount of such imprisoned divine lights in their midst. When more sparks fall and are captured in the Satanic realm, cosmic evil becomes stronger. When such sparks are liberated and uplifted, evil is weakened. If a complete separation can be achieved, and all the sparks liberated and returned to the realm of divine light, than evil will cease to exist for lack of support and sustenance. The uplifting of the sparks becomes, therefore, the main aim of the divine powers. When this process is completed, redemption will arrive, and the *tikkun* will be achieved.

When Man was first created in the Garden of Eden, his duty was to complete the process of redemption. As his structure symbolically represented the cosmic dualism of good and evil, he had the power, in a symbolic way, to bring about the complete victory of good over evil, had goodness prevailed and directed all his actions. When Adam sinned, the process of the *shevirah* was repeated, strengthening evil instead of restoring the sparks of goodness to their rightful place. The "original sin" was, therefore, a mythical event, in which divine sparks from Adam's soul fell into captivity in the Satanic realm, instead of serving to uplift the previously captured divine lights of the original breaking of the vessels. This was the first attempt of the Godhead to correct the *shevirah* after the creation, and it failed completely when Adam and Eve sinned in the Garden of Eden.

Since that original sin, evil was intensified and strengthened throughout the cosmos, and the Godhead repeatedly tried to overcome it. The greatest attempt, which was almost successful, was the Mount Sinai theophany. When the Israelites announced *"na'aseh ve-nishma,"* expressing their unconditional acceptance of the Torah and their readiness to yield to it completely, the process of the *tikkun* was completed, all the sparks uplifted by this profound religious devotion to the Godhead, and the cosmos was about to be redeemed. Then came the enormous sin of the worshippers of the Golden Calf, another *shevirah* occurred, countless new sparks were captured by the evil powers, and evil was again strengthened and envigorated, making the next attempts to achieve the *tikkun* more difficult.

History, therefore, according to Lurianic mythology, is the story of the repeated attempts of the divine powers to achieve the separation between good and evil, to uplift the fallen sparks and correct divine existence, and then bring forth the redemption. The means for achieving this are the Torah and the Commandments. The various *mitsvot,* the religious and ethical demands made of every Jew, were devised by the divine powers in a way that every good deed or thought helps to redeem one divine spark which is in Satan's captivity. When a Jew follows the way of the Torah, his life is dedicated to this mythical struggle of good against evil, and everything he does contributes to the enhancement of the process of the *tikkun* and the weakening of the evil powers.

However, every sin, every misdeed, every unethical act or thought, makes another divine spark in the Jew's soul fall and be captured by the evil powers. Sins are thus the source from which these evil powers receive their daily sustenance and vigor.

An act of repentance means that the sparks which fell down because of the previous sin can rise up and serve to strengthen goodness instead of evil. There is an automatic element in this process, for a man does not have to be aware of the cosmic significance of his deeds and misdeeds; the impact on the mythological process of the enhancement or obstruction of the *tikkun* happens anyway, though, according to Luria, the knowledge of the divine significance of such deeds helps to increase their impact. The Lurianic *kavvanot,* the "intentions" which he added to the performance of the various commandments and the prayers, are intended to strengthen this impact, though they do not form a condition for a mystical meaning of everyday actions.

This is why the disciples of Luria could demand that his teachings remain esoteric. If the knowledge of Lurianic kabbalah was conditional for the effectiveness of the process of the *tikkun,* it could not be kept a secret, for it concerned the behavior of every Jew every moment of his life. But as, according to them, the process can proceed even when its full meaning is not known to the participants, it was not the duty of the disciples to publish it and preach it. As stated above, Lurianic kabbalah spread in spite of the attempts of

GERSHOM SCHOLEM

the disciples, and especially of Rabbi Hayyim Vital, to keep
it a secret. The history of the spread of Rabbi Hayyim's books
is the proof of the correctness of Rabbi Isaac the Blind's ancient warning: "A book which is written cannot be hidden
in the cupboard."[41]

The major transformation which Lurianic kabbalah brought
into Jewish mysticism, an element which Scholem emphasized repeatedly, is the dramatic change that it brought into
the Jewish mystic's attitude toward history and historical activity.

Early kabbalah, including Zoharic kabbalah, tried to show
the way toward the Godhead through the ladder of the *sefirot*.
The ascension of the mystic on this ladder was a repetition,
only in the opposite direction, of the process of the emanation of the *sefirot*. Therefore, the ancient story of the "secret
of the creation," the way that the various divine powers were
separated and emanated from the Godhead, was the main
interest of the mystics. These were their directions concerning the mystical ascension back toward the ancient divine
unity which no longer existed in the world of the enormous
plurality after the creation. They turned their backs toward
the future, toward current, unfolding history, and concentrated on the mystical return to the unity of the process of
genesis.

In the Lurianic kabbalah there is no ancient unity toward
which the mystic can ascend. The early history of the deity
and of the cosmos is one of dualism, struggle, and catastrophe. From its very beginning the world, including the divine
world, was the stage for the drama of the conflict between
the eternal elements of good and evil within the Godhead.

272

True unity, complete harmony, divine perfection—all these can be found only in the future, after the *tikkun* is completed and redemption achieved. The mystic can achieve his personal, individual fulfillment only in the future, together with the correction of the world, of the cosmos, and of the divine *sefirot* themselves. Therefore, his mystical endeavors become united with the historical needs of the earthly community, of the nation, and of the divine sparks now in exile within the realm of the evil powers seeking redemption. Jews who are in exile share the fate of these divine lights in exile, and together they must strive for their own deliverance from their oppressors. Mystical fulfillment and historical messianic redemption become one and the same, and nothing separates the religious efforts of the mystic from those of the common worshipper. Though the disciples of Luria tried to keep his teachings esoteric, the barrier fell, and the separation between Jewish mysticism and Jewish everyday religious practice vanished. The gates toward the active participation of the mystics in the formulation of Jewish history were opened, and nothing could close them again. Lurianic kabbalah thus became the power which transformed Jewish mysticism from the realm of the few mystics who seek individually their soul's salvation, to a historical force which has direct and meaningful impact on the lives of the common people. It showed the direction of development toward communal and national redemption.

In Lurianic theology, the difference between the individual and the community is minimized. Religion cannot be relied upon to achieve individual perfection. The meaning of worship becomes the concern of the whole community, the whole nation, for the process of *tikkun* is carried on by all of them together. When a person performs a *mitsvah,* the freed spark strengthens everybody, and all profit from the weakening of the powers of evil. When a person commits a sin, the fallen spark hinders the redemption for everybody, delaying or preventing the redemption of the nation as a whole, as well as the salvation of divinity itself. An individual cannot withdraw from the community and seek his own religious perfection while disregarding his fellow men; their sins, as well as their good deeds, have a direct impact on him, and vice versa.

The religious organization of the community is, therefore, described very much like a fighting unit on the battlefield. Individual salvation is impossible; everybody is dependent on all the others and all the others depend on each individual. Communal effort is needed in order to achieve the *tikkun,* and therefore the community should help each individual and strengthen him in his struggle against the evil inside him. Whether an individual observes the Sabbath or not is no longer a personal matter between the worshipper and God; all the community cares and is dependent on the individual's behavior concerning every commandment. All the nation is hurt when an individual does not conform to the religious commandments. We have evidence that in Safed, even before the appearance of Luria, there were tendencies toward communal pressure on individuals to preserve to perfection all the commandments and ethical demands.[42] Lurianic theology was probably the result of these tendencies, and strengthened them by giving them a cosmic, mythological justification.

The meaning of repentance also changed completely following the impact of Lurianic kabbalah. Repentance no longer could be regarded as the personal return of the sinner to his God, and the absolution of his personal misdeeds so that he could receive his reward from God. All sins had to be repented in order that the *tikkun* be achieved and all the sparks delivered from captivity. One person can, and even must, perform the ritual of repentance over the sins of others, whether they are his fellows in the community or sinners long dead and buried. The responsibility cannot be divided, and cannot be regarded as personal. The weight of all worldly evil lies on the shoulders of every individual, and he has to do everything he can in order to include in his repentance all the sins of previous and present generations. Repentance thus becomes a never-ending process. The *ba'al teshuvah,* the "repentant," is not a sinner returning to God after his personal misdeed, but one who dedicates all his religious powers to the correction of all sins, his own and others. This attitude toward the process of repentance was known in Safed before Luria.[43] Lurianic theology only explained to the Safed mystics why they were doing what they were doing independently of this theology.

VII

One of the most profound characteristics of Lurianic kabbalah which had great impact on Jewish thought and history is that it served as an enormous conservative force. Although the radical symbolism, the dramatic mythology seemed new and revolutionary, and though the close parallels between Lurianism and ancient gnostic ideas may indicate that this theology was foreign to traditional Judaism, in fact it brought few changes in old Jewish beliefs and practices.

Lurianic theology not only did not change anything in the old, accepted Jewish way of worship, but strengthened it. This is because the main thrust of Lurianic theology is one of explanation and not of change. It deals with the reasons one should perform the Jewish commandments, and not whether there is another way to practice religion. The enormous process of the *tikkun* and the redemption is dependent on the simplest, most commonplace demands of Jewish tradition. The blessing that a Jew is required to say before almost every deed, every bite of food, the "hundred benedictions to be said every day"—these are the forces which are destined to deliver the divine sparks from captivity. Indeed, Luria and his disciples added several customs and demands to the accepted Jewish traditional worship, some of them recognizable by their name—*tikkunim*.[44] His main contribution was the explanation why all these seemingly mundane and material deeds are so important. They are needed not only for assisting the individual Jew to achieve personal religious perfection; they are necessary for the salvation of the nation, the community, the world, the cosmos, and even the divine powers themselves. The individual performing the *mitsvot* is by his deeds shaping the fate of divinity itself. One can never be certain what the cosmic balance is at a specific moment. Every human deed or misdeed may change the whole universal balance between good and evil and be decisive concerning the fate of the earth and the heavens together. It is always possible that redemption is just minutes away, and that the redemption of the one spark that one may free by one's next prayer may bring forth messianic, cosmic salvation. It may also be that the world is at any one moment just one step away from the complete redemption, and a minute sin performed at that very moment by some individual would prevent and delay the redemption. The observance of the commandments thus achieves a level of importance never dreamed of before, and religious life suddenly acquires a new meaning, a much stronger relevance, in mythological dimensions.

The practical outcome of the acceptance of the Lurianic kabbalah can therefore only result in stronger adherence to even the most minute details of religious commandments, ethical behavior, and Jewish ritual, for these carry the world onward in the process of *tikkun*. New vigor can be found in the way Jews performed the millennia-old commandments following the spread of this new mythology.

Besides its contribution to the renewed adherence to the performance of the commandments, there were other conservative elements in Lurianism. One of the most important was its treatment of all worshippers as equal. Luria did not see himself as a religious leader, and his disciples also did not seek positions of leadership because of their mystical knowledge. The actual performance of the religious deeds is decisive concerning the cosmic struggle between good and evil; who performs them is of secondary importance. Every Jew, be he educated or not, with knowledge of the mystical meaning of his deeds or not, has a role in the universal process of the *tikkun*. The instructions for successfuly accomplishing one's role in redeeming the divine powers are found in the simplest and most commonplace Jewish books of *halakhah* and ethical instruction. Knowledge of the Lurianic *kavvanot* is helpful, but does not constitute a condition to the performance of the mystical goal. Every Jew is, in this sense, a mystic, even if he does not know it himself. This lack of the spirit of mystical or intellectual aristocracy, and the enhancement of the role of the common people in the enormous mythological process, contributed to the acceptance of Lurianic theology as a conservative, constructive force within Judaism.

This element is also apparent in the messianic message of the Lurianic kabbalah. This mythology is intensely messianic or redemptive, for it concentrates all the powers, deeds, and thoughts of every worshipper toward the achievement of the messianic goal. It does not strive for the restoration of an ancient past, but toward the creation of a new world, a redeemed and perfect one. Never before did Judaism produce such an intense theology, which concentrated all Jewish practice in the one direction of messianic redemption. With Lurianic theology, a new chapter in the history of Jewish messianism was opened, a most powerful and intense one.

But what about the role of the messiah himself? According to Lurianic theology, redemption is not achieved by the deeds of a man, be he even the messiah himself. It is the communal, or national, effort of generations of worshipping Jews which uplifts and frees the fallen sparks and thus deprives the evil powers of their source of sustenance. The coming of the messiah is not the cause of the redemption but its outcome. The appearance of the messiah is the result of the countless good deeds of the whole people, and this appearance signifies the successful completion of the process of the *tikkun*. This is why it was possible for Rabbi Hayyim Vital to believe for five decades in his own messianic role as the messiah son of

David without doing anything to fulfill that role. The messiah does not have any special duties before the redemption; after its achievement by the nation as a whole, he becomes its crowned leader.[45]

That Luria and his disciples never demanded any special role for themselves or their beliefs in the affairs of the community, and did not suggest any institutional or devotional changes besides stricter adherence to accepted norms, made them a conservative and unthreatening power within the history of seventeenth-century Jewish communities, and facilitated the rapid spread of this doctrine and its acceptance by Jewish communities all over the world.

Among all the elements of Lurianic mysticism, none was more potent and profound than the image of exile as the plight of the divine powers themselves. When a Jew experienced the hardships of exile he could now remember that God had been in exile long before him; even more, that God's redemption was dependent upon the actions of every individual Jew. Exile was a cosmic phenomenon after the "breaking of the vessels," and redemption involved the restoration of the divine powers to their rightful place. By placing the Jewish experience of exile in the heart of the divine world itself, Lurianic theology acquired power and impact unseen before in the history of Jewish thought.

For the first time in the history of the Jews in the diaspora, Judaism as a whole was united in the belief in one theology, one set of symbols, and one basic terminology. The few who did not accept the mythology presented by Luria still acquiesced to the current spirit of their world and expressed their admiration to Luria as a unique personality, as presented in the hagiography around him, and used the terminology of the Lurianic kabbalah even if they did not share the mystical implications. This common basis, fresh and vigorous, revolutionary in thoughts, pictures, and symbols while extremely conservative in deeds and social institutions, shaped the history of Jewish thought for centuries to come.

NOTES

1. Two studies by H. H. Ben-Sasson have contributed a great deal to the understanding of this period. See his "Exile and Redemption in the Eyes of the Exile Generation" (Hebrew), in S. Ettinger et al., eds., *I. Baer Jubilee Volume* (Jerusalem, 1961), pp. 216–27; and "The Generation of the Exile from Spain Describing Itself" (Hebrew), *Zion,* 26 (1961). Cf. J. Dan, *Hebrew Ethical and Homiletical Literature* [Hebrew] (Jerusalem, 1975), pp. 167–82.

2. The most important work of the period expressing these sentiments is R. Joseph Ya'abetz's *Or ha-Ḥayyim.* See J. Dan, *Hebrew Ethical and Homiletical Literature,* pp. 180–89.

3. A vast amount of scholarly research has been written about the Marranos. See esp. I. Baer, *A History of the Jews in Christian Spain,* translated by L. Schoffman (Philadelphia: Jewish Publication Society, 1961) vol. 2, pp. 210–99; H. Beinart, *Conversos on Trial: The Inquisition in Ciudad Real,* translated by Yael Guiladi (Jerusalem: Magnes Press, 1981). See also H. Beinart, *Records of the Trials of the Spanish Inquisition in Ciudad Real, vol. 1–3* (Jerusalem: Israel Academy of Sciences and Humanities, 1974–81).

4. See Gershom Scholem, "The Kabbalah in Spain on the Eve of the Expulsion" (Hebrew), *Tarbiz,* 24 (1955), pp. 167–206.

5. See G. Scholem, *Major Trends in Jewish Mysticism,* 3rd rev. ed. (New York: Schocken, 1954), pp. 248–49, and his study "The Maggid of Rabbi Joseph Taitazak" (Hebrew), *Sefunot,* 11 (1968), pp. 47–112. See also M. Idel, "Inquiries into the Doctrine of *Sefer ha-Meshiv*" (Hebrew), *Sefunot,* 17 (1983), pp. 185–266.

6. According to Scholem, Abraham ben Eliezer ha-Levi was the author of the commentary. See "The Kabbalist R. Abraham ben Eliezer ha-Levi" (Hebrew), *Kiryat Sefer*, 2 (1925–26), pp. 115–19, 135–36. Cf. J. Dan, "Notes on the Prophecy of the Child" (Hebrew), *Shalem*, 1 (1974), pp. 229–34.

7. For references, see above ch. 1, n. 21.

8. See R. Elior, *Galya Raza*, critical edition with introduction, variant readings, and notes (Jerusalem: Hebrew University, 1981).

9. See G. Scholem, *Kabbalah* (Jerusalem: Keter, 1974), pp. 69, 73. (For a detailed study of this kabbalist, see Roland Goetschel, *Meir Ibn Gabbay: Le Discours de la Kabbale Espagnole* [Leuven: Peeters, 1981].)

10. See G. Scholem, "The Maggid of Rabbi Joseph Taitazak," pp. 47–112.

11. See Maimonides, *Mishneh Torah, Hilkhot Sanhedrin* 4:11.

12. This historical controversy was studied in detail by J. Katz, "The Controversy on the Semikha (Ordination) between R. Jacob Bei-Rav and the Ralbah" (Hebrew), *Zion*, 16 (1951), pp. 28–45.

13. The continuous process of ordination in Safed was described by M. Benayahu, "Ḥiddush shel ha-Semikha," S. Ettinger et al., eds., *I. Baer Jubilee Volume* (Jerusalem, 1961), pp. 248–69.

14. For a study of Alsheich's homiletical writings, see S. Shalem, *Rabbi Mosheh Alshekh*, edited by M. Benayahu (Jerusalem: Ben-Zvi Institute, Hebrew University, 1966).

15. Joseph Karo's kabbalistic views were analyzed in detail by R. J. Z. Werblowsky in his *Joseph Karo: Lawyer and Mystic*, 2nd ed. (Philadelphia: Jewish Publication Society, 1977). Werblowsky devoted a chapter in his book to a study of the spiritual atmosphere in Safed in the time of Karo; see pp. 38–83. Cf. S. Schechter, "Safed in the Sixteenth Century," in his *Studies in Judaism*, 2nd series (Philadelphia: Jewish Publication Society, 1977), pp. 231–97.

16. The phenomenon of the maggid was central to the kabbalah of the sixteenth and seventeenth centuries. See above, no. 5 for reference to Scholem's article on the subject. See also I. Tishby, "R. Moses Hayyim Luzzato's Relationship to Sabbatianism" (Hebrew), in I. Tishby, *Netivei ʾEmunah u-Minhut* (Ramat Gan, 1964), pp. 169–85; M. Benayahu, "The Maggid of R. Moses Hayyim Luzzato" (Hebrew), *Sefunot*, 5 (1961), pp. 299–336. (See also L. Fine, "Techniques of Mystical Meditation for Achieving Prophecy and the Holy Spirit in the Teachings of Isaac Luria

GERSHOM SCHOLEM

and Hayyim Vital" [Ph.D. thesis, Brandeis University, 1976], esp. pp. 18–42.)

17. Concerning the tragic figure of Molcho, see A. Eshkoli, *Jewish Messianic Movements: Sources and Documents on Messianism in Jewish History,* edited by Y. Even-Shemuel (Jerusalem, 1956), pp. 250–79, 360–412. See also M. Idel, "Shlomo Molkho as a Magician" (Hebrew), *Sefunot,* 18 (1985), pp. 193–220.

18. The thought of Cordovero was studied in detail by J. Ben-Shlomo, *The Mystical Theology of R. Moses Cordovero* [Hebrew] (Jerusalem: Mosad Bialik, 1965).

19. To date 12 volumes of Cordovero's *'Or Yaqar* on the *Zohar* (Genesis to parts of Leviticus) have been published together with three volumes on *Tiqqunei ha-Zohar.* (The kabbalistic thought of Cordovero in his commentary *'Or Yaqar* has been the subject of several articles by B. Sack. See, for instance, "The Exile of Israel and the Exile of the Shekhinah in *'Or Yaqar* of R. Moses Cordovero" [Hebrew], *Jerusalem Studies in Jewish Thought,* 4 (1982), 157–78; "Ha-Qelipah Zorekh ha-Qedushah," *Studies in Jewish Mysticism Presented to Isaiah Tishby on his Seventy-fifth Birthday, Jerusalem Studies in Jewish Thought,* 3 (1983–84), pp. 191–206.)

20. Cordovero, *Pardes Rimmonim,* ch. 23, "Sha'ar Erkhei ha-Kinnuyim," is an alphabetical dictionary of the main Zoharic symbols.

21. See the detailed analyses in J. Ben Shlomo, *The Mystical Theology of R. Moses Cordovero.*

22. See J. Dan, " 'No Evil Descends from Heaven'—Sixteenth Century Jewish Concepts of Evil," in B. Cooperman, ed., *Jewish Thought in the Sixteenth Century* (Cambridge: Harvard University Press, 1983), pp. 89–105.

23. Tishby analyzed this element in Cordovero's thought. See his "Paths of Mythologization and Systematization in the Kabbalah" (Hebrew), *Netivei 'Emunah u-Minhut,* pp. 26–27.

24. See B. Sack, "The Mystical Theology of Solomon Alkabez" (Ph.D. thesis, Brandeis University, 1977).

25. See the English translation by L. Jacobs, *Tomer Devorah* (London: Valentine, Mitchell, 1960).

26. The fascinating subject of the ethical literature of Safed has received increased attention in the last decade. See M. Pachter, "Ethical and Homiletical Literature in Safed" (Ph.D. thesis, Hebrew University, 1975); J. Dan, *Hebrew Ethical and Homiletical Literature,* pp. 202–29. See

282

also M. Pachter, "The Theory of Devekut in the Writings of the Sages of Safed in the Sixteenth Century" (Hebrew), *Jerusalem Studies in Jewish Thought,* 3 (1982), pp. 51–121.

27. The intricate process of the Lurianic kabbalah's replacing that of Cordovero has been the subject of several studies by Tishby. See his *Studies in Kabbalah and Its Branches* (Jerusalem: Magnes Press, 1982), vol. 1, pp. 131–267.

28. The material concerning the hagiography surrounding Isaac Luria was studied by M. Benayahu in his edition of *Toldot ha-ʾAri* (Jerusalem: Ben Zvi Institute, Hebrew University, 1967). Cf. J. Dan, *The Hebrew Story in the Middle Ages* [Hebrew] (Jerusalem, 1974), pp. 238–51.

29. Concerning Ibn Tabul's works and their relationship to those of Vital, see G. Scholem, *Major Trends,* pp. 254–63; I. Tishby, *The Doctrine of Evil and the "Kelippah" in Lurianic Kabbalism* [Hebrew] (Jerusalem: Magnes, 1984), esp. pp. 22–27, 57–58.

30. M. Pachter published a homily given on Luria's grave. From this source we can gather what his image was among his contemporaries. It appears that when he died Luria was not regarded as an outstanding figure in Safed.

31. On the messianisn in Luria's circle, see D. Tamar, "An Epistle from Safed, Dated 1525 or 1625, dealing with the Ten Tribes" (Hebrew), *Sefunot,* 6 (1962), pp. 305–10.

32. See Hayyim Vital, *Sefer ha-Ḥezyonot,* edited by A. Eshkoli (Jerusalem: Mosad ha-Rav Kook, 1954).

33. Genesis 49:10 ("until Shilo comes and nations will adhere to him;" in Hebrew the equivalent of 335, the year 1575).

34. See G. Scholem, "Shtar ha-Hitkashrut shel Talmidei ha-ʾAri," *Zion,* 5 (1940), pp. 133–60.

35. Shlumil's three letters were published in the book *Taʿalumot Ḥokhmah* by Y. S. Delmedigo of Crete in a chapter entitled "Letters of Praise to the Greatness of Luria." Later they were published as a separate book entitled *Shivḥei ha-ʾAri.* A fourth letter was published by S. Asaf in *Qovez ʿal Yad,* 13, pp. 118–31.

36. This process of the gradual replacement of Cordoverian kabbalah by that of Luria was felt especially in Italy. See references to Tishby's studies in n. 27, above.

37. The most important opponent to kabbalah in seventeenth-century Italy was R. Judah Aryeh of Modena whose polemic against the kabbalah

was entitled *'Ari Nohem* (1648). Only a few of Modena's contemporaries supported him, although some, like Y. S. Delmedigo of Crete, may have secretly sympathized with his position. Modena mainly attacked the *Zohar*, although he knew of Luria. A more representative attitude can be found in the works of Manasseh ben Israel of Amsterdam, especially in his *Nishmat Hayyim*, a work on psychology and demonology. The author praised the *Zohar* and Luria, but presented a theology in complete disregard of their teachings. See J. Dan, "The Concept of Evil and Demonology in Rabbi Mannaseh ben Israel's *Nishmat Hayyim*" (Hebrew), *Dov Noy Jubilee Volume* (1983), pp. 263–74.

38. Scholem's main discussions of Lurianic kabbalah are to be found in *Major Trends*, pp. 260–86; see also "Kabbala und Mythos," *Eranos Jahrbuch*, 17 (1949), pp. 287–334 [English translation in *On the Kabbalah and Its Symbolism*, translated by Ralph Manheim (New York: Schocken, 1965), pp. 87–117.] A detailed presentation of the processes of *tzimtzum*, *shevirah*, and *tikkun* in Lurianic theology is to be found in I. Tishby, *The Doctrine of Evil and the "Kelippah" in Lurianic Kabbalism*.

39. See *Exodus Rabbah* 25:10 and *Leviticus Rabbah* 25:24. See Scholem's analysis in *Major Trends*, pp. 260 and 410, ns. 41–43.

40. On the myth of *shevirah*, see G. Scholem, *Major Trends*, pp. 266–68; I. Tishby, *The Doctrine of Evil*, pp. 21–51.

41. See reference above, ch. 6, p. 173.

42. Customs like the public announcement of the approaching Sabbath, and even a check of homes to see if all fires had been put out and all cooking ceased, were practiced in Safed before Luria, giving expression to the idea of mutual dependence of the members of the community, and probably denoting the ambition of Safed's righteous rabbis to create a perfect community *(qehilat qodesh)* in order to enhance the redemption. See S. Assaf, *Qovez 'al Yad*, 13, pp. 122–24; J. Dan, *Hebrew Ethical and Homiletical Literature*, pp. 207–11. See also R. J. Z. Werblowsky, *Joseph Karo: Lawyer and Mystic*, pp. 38–56.

43. Safed kabbalists organized groups of righteous people to assist each other in redemptive processes before Luria as is attested by books like *Sefer Haredim* by Eleazar Azikiri who discussed a group *dusat shalom* in his introduction. Hayyim Vital in his *Sefer ha-Hezyonot* likewise tells of such an experiment. Some of the Safed repentants practised self-torture for the sake of repentance. See S. Assaf, op. cit., p. 13; cf. J. Dan, *Hebrew Ethical and Homiletical Literature*, pp. 208–09.

44. See G. Scholem, "Tradition und Neuschopfung im Ritus der Kabbalisten," *Eranos Jahrbuch,* 19 (1950), pp. 121–80. [English translation in *On the Kabbalah and Its Symbolism,* translated by Ralph Manheim, pp. 118–57; Hebrew translation in J. Ben Shlomo, ed., *Pirqei Yesod be-havanat ha-Qabbalah u-semaleha* (Jerusalem: Mosad Bialik, 1976), pp. 113–52.]

45. Jewish messianism in general, and kabbalistic messianism in particular, especially that of the Lurianic school, were described by Scholem in his studies "Toward an Understanding of the Messianic Idea in Judaism" and "The Messianic Idea in Kabbalah" in G. Scholem, *Devarim Be-Go,* (Tel Aviv: Am Oved, 1976), pp. 155–216. [English translations in G. Scholem, *The Messianic Idea in Judaism* (New York: Schocken, 1971), pp. 1–48.]

CHAPTER 11

THE SABBATIAN UPHEAVAL

I

NO PART OF Scholem's voluminous scholarly works had a greater impact on modern Jewish historiography than his studies of the Sabbatian movement of the seventeenth century. Perhaps it was the unique, dramatic, and profound nature of the movement itself that interested so many.

A number of scholars followed Scholem in the study of the Sabbatian movement. While only a few of his students continued his work in the history of *Hekhalot* mysticism, early kabbalah, the *Zohar* and other subjects, his work on the Sabbatian movement is continued today by many historians in Israel and abroad. The advances in the study of this movement were very rapid; many new sources were revealed and published.[1] Sabbatianism in specific countries, areas, and towns was studied in many monographs.[2] The whole subject has acquired an importance for the understanding of Jewish history before and after the movement as well as during the centuries of its development and decline.

II

Historians of Judaism have a unique problem in adjusting European accepted chronological designations to Jewish history. When do the Middle Ages start and when is their conclusion? While most European scholars associate the beginning of the Middle Ages with the fall of the Roman Empire, this event had very little meaning for Jewish history, for few Jews lived at that time in the western Roman Empire, and the history of Byzantium and Persia—under whose rule most Jews lived—was little affected by the events of the year 476. Because of this, most Jewish historians begin the Middle Ages with the conquests of Islam in the beginning of the seventh century, conquests which united most of the Jewish world under the rule of Islam and opened a new chapter in the political and cultural history of Judaism.

Concerning the ending of the period of the Middle Ages much confusion existed. The fall of Constantinople in 1453 did not mean much to Jewish communities in the Netherlands or in Poland. The discovery of America in 1492 was very meaningful to Jewish history, but its impact was not felt for centuries. The Renaissance in Italy was meaningful to the culture of a small group of Jews in Italy and western Europe, while the majority in eastern Europe and the Near East were not affected by it at all. As for Jewish events, the most important was the expulsion from Spain, in 1492, but this also had an impact only on a part of Judaism and not on the nation as a whole.

Scholem's view was that the beginning of the Sabbatian movement in 1665 and 1666 should be seen as the end of medieval Jewish history and the beginning of modern Jewish history.[3] His main argument to support this view was that this event had important, meaningful, and permanent effects on every Jewish community throughout the world. Sabbatianism was, for him, the culmination of medieval Judaism and the point of departure for all major forces which shaped modern Jewish history, including Hasidism and Enlightment, messianism and the participation of the Jews in European culture. Scholem saw the Sabbatian movement as a key to the development of Jewish society, culture, and beliefs in modern times.

III

The relationship between the two dominant figures in the beginning of the Sabbatian movement, Sabbatai Zevi himself and his prophet, Nathan of Gaza, was studied in detail by Scholem,[4] who reached the conclusion that the success of the movement and its spread in the early phases of its history depended more on the prophet than on the messiah. Sabbatai Zevi himself was in his early forties when the movement began. His messianic pretensions were well known in several Jewish communities in Eretz Israel and Turkey and he was regarded by those who heard his messianic claims as an unbalanced scholar, sometimes tolerated but driven out when patience with his strange behavior was exhausted. Scholem came to the conclusion that Sabbatai Zevi was manic-depressive. This was expressed by his transition, every few months, from a state of extreme self-confidence and certainty of his supernatural powers and status to a state of melancholy and depression. A handsome man and a good singer, on first meetings he used to impress people, until they became familiar with his strange delusions.

The Jews of the seventeenth century were used to messianic pretenders; the appearance of Sabbatai Zevi himself did not create any noticeable stir, and certainly the beginning of the movement cannot be attributed to anything he did.[5] The event that occurred in 1665 was the sudden revelation of the prophet Nathan in Gaza.

Pretenders to prophecy can be found in Jewish history in the Middle Ages, though not many. Nathan of Gaza was unique: he came from Eretz Israel. The Talmudic sources emphasize that prophecy is impossible anywhere but in Israel, and they did their best to explain, for instance, that Ezekiel prophesied in the temple in Jerusalem, and only revealed his prophecies on the river Kvar in Babylonia.[6] There is no precedent for the appearance of a prophet in Israel since biblical times, and the impact of Nathan's appearance was great.

Nathan did not only declare that he had seen visions portraying Sabbatai Zevi as the messiah. He also created a literature, some of it pseudepigraphic. These were works of antiquity which he claimed to have discovered which described the arrival of the messiah in the form of Sabbatai Zevi.[7] Nathan wrote many letters announcing the arrival of the messianic age,[8] and used most skillfully the network of communications which existed then between synagogues and communities to spread the message of the messiah's arrival far and wide. In only a very few months Nathan's messages spread around most of the Jewish world.

The nature of the connection between the messiah and his prophet is not completely understood. What was it in Sabbatai Zevi's personality which so attracted and fascinated the young scholar in Gaza? What made the young kabbalist, who undoubtedly had also worldly and practical talents, decide to dedicate everything to preaching the messianic message of Sabbatai Zevi?

Nathan wanted to create a unity between the dominant theology of the time, the Lurianic kabbalah, in which he was a well-versed and creative adherent; the ancient Jewish messianic myth, as presented, for instance, in the *Sefer Zerubavel,* the early medieval apocalypse describing in detail the appearance of the messiah and his endeavors, which was a most popular work; and Sabbatai Zevi himself. Nathan set out to show that all these three elements were one and the same, that Lurianic myth and messianic myth carried the same message in different terminology, and that the individual characteristics of Sabbatai Zevi were the embodiment of both of them.

The early Sabbatian movement met with great success. The old messianic myth described the messiah as wandering between the lowly state of a beggar at the gates of Rome, dressing his terrible wounds, and one of a great leader of Israel, the beloved representative of God. His career, according to that old apocalypse, included terrible defeats as well as great victories. Nathan could show that these dramatic changes in the messiah's status were the allegorical expressions of the moods of Sabbatai Zevi, the manic-depressive. All the prophecies concerning the appearance of the messiah and his sufferings were present in the mannerisms of Sabbatai Zevi.[9]

Nathan created a unity between his messiah and Lurianic theology. Lurianic mythology did not contain a specific role for the personal messiah before the process of the *tikkun* was achieved; the messiah was to appear as the result of the successful struggle of the whole Jewish people to uplift the sparks and return them to their rightful place in the divine realm, depriving evil of its sustenance and thus achieving its abolishment. There is no place in this theology for any form of leadership, and no specific duties for the messiah. This created a most heavy burden on the shoulders of every individual Jew; his every misdeed could delay the redemption, and the fate of the whole world, of the divine world, rested on his ethical and ritualistic behavior.

The Lurianic system was the product, and the way of life, of a selected, pioneering group of scholars in Safed, who settled in that community because of their deep commitment to the kabbalah and to messianic expectations. It was far less suitable for the normal social structure of other Jewish communities.

Nathan's messianic theology is based on complete, unqualified acceptance of the Lurianic myth. He used its terminology and his works are developments of Lurianism. But Nathan introduced one major change into the Lurianic picture: a realm within the structure of evil, the deepest and most difficult part, described as the "heels" of the evil *"Shiur Komah,"* which cannot be changed by the usual worship of every Jew. Thus overcoming evil cannot be completed by the people alone; direct divine intervention is also needed. That intervention, according to Nathan, is provided by the messiah, who is an incarnation of a divine power (the sixth *sefi-*

rah, tiferet). Sabbatai Zevi, said Nathan, appeared in order to make the completion of the process of Lurianic *tikkun* possible by fighting and overcoming the "heels" of the world of impurity and evil.

To uplift the divine sparks kept in darkest captivity in that sphere within the Satanic world, Sabbatai Zevi had to descend into the depth of evil, fight it, free the sparks and then lift them up to their original place in the divine world. The prophesied and actual changes of the state and the mood of the messiah are the result of this necessary process. When the messiah is fighting evil at its core, his external melancholy is the result; when he approaches the divine world with the redeemed sparks he is exalted, happy, in a state of enlightenment. Thus all parts of the picture come together, each supporting the other and serving as a proof to the veracity of the others. That Sabbatai Zevi was obviously the savior described by ancient messianic apocalyptic works, and Lurianic theology, as interpreted by Nathan, is the explanation why a messiah is necessary and how he enhances redemption.

IV

The rapid spread of the Sabbatian movement, which in less than a year engulfed the whole Jewish world, in the east and in the west, without almost any voice of opposition, puzzled nineteenth-century Jewish historians. They were somewhat embarassed by the phenomenon of the departure of a whole people from rational thinking, or so it seemed, and they sought various explanations, some of them crudely denying the known facts. For instance, some connected the spread of Sabbatianism with the upheavals and massacres of the Jews in Poland and in the Ukraine in 1648 to 1649 *(gezerot tach)*. The Chmelnitzki massacres served as an explanation for the dramatic eruption of Jewish messianism a decade and a half later.

Scholem studied this problem and concluded that no such explanation could be supported by the historical facts. Rather, the Sabbatian movement grew and was strongest in communities, especially those in Turkey, which were remote from events in eastern Europe and where information concerning the massacres was scant. In contrast, the Jewish communities in Poland were among the last to accept Nathan's messages and were the least impressed by them.[10] Nothing in the history and development of the Sabbatian movement shows any connection to the upheavals in Poland and the Ukraine. Scholem regarded the theory that messianism was the direct result, and refuge, of Jews during periods of extreme hardship as false. Messianism often flourished where Jews lived relatively in a secure and prosperous state (like the Ottoman Empire in the seventeenth century), and often was completely absent when Jews were persecuted in the worst fashion.[11] Nineteenth-century historians often tried to connect messianism with suffering as an apology to excuse the Jews for their "irrational" behavior, refusing to admit that messianism, in various degrees, was a constant creative power within Jewish religion and culture.

Another attempt to explain the spread of Sabbatianism was made in this century by scholars who tried to find a social and economic background to the movement. According to them, Sabbatianism arose from the rebellion of the Jewish lower masses against the social and economic leadership; that is, messianism was but a cover to intense social struggles.[12] Again, as Scholem proved, the facts completely deny this explanation. The participation of the prosperous in the Sabbatian movement was no less than that of the poor. Never did Sabbatianism assume characteristics of a populist movement, and it did not contain any elements of a class struggle. Sabbatianism was the direct result of the development of Jewish mysticism in the previous century.

Scholem emphasized the role of the Lurianic kabbalah in the spread of Sabbatianism.[13] That the Jewish world was united at that time around the symbolism and the terminology of the Lurianic teachings is important to understanding the rapid spread and ready acceptance of Nathan of Gaza's prophecy. Luria described the imminence of the redemption, and his myth strengthened the existing beliefs that the messiah was about to appear at any moment. The Jews were ready to accept a messianic message, especially if it was expressed in Lurianic symbolism and delivered by a prophet from Eretz Israel. That Nathan employed so many other motifs from ancient Jewish sources, especially the messianic myth of the *Book of Zerubavel* and other ancient apocalyptic works, facilitated the spread of his teachings. The close contacts that existed at that time through networks of communities, synagogues, traveling preachers, and the exchange of letters made his task easier, and he skillfully employed all these means. Thus, by the end of the next year, 1666, the whole Jewish world was awaiting the imminent redemption, which Nathan said was about to start within a few months. Almost everybody believed Sabbatai Zevi was going to remove the crown of the sultan of the Ottoman Empire, crown himself, and lead the Jewish people wherever they were to the land of Israel. He would rebuild the temple and messianic times would start. He even allotted the governorships of various parts of the country to his friends, whom he described as representatives of the twelve tribes.

V

Sabbatai Zevi did indeed meet the Ottoman emperor, who investigated the excitement and turmoil among his Jewish subjects. But instead of lifting the emperor's crown Sabbatai Zevi came out of that meeting wearing the Moslem turban, signifying that he had converted to Islam.[14] Thus began the deepest spiritual crisis of modern Judaism. But according to Scholem, Sabbatai Zevi's conversion to Islam was not the end of the Sabbatian movement but rather its beginning. Before the conversion, Sabbatianism was just an awakening of messianic hope, expressed in the most traditional fashion of repentance (Nathan's most popular work of that period was a series of instructions on how to perform repentance)[15] and devotion to traditional worship. There was nothing that marked it as an innovative power within Jewish society. Only when Judaism was suddenly faced with an impossible and paradoxical situation did the spiritual power unleashed by Nathan and Sabbatai Zevi create a new movement, a new theology, and a new phase in Jewish history.

Previous historians described the Sabbatians after the conversion as "remnants" of the destroyed movement. These remnants, Scholem pointed out, existed throughout the seventeenth century. Major movements of the eighteenth century were influenced by Sabbatians, who included some of the greatest leaders of eighteenth-century Judaism. Some echos of Sabbatian groups are found in nineteenth-century European Judaism, and a Sabbatian-Moslem sect, the Dönmeh, probably exists in Turkey today.

Had Sabbatianism been destroyed in 1666, it could not continue to exert such profound influence on the minds of diverse Jewish communities for 200 years, insisted Scholem. We must analyze what happened in 1666 and subsequent years in order to understand the power and fascination that Sabbatianism had for so many years for so many people, many of them among the most prominent and best educated in Jewish society.

Scholem explained that religion is not necessarily the realm of the rational. Paradoxes do not destroy religions; sometimes they build them. The paradox of the suffering righteous is not destructive to religious belief; to the contrary, it is the power that upholds faith in the hereafter. The paradox of the crucified messiah did not destroy nascent Christianity but built it. In the same way, the paradox of the converted messiah is the spiritual source of the development of the Sabbatian movement after 1666. Historians must study carefully the ways that the Sabbatian believers struggled with the conversion of the messiah in order to perceive the sources of the powers which the belief in Sabbatai Zevi obviously held for such large sections of Judaism for so long a time.[16]

The crisis, Scholem explained, was the result of the clear contradiction between external appearances and internal faith in the hearts of the Jews. Externally, nothing had changed. The world continued to be ruled by the gentile powers as it had been before; Israel was oppressed as it had been before. Even the messiah had converted to Islam. Nevertheless, internal faith held that the redemption was imminent and that Lurianic theology and apocalyptic myth denoted that Sabbatai Zevi was the messiah who would deliver Israel and return the Jews to their homeland. The problem with which the conversion presented Judaism was whether to believe the external appearances, or to follow the faith in the prophecy of Nathan of Gaza, of Luria, and of Zerubavel.

It should not be surprising, wrote Scholem, that so many Jews preferred to adhere to inner convictions than to external appearances. The insistence of Lurianic theology upon parallel symbolic connections between heaven and earth, between the divine world and the material one, made Jews regard earthly events as remote symbols of divine processes. The difference between Nathan's prophecy of redemption and the unchanged state of the material world only proved that the changes in the divine realm were not yet transformed into their material symbols; the divine causes existed, while the earthly effects did not. One should not throw away the ancient traditions of Judaism as presented by Luria and the other sources, included in Nathan's prophecy, because of the delay in the apparent (and therefore less important than the hidden) phenomena of the redemption.

The crucial point was, of course, the explanation of the conversion of Sabbatai Zevi. For generations Jews were educated in the belief that there could be no worse crime for a Jew than to convert to another religion. The whole concept of *kiddush ha-shem* expressed the martyrological belief that it was better to sacrifice one's life than to yield to conversion. And now, so it seemed, the messiah himself committed the worst possible transgression, forsaking the opportunity of martyrdom and yielding, without a struggle, to the emperor's demand of his conversion. This was a paradox that was the source of a diverse range of explanations.

The most basic explanation which was accepted by all Sabbatians was that the conversion was necessary in order to enable Sabbatai Zevi to penetrate into the depth of the realm of evil in order to free the sparks imprisoned there. He had to assume the garb of the evil powers themselves so that he could gain access into their dominions. His conversion was nothing but a pretense, so that he could destroy evil from within. Sabbatian literature often uses the picture of the tree of the evil powers which is being eaten from within by the messiah like worms eating the interior of a tree. The outside appearance of the tree is not changed. It seems to be strong and blooming, but it is empty within and will crumble at the slightest touch. Other metaphors include the motifs of the necessity of waste and rot before a new blooming is possible. All served to explain that the messiah had to be identified externally with evil in order to achieve its destruction, which was his divine mission.[17]

We find in Sabbatian literature other, more politically oriented explanations, like the claim that in order to overcome the worst evil element in the world, which was Christianity, a coalition had to be devised between Islam and Judaism. This coalition to overcome, in the first stage, the common enemy, is symbolized by the messiah's conversion to Islam.

Another subtle but important reason given by the Sabbatians for Sabbatai Zevi's conversion is one related to the traumatic Jewish experience of the *marranos* in Spain and Portugal. The reports of the Inquisition's horrors made a deep impression on Jews, and in the seventeenth century many families and individuals whose forefathers had converted to Christianity two centuries before fled from Spain and Portugal and returned to Judaism in Holland, Italy, and other countries. Many of these were well educated, and they were readily integrated into Jewish intellectual society. One of these was Rabbi Michael Abraham Cardozo, who fled from Spain, who became one of the greatest theologians of the Sabbatian movement, second only to Nathan of Gaza.[18] According to Cardozo, Sabbatai Zevi had to convert in order to identify with the sufferings of the *marranos*. He had to become a *marrano* himself, a Jew who keeps his Jewish devotion a secret while pretending to be something else. There is a deep religious meaning to the frightful experience of the *marranos*, and the conversion of Sabbatai Zevi is a retroactive identification with their sufferings. Not many of the Sabbatians believed this, but it had an impact on the formulation of Sabbatian beliefs and ways of life in subsequent years.

VI

Sabbatianism sprang from the paradox of a converted messiah, as Christianity had sprung from the paradox of a crucified messiah. But, Scholem pointed out, there is a great difference between these two paradoxes. There are many constructive human values which can be derived from the Christian messiah, especially those of devotion and martyrdom. But what was to be done with the Sabbatian messiah, the cowardly sinner, who betrayed the tradition of thousands of Jewish martyrs who chose the opposite way in a similar situation?

One obvious thing to do was to follow Sabbatai Zevi, in *imitatio dei* and convert to Islam. A few of his followers indeed did that immediately after his conversion, and a group of several thousands was converted two decades later to create the Jewish-Moslem sect of the Dönmeh.[19]

But most remained within Judaism and practiced their Sabbatian beliefs within the framework of Jewish society. The basic ideas and symbols which provided them with a theology and justification for their behavior were developed by Nathan of Gaza.[20] The key symbol was that of the *torah de-azilut*.

While exile continues and history has not reached the stage of redemption, a Jew must follow the commandments of the Torah and the Talmud, as presented by the halachic authorities. But what will happen in messianic times? Will the Torah remain unchanged? Most Jewish philosophers in the Middle Ages insisted that it would never be changed, most emphatically Maimonides, who viewed Christianity as the result of the belief that the appearance of the messiah signifies a new Torah, in which most of the earlier prohibitions are lifted. He categorically stated that the messiah will not change one word in the Torah. He will be recognized by the fact that he will teach the Torah to all Israel, making them repent their sins and creating a Jewish community which will be completely governed by the laws of the Torah as given to Moses on Mount Sinai for all eternity.[21]

One of the few examples of a different way of thought is found in the early kabbalistic work *Sefer ha-Temunah (The Book of the Picture)* (of the letters of the alphabet and of the Deity). In this work, the author presents a system according to which God creates a succession of worlds, each replacing the previous one after its ending and destruction, and each world governed by one of the *sefirot*.[22] The Torah of each world is a version of a "basic" Torah, according to the characteristics of that *sefirah*. The world in which we live is undoubtedly governed by the fifth *sefirah, din,* which is the power of law and justice. Because of this our Torah is constructed of exact rulings concerning what to do and what not to do. The next world, governed by the sixth *sefirah, tiferet,* which is the power of mercy and compassion, will have a Torah reflecting these values.

Nathan of Gaza followed the ideas of the ancient kabbalist who wrote the *Sefer ha-Temunah,* in a spirit very similar to that of Joachim of Fiore. The Torah given by God to Moses on Mount Sinai was not the perfect Torah, the truly divine one. It was the *torah de-beriah,* "the Torah of creation," according to the kabbalistic system of the succession of worlds, the one just below the divine *sefirot.* The Torah of messianic times is the truly divine Torah derived from the world of emanation, *torah de-azilut.* The coming of the messiah signifies the transition from one Torah to another. This is why Sabbatai Zevi behaved as if he were not bound by the laws of the traditional Torah, which was not his; his strange actions were the results of his living by the laws of the supreme, spiritual, and divine Torah of the redemption, the one to be revealed when the Lurianic *tikkun* is completed.

This idea opened the gates for antinomian tendencies within Sabbatian thought and practice, because the new messianic Torah is one in which many of the older prohibitions are lifted and spiritual, rather than ritualistic, ways of worship are expected. The Sabbatians differed considerably from each other in their understanding of the laws of the *torah de-azilut*.

The main answer that Nathan of Gaza gave the Sabbatians was how to follow Sabbatai Zevi into conversion, imitating his state. According to this belief, a Jew does not have to convert to another religion, Islam or Christianity, to immitate Sabbatai Zevi and become a *"marrano"*; he can do it within Judaism, by pretending to believe in the old, traditional Torah, while inwardly believing in the true Torah, the current one, the messianic Sabbatian one. In this way one can be a "convert" or a *marrano* within traditional Judaism, pretending to believe in its norms and commandments, and secretly follow the new messianic revelation of Sabbatai Zevi and Nathan of Gaza. Scholem characterized this attitude as one of "holy hypocrisy." It does not matter in which religion or society one lives as long as one behaves hypocritically, pretending to believe in one thing while believing another.

How does one follow the *torah de-azilut?* What does one actually do to express one's disbelief in old traditional values and one's adherence to the messianic Torah? The answers that Sabbatians gave included a whole range of religious possibilities. One could espouse the completely antinomianistic claim that the spiritual Torah is the direct opposite of the old one, and everything prohibited in the old is a commandment in the new—"the negation of torah is its upholding," or one could adhere strictly to the old Torah with only minor variations.

The symbolic nature of both Lurianic and Sabbatian mysticism naturally enabled many Sabbatians to employ symbolic means to express their faith in the new Torah. One of the most frequent was the celebration of the ninth day of the month of Av, the day in which the temple in Jerusalem was destroyed, a traditional day of mourning and fasting, which was also regarded as the messiah's birthday. (Indeed Sabbatai Zevi was born then.) While all other Jews fasted and wept, the Sabbatian would secretly celebrate the messiah's birthday, thereby signifying his freedom from the old commandments and his faith in the messiah. These celebrations need not be public or elaborate. Sometimes it would suffice just to eat a bite of fruit, giving only a symbolic expression to the faith in Sabbatai Zevi. The hypocrisy, the duplicity were the important elements, not the hedonistic pleasures. Thus some Sabbatians would express the freedom that the *torah de-azilut* gave by eating a piece of lard, prohibited in the Torah but symbolically practiced by Sabbatai Zevi himself.

Some Sabbatians, especially in the eighteenth century, went even further to explain Sabbatai Zevi's conversion. He had to convert because of the enormous strength of the powers of evil which he set out to vanquish. The redemption thus was delayed, even for many years after Sabbatai Zevi's death, because of the struggle that is going on and the stiff resistance of Satan. The duty of the faithful in these circumstances is to support the messiah with all their strength. This support can

303

be given only through the old Torah, which, according to Luria, includes the laws which symbolically bring about the *tikkun* of the divine world. The faithful have, therefore, to observe strictly all the commandments and ethical demands of the traditional Torah, in order to uplift as many sparks as possible and make the messiah's struggle against evil somewhat easier. These Sabbatians were the most devout and strict observers of the Torah, often called *hasidim*, "pious." Paradoxically, to find the Sabbatians in an eighteenth-century Jewish community one would seek the most pious, strict observers of Jewish traditional laws, customs, and ethical demands.

Two practices were common for all Sabbatian followers of the messianic Torah to observe. One was duplicity; they kept their messianic faith in Sabbatai Zevi a secret, thus creating the false impression that Sabbatianism vanished or considerably diminished after the conversion. It did not vanish, it voluntarily went underground in order to fulfill their concept of *imitatio dei*. The second was honesty; they expressed their belief in a new Torah which would free them from the old traditional requirements even if in practice they still followed diligently all its commandments. The freedom was not an external physical one, but an inner spiritual freedom that only few of the Sabbatians expressed openly by antinomianistic behavior. This sense of freedom, however, had a profound impact upon Jewish behavior when Jews faced European culture as the time of emancipation approached.

VII

The Frankist movement of the middle of the eighteenth century was the most extreme expression of Sabbatianism. It had an impact upon later Jewish history.[23] Jacob Frank was a Sabbatian from Poland who followed a Turkish Jew, Baruchya, who claimed to be the incarnation of Sabbatai Zevi.[24] When Frank returned to Poland (after Baruchya's death), he himself claimed to be the continuation of that line and to be the current (and final) incarnation of the messiah. Around him gathered a few thousands of Jews, who believed in his messianic role. However, rumors spread among the Jewish communities that the Frankists were promiscuous, performed orgies, required incest and the exchange of wives and other crimes.[25] Rabbis gathered to denounce them, to declare them out of bounds of Jewish communities, and even to "allow their blood," meaning that killing them did not constitute a religious crime. Outcast from Judaism, the Frankists sought the assistance of the Catholic church in Poland. The Church was agreeable because it saw this as an opportunity to start the large-scale conversion of a number of Jews to Christianity. The Frankists insisted on their conversion as a separate group, keeping their own identity, their own community, their books, and even their beards. The Church agreed but demanded that they face the Jews in a religious dispute to convince other Jews that conversion to Christianity was the right way.

Two such disputations were held, one in Kaminietz in 1757 and the other in Lvov in 1760; and after the second the Frankists were allowed to be converted.[26] A unique and traumatic event marked this dispute: The Frankists supported the Christian claim that the Talmud required Jews to use the blood of Christian infants for religious purposes. This is the only time in Jewish history that people who were technically Jews supported, in public, the blood libel, thus claiming that the Jewish people were ritual murderers. It is said that Jacob Frank told the rabbis: "You wanted blood, I gave you blood."

This fate of a large group of Jews, who put the blood libel on their brothers and converted to Christianity, was a most traumatic event for rabbinic Judaism. It showed that there was no limit to the evil consequences of Sabbatianism. From then on, Jewish rabbis insisted on the strictest adherence to every detail of the traditional commandments and opposed every innovative idea as dangerous. The reaction to the Frankist trauma also contributed to the vehement opposition of many rabbis to Hasidism in the eighteenth and nineteenth centuries, and to Zionist activity at the end of the previous century and the present one. Even the wish to come to the land of Israel was suspicious, for there had been several immigrations of Sabbatian believers from Europe to Eretz Israel, inspired by Sabbatian messianic expectations.[27]

The teachings of Jacob Frank also were used by some sectarians to explain their destructive tendencies. They interpreted Frank to say that what hinders redemption is the actual existence of the present world. The new, spiritual, and free stage of historical existence cannot be reached until the previous one is destroyed. As the true way to follow the old traditional Torah is to destroy it, so the true way to build a new world of freedom is to destroy the old one.

VIII

There is no doubt that the Frankist movement was a traumatic one for Judaism, but another one was no less upsetting.

This was the controversy concerning the Sabbatianism of Rabbi Jonathan Eibschutz, the great scholar, preacher, and rabbi of Prague in the eighteenth century.

When Sabbatianism went underground and its adherents practiced their belief in secret, a group of Jewish rabbis, scattered in many countries, made it their business to expose and denounce them, especially if they acquired positions of leadership and influence in Jewish communities. One of the most prominent among these was an important kabbalist and writer, Rabbi Jacob Emden,[28] whose father was a very well known and influential halachist.

Rabbi Jacob Emden was an arrogant, aggressive person. He believed that he was persecuted because of his zeal in exposing Sabbatians, but he had a very keen sense of what Sabbatianism was and how its believers behaved. He published many accusations against many different people, and in most cases historical study seems to uphold his accusations as based on fact. None of these attracted so much attention and created such a deep controversy as his claim that Rabbi Jonathan Eibschutz was a secret believer of Sabbatai Zevi and his messianism.

The basis for Emden's argument was a handful of amulets written and given by Rabbi Jonathan to members of his community, as was the custom at that time. Rabbi Jacob Emden analyzed these amulets and came to the conclusion that they included holy names that were computations of the name of Sabbatai Zevi, presented as a divine power. Eibschutz categorically denied these accusations, but Emden published the content of the amulets and the proofs were quite convincing. Emden also claimed that a clearly Sabbatian book by the name

And I Shall Come Today to the Fountain was written by Rabbi
Jonathan.[29]

The conflict divided East European Jewry into two factions, the supporters and the opponents of Rabbi Jonathan.
Each side produced pamphlets and books to prove its case.
Those defending Sabbatianism attacked Emden's character severely and claimed that his accusations were the result of
personal jealousy and hatred of the successful Rabbi Jonathan. The controversy became very bitter and acrimonious,
and continued for many years. Scholem studied this matter
and seemed to prove conclusively that Rabbi Jonathan was
indeed a believer in Sabbatai Zevi and the author of the Sabbatian book.

When Scholem published his conclusions concerning this
controversy he was attacked by traditional rabbis in Jerusalem
in the most vehement manner.[30] Some used this opportunity
to attack his scholarly work as a whole, and his personality
and erudition came under fire. His book *Major Trends in Jewish Mysticism* contained scores of statements that could arouse
opposition and anger among orthodox rabbis, but neither his
conclusion that Rabbi Shimeon bar Yohai did not write the
Zohar, nor his description of the *Hekhalot* literature of Rabbi
Akiba and Rabbi Ishmael as gnostic in character invoked such
anger. Scholem's support of the accusations against Rabbi
Jonathan Eibschutz represented the one thing that the orthodox rabbis of Jerusalem could not tolerate.

Why such anger concerning this matter among so many
for such a long time? It seems that what was, and is, at issue,
is traditional Jewish education. It is possible, or even imag-
inable, that a person who was educated in the most tradi-

tional way, who studied the Talmud for many years and understands it well, somebody who knows the most minute details of Jewish law and is declared a rabbi who can teach and instruct in the *halakha*, a person who preaches in the synagogue and serves as his community's guide in ethical matters could entertain the idea that Sabbatai Zevi was the messiah? This was and is unthinkable and unacceptable to orthodox Judaism. The deep conviction of the intrinsic purifying power of the Torah—meaning, practically, the systematic study of the Talmud in the traditional manner—is one of the deepest convictions of traditional Judaism, and following the example of Rabbi Jonathan Eibschutz could shatter it.

Even today, books are written to prove how impossible Rabbi Jacob Emden's charges were, and how close his intellectual world was to that of Rabbi Jonathan. The trauma has not passed, for it affected one of the most basic foundations of traditional Judaism. For Scholem, this was one more example of the deep changes imposed on Judaism by the Sabbatian movement.

NOTES

1. In his essay "Redemption Through Sin" (Gershom Scholem, *The Messianic Idea in Judaism* [New York: Schocken, 1971] pp. 70–80) Scholem stated that almost no original sources from the Sabbatian movement remained after having been systematically destroyed in years following the rise of the movement. This proved to be untrue. Scholem himself was amazed in later years by the wealth of historical, literary, and theological material which survived and which was utilized by him and others in order to describe the movement. It seems that scholarly neglect, even more than systematic destruction, was responsible for ignorance concerning Sabbatianism until Scholem began his investigations.

2. For the most recent bibliography of scholarship on Sabbatianism, see Scholem's encyclopedia article on the movement reprinted in G. Scholem, *Kabbalah* (Jerusalem: Keter, 1974), pp. 244–86.

3. Concerning the beginning of modernity in Jewish history, see B. Z. Dinur, *Be-Mifneh ha-Dorot* (Jerusalem: Mosad Bialik, 1955).

4. See G. Scholem, *Sabbatai Sevi—The Mystical Messiah,* translated by R. Z. Zwi Werblowsky (Princeton: Princeton University Press, 1973), index, s.v. "Nathan of Gaza."

5. See Tishby's criticism in his "Gershom Scholem's Study of Sabbatianism" (Hebrew), in I. Tishby, *Netivei 'Emunah u-Minhut* (Ramat Gan, 1964), pp. 235–75.

6. The fact that Ezekiel was a priest was used to strengthen this view.

7. Some of the texts were published by Scholem in *Be-ʿIqvot Mashiaḥ* (Jerusalem: Sifrei Tarshish, 1944).

8. An important anthology of Nathan's letters is found in an anti-Sabbatian work by Ya'akov Saporta, *Tzitzat Novel Zevi.* A critical edition of the work, with a detailed introduction, was published by I. Tishby (Jerusalem, 1954).

9. An important study of the theology of Nathan of Gaza was published by C. Wirszubski, "The Sabbatian Theology of Nathan of Gaza" (Hebrew), *Keneset,* 8 (1944), pp. 210–46.

10. See G. Scholem, "The Sabbatian Movement in Poland" (Hebrew), *Bet Yisraʿel be-Polin,* 2 (1954), pp. 36–76. [French translation by G. Vajda in *Revue de l'Histoire des Religions,* 143 (1953), pp. 30–90, 209–32; 144 (1953), pp. 42–77.]

11. See G. Scholem, "Toward an Understanding of the Messianic Idea in Judaism, in G. Scholem, *The Messianic Idea in Judaism,* pp. 1–36.

12. The most important exponent of this view was the late Marxist historian Rudolph Mahler. See his *History of the Jewish People in Modern Times* [Hebrew], vol. 1, 4 parts (1952–62); vol. 2, 3 parts (1970–80).

13. Scholem saw the relationship between Lurianism and Sabbatianism as a crucial one: it stands in the center of all his studies regarding the rapid spread of Sabbatian ideas and their historical impact. See G. Scholem, *Sabbatai Sevi,* p. 15ff.

14. The detailed description of this meeting was given by Scholem in *Sabbatai Sevi,* pp. 668–86.

15. Nathan's orthodox demands concerning repentance are found in several manuscripts. The text was published by Tishby in *Netivei 'Emunah u-Minhut,* pp. 30–51.

16. The power of paradox as a creative force in religion is expressed in the motto which Scholem chose for *Sabbatai Sevi—The Mystical Messiah:* "Paradox is a characteristic of truth. What *communis opinio* has of truth is surely no more than an elementary deposit of generalizing partial understanding, related to truth even as sulphurous fumes are to lightning" (from the correspondence of Count Paul Yorck von Wartenburg and Wilhelm Dilthey).

17. See C. Wirszubski, "The Sabbatian Theology of Nathan of Gaza," pp. 210–46.

18. The biography of Isaac Cardozo was studied in detail by Y. Yerushalmi, *From Spanish Court to Italian Ghetto; Isaac Cadoso: A Study in Seventeenth-Century Marranism and Jewish Apologetics* (New York: Columbia University Press, 1971). Yerushalmi dealt with the relationship between the two brothers, and their exchange of letters concerning Sabbatianism. It seems that Isaac Cardozo saw in his brother's messianic belief a product of their common Catholic education in Spain before their emigration and return to Judaism.

19. Concerning the Dönmeh sect, see G. Scholem, "Die Krypto-jüdische Sekte der Dönme (Sabbatianen) in der Türkei," *Numen,* 7 (1960), pp. 93–122; G. Scholem, "The Sprouting of the Horn of the Son of David: A New Source from the Beginnings of the Dönme Sect in Salonica" (Hebrew), *Tarbiz,* 32 (1962), pp. 62–79 [English version in *In the Time of Harvest: Essays in Honor of Abba Hillel Silver* (New York, 1963), pp. 368–86]; G. Scholem, "A New Text from the Beginnings of the Dönmeh Sect in Salonica" (Hebrew), *Sefunot,* 9 (1964), pp. 193–207. See also G. Scholem, *Sabbatai Sevi,* index, s.v. "Dönmeh sect."

20. Nathan's theology after the conversion of Sabbatai Zevi was discussed by Wirszubski; for reference, see above, n. 17.

21. Maimonides, *Mishneh Torah, Hilkhot Melakhim* 12:1-2.

22. Concerning the book, *Sefer ha-Temunah,* see above, ch. 7, pp. 194–95.

23. Scholem's most recent exposition of the study of the Frankist movement, including a detailed bibliography, is to be found in his encyclopedia article reprinted in G. Scholem, *Kabbalah,* pp. 287–305.

24. See G. Scholem, "Barukhya, the Leader of the Sabbatians in Salonica" (Hebrew), *Zion,* 6 (1941), pp. 119–47, 181–202.

25. The Frankist movement relied on a talmudic saying which seems to imply that the messiah will not come until all the souls created by God have had the chance to enter bodies and come into the world [cf.

Yevamot 62a]. If so, then the more children that are born, the closer is the redemption.

26. The documents concerning these disputations were published and studied by M. Balaban in *The History of the Frankist Movement* [Hebrew] (Tel Aviv: Davir, 1934–35), pp. 137–51, 209–24.

27. The most important Sabbatian emigration to the land of Israel was that led by R. Yehuda he-Hasid (no connection to the thirteenth-century sage of the Ashkenazi Hasidim) and R. Hayyim Malakh ("the angel") in 1700. Most of the immigrants who came to Jerusalem, including R. Yehudah, died soon after their arrival in a plague and left an unfinished synagogue (the *"ḥurva,"* ruin, of R. Yehudah in the old city, Jerusalem). Hayyim Malakh returned to Poland and continued his Sabbatian activity. See G. Scholem, "The Sabbatian Movement in Poland," pp. 48–64.

28. See Y. Liebes, "The Messianism of R. Jacob Emden and his Attitude towards Sabbatianism" (Hebrew), *Tarbiz,* 49 (1980), pp. 122–65. Liebes suggests that the controversy had an element of personal rivalry; Emden himself had messianic aspirations.

29. This controversy was described by Scholem in G. Scholem, *Major Trends in Jewish Mysticism,* 3rd rev. ed. (New York: Schocken, 1954), p. 321.

30. The most noteworthy example was that of Reuven Margaliot in his pamphlet "The Cause of R. Jacob Emden's Opposition to R. Jonathan Eibeschutz" [Hebrew] (Tel Aviv, 1941). This critique prompted Scholem to respond with his one little pamphlet entitled *Leqet Marqaliot* (Tel Aviv: Schocken, 1941), i.e. "a collection of pearls," an obvious play on words with his critic's name.

CHAPTER 12

HASIDISM AND THE
MODERN PERIOD

I

GERSHOM SCHOLEM studied the modern Hasidic movement in several articles. Founded by Rabbi Israel ben Eliezer, known as the Besht *(ba'al shem tov),* the acronym for the traditional Hebrew term for a magician and popular healer,[1] as the latest phase in the development of Jewish mysticism, which began with the expulsion of the Jews from Spain. It continued with the intensification of Jewish messianism and the emergence and spread of the Lurianic kabbalah; it became a major historical crisis for Jewish culture with the Sabbatian movement. Hasidism was one of the answers that the Jewish religious community, suffering from the effects of the Sabbatian heresy and faced with modern challenges, developed to confront the physical and spiritual circumstances of the late eighteenth and the nineteenth century.

Scholem was concerned with the reliability of the sources concerning early Hasidism. There are very few historical references to Hasidism in non-Hasidic sources before the great controversy and the anti-Hasidic polemic which began in 1772. Most of the Hasidic material concerning the early period is relatively late. The Besht's legendary biography, which is a collection of hagiographic stories, was published in 1815, 55 years after his death.[2] Its value as a historical source is very doubtful. Scholem dedicated his efforts to discovering early evidence concerning the emerging Hasidic movement in non-Hasidic sources, and looked for early opposition to Hasidism in the writings of Jewish preachers and in Hebrew ethical works from the middle of the eighteenth century. His work presented the Besht as a charismatic leader, who attracted a certain type of preacher and religious thinker by his ideas. According to Scholem, there were probably proto-Hasidic groups in some major cities of eastern Europe before the Besht began his traveling and preaching (about 1736). Some of them probably were connected in various ways with Sabbatian groups which operated in the same geographical areas and the same social strata. The Besht's innovative ideas were, therefore, part of the cultural and historical setting of that period, and should be viewed as such. Also, the legendary biography *Shivhey ha-Besht (In Praise of the Besht)* contained, according to Scholem, some historical material obscured under the fictional and late legends.

Scholem dedicated to Hasidic theology some important studies which were incorporated in his thematic essays concerning major problems in Jewish mystical thought. As these essays are constructed in a historical sequence, describing the subject chronologically from ancient times on to modern, Hasidism is usually the concluding subject.[3]

Scholem's one comprehensive description of Hasidism was

published in *Major Trends in Jewish Mysticism* as the brief concluding chapter.[4] Two of his most important discussions of central problems concerning Hasidism were written in the framework of a controversy with his colleagues Isaiah Tishby and Martin Buber. A brief analysis of these controversies will enable us to examine Scholem's most important ideas about the Hasidic movement and its role in the history of Jewish mysticism.

II

In the chapter on Hasidism in *Major Trends,* Scholem discussed the position of Hasidism concerning messianism, especially compared with the heretic messianism of the Sabbatian movement and the older messianism of the Lurianic kabbalah. Furthermore, Professor Ben Zion Dinur (Dinaburg) claimed that the Hasidim, and especially the Besht, were intensely messianic, and that Hasidism intended its teachings and its organization to enhance the coming of the messiah.[5] Dinur relied on a letter by the Besht, published in Rabbi Jacob Joseph of Polonoi's *en Porat Yosef* in 1781,[6] in which the Besht told his brother-in-law in Eretz Israel about a mystical experience he had had. The Besht met the messiah when his soul ascended to heaven. During this meeting he asked when the messiah would come. The answer he received was interpreted by Dinur to mean that the messiah would come when the Besht's teachings had spread to all the Jewish people.

Dinur's interpretation was not accepted by many. Martin

Buber, in his many works of Hasidism, took an opposite view,[7] explaining that the Hasidic movement saw redemption in everyday life, rejecting completely Sabbatian messianism. Buber, however, did not support his views with a detailed scholarly study of the sources, and his presentation relies on impressions rather than an exhaustive examination of the documents.

Scholem disagreed with Dinur. He believed that Hasidism neutralized the intense messianic pressures upon Judaism from the Sabbatian movement, and chaneled them to new religious paths. The new ways involved the concept of communion with God, so important and central to Hasidic thought and life. This was in fact a transformation of the Lurianic teachings concerning the *tikkun* and the "uplifting of the sparks." The new ways also involved the belief that the Zaddik was an intermediary between the Hasid and God, fulfilling a messianic function by protecting the Hasid from divine punishment, helping him to achieve complete repentance, and as assisting the acceptance of his prayers before the throne of glory. In these and other central elements in Hasidic theology Scholem saw a neutralization of the messianic drive. Hasidism, according to him, presented a theology which found divine revelation and contact with the divine in the everyday performance of man's religious and human duties, thus making the pressure for a universal, national redemption less acute.

At the Fourth World Congress of Jewish Studies in Jerusalem in August 1965, Isaiah Tishby delivered a major paper on the problem of the messianic element in Hasidism. Tishby did not accept Dinur's view that messianism was the real motive behind the Hasidic movement, but he also rejected

Scholem's view that Hasidism neutralized the messianic element.[8]

Scholem later published his most detailed paper on Hasidism as a response to Tishby's paper.[9] In this response Scholem clarified his views concerning the nature of Hasidism as a conservative, nonrevolutionary movement which transformed the messianic drive to a kind of personal and communal mystical experience that replaced the apocalyptic redemptive vision. This explained, according to Scholem, the Hasidic attitude toward emigration to Eretz Israel, which they did not encourage after an initial enthusiasm,[10] and the fierce opposition of most Hasidic leaders to Zionism and even to emigration to the New World. Salvation and redemption were to be reached in exile, but within the community, by the process of *devekuth*, "communion," and close contact with the leader of the community, the Zaddik, and not by the historical activity demanded by the Sabbatians and their many followers.

III

Scholem's controversy with Martin Buber was centered around the value of Hasidic stories as a historical source and their relevance for understanding Hasidic thought.

For Martin Buber, the true characteristics of Hasidism and the teachings of each individual Zaddik could be gleaned from an inspired reflection upon the stories and the sayings of the teachers of Hasidism.[11] Thus, according to Buber there was a popular and intuitive element in this movement; it did not present its teachings in the systematic, theological manner of earlier Jewish mystics. He regarded it as somewhat remote from the kabbalah. Buber did not rely in his presentation of Hasidism on the voluminous collections of sermons by the Hasidim; he preferred the brief anecdotes, the homilies, and the hagiographic stories that the Hasidim told about their rabbis. He even went so far as to draw some parallels between Hasidism and Zen Buddhism, claiming that the two movements were united in their use of stories and anecdotes that are seemingly incomprehensible, but which convey, in a most profound and paradoxical manner, the true essence of Hasidism. The Zen koan was similar to the Hasidic anecdote in that they both contained in a concentrated form the innermost vision of the teacher. The Hasidic story is a pedagogic instrument by which the intuitive truth is transmitted from teacher to disciple. No scholarly analysis of historical texts will reveal what Hasidism really says and means, according to Buber. The reader must concentrate his reflection on the stories and glean from them undreamed-of levels of human and religious truth.

Scholem rejected Buber's approach.[12] According to Scholem, Buber's methods relied almost completely on the intuition of the reader, thus making every conclusion basically a subjective one. Scholem could not accept Buber's disregard for the main literary and ideological tool of the Hasidic teachers: homilies published in special collections. Thousands of volumes of Hasidic homiletics have been printed, and Scholem collected them carefully. While Buber published a version of the stories of Rabbi Nahman of Bratzlav, the Besht's great-grandson and one of the most profound Hasidic teachers, which he translated from Hebrew into German and reedited, cutting out whatever he did not like,[13] Scholem collected the scattered works of Rabbi Nahman and published a definitive, thorough, and detailed bibliography of them.[14]

The comparison Buber suggested between Hasidism and Zen Buddhism was completely erroneous, according to Scholem. Zen Buddhism can be studied by its koans, because that is the major vehicle used by the Zen scholars to express themselves. The Hasidic teachers, on the other hand, expressed themselves in great length in their homiletical works, while most of the stories and the anecdotes were written by disciples a long time later, and published in unreliable collections.

It seems that this is the one field in which, to date, Scholem's views have not been accepted by the wide public, and Buber's still prevail. While all historians of Hasidism adopt Scholem's historical approach, the public still follows the Buber approach. The popularity of Buber's *Hasidic Stories* and the identification of this movement with nostalgic pictures of the Jewish past in Eastern Europe which was destroyed, seem to make scholarly, methodical study of Hasidism far from popular.

IV

Scholem regarded Hasidism as the last phase in a long process of development. On the one hand, Hasidism was a direct continuation of the chain of tradition and innovation of Jewish mysticism, which started a millennium and a half before the eighteenth century and the Besht. On the other,

Hasidism was the modern stage in the long historical process which started in the fifteenth century and made Jewish mysticism a historical force, influencing and sometimes shaping the fate of Jewish communities facing the non-Jewish world.

Hasidism returned to devotional mysticism, based on the idea of *devekuth,* communion with God, which seemed to weaken the gnostic element in the Hasidic kabbalistic world view. Hasidism continued the use of kabbalistic gnostic symbols, but their most radical meanings lost their edge when the emphasis was put on individual perfection and closeness to God.[15]

Hasidism also preserved one of the most radical Sabbatian ideas, that of the intermediary between the divine world and the earthly one. In Sabbatianism, the task of redemption was laid on the shoulders of the messiah, Sabbatai Zevi, who received from his believers their faith and transformed this spiritual power into a force to overcome evil and bring forth the messianic age. Hasidism, which did not believe in the presence of an individual messiah in the world in the present time (with the exception, perhaps, of believers in Rabbi Nahman of Bratzlav),[16] still held to the idea that there is an intermediary force between the divine world and the Hasidic community—the Zaddik, the rabbi of the Hasidic community. The Zaddik is conceived as a redeemer, an earthly revelation of a supreme divine spark. His mission is not the redemption of the whole people of Israel, but only that of the Hasidic community which adheres to him.

Hasidism neutralized the fierce messianism which accompanied the idea of the intermediary in the Sabbatian movement by limiting the role of the Zaddik as redeemer only to his time, his place, and his specific community. In this way, the redemption brought by the Zaddik is not universal or cosmic, but everyday, step-by-step redemption. The Zaddik helps his adherents absolve themselves of sin, repent, and make their prayers accepted in the divine world before the throne of glory; he protects them from historical upheavals and the persecution of their non-Jewish neighbors, helps them in their material need, and prays with them for the birth of sons and for good health and long life. In exchange for this daily religious and material care, the believer in the Zaddik supports him with his faith and materially cares for his worldly needs.

This ideology created very strong Hasidic communities, united around their leaders and completely faithful to them in the belief that they represented a divine power which protected and assisted them; but these communities, unlike the Sabbatians, were not oriented toward historical change and radical activity. Their orientation was toward daily existence in tolerable religious and material circumstances. This proved to be one of the strongest forces in modern Jewish history. The decline of Hasidism was announced by their opponents and by scholars from early in the nineteenth century onward. Hasidism, however, paid no heed to the prophecies of its decline and disintegration, and proved its durability when its communities overcame crisis after crisis, preserving their identity in Russian labor camps and in Nazi deathcamps, overcoming the upheavals of being transferred from continent to continent, and always regrouping in their own neighborhoods, constructing their schools and social institutions, preserving their belief in their Zaddik, and bringing forth a new generation of Hasidim. Even today, a century and a half after Hasidism was announced to be an anachronistic remnant of medieval superstition rapidly declining in the modern age, Hasidism is still the strongest, best-organized group within orthodox Judaism, and, as far as one can judge, is destined to remain so for a long time to come.

Scholem also saw in Hasidism the modern stage in the long process of spreading the kabbalah. When the kabbalah emerged in the end of the twelfth century it was practiced by very small, closed, and esoteric groups of mystics who kept their mystical experiences and writings a secret. During the Middle Ages interest in the kabbalah and its cultural impact gradually increased, but it was still restricted to closed circles of the elect. After the expulsion from Spain the kabbalah spread rapidly, especially after the Lurianic revolution, but still it was part of Jewish intellectual life rather than the belief of the masses. Sabbatianism brought kabbalistic terminology to almost every Jewish household, but the emphasis was on messianic expectations and not on mystical symbolism. With Hasidism, the kabbalah reached the stage in which every homily in the synagogue, every table discussion in the court of the Zaddik, was based on its terminology and symbolism. Only in the modern period did Jewish mysticism become an integral part of Jewish everyday experience and belief. [17]

But above all, Scholem saw in Hasidism a stage in the historical drama which began on the eve of the expulsion from Spain, when the messianic element in the kabbalah increased rapidly and the historical message of Jewish mysticism for the people as a whole became more and more meaningful. The Lurianic kabbalah was the culmination of this process, when the people of Israel were regarded as collectively toiling to bring forth a dramatic change in the history of the universe and their own fate. Sabbatianism concentrated this energy around the figure of the messiah, and changed Jewish life and self-image in the most radical manner. Hasidism, according to Scholem, was the next step, in which the kabbalah, in self-defence against Sabbatian extremism, neutralized the messianic element and returned to individual, devotional mysticism, organized in the Zaddik-led communities and fortified by the Sabbatian idea of the intermediary between the world of the divine powers and the earthly communities, but concentrating on immediate, day-to-day redemption rather than on an apocalyptic, cosmic one.

While the controversy concerning the messianic element in Hasidism still goes on among scholars, the general outlines of Scholem's studies is almost universally accepted. Hasidism is no longer regarded by historians either as a reactionary remnant of the Middle Ages, nor as a romantic reminder of a nonexistent past. It is the modern aspect of creative Jewish mysticism and it has become a major force in the shaping of Jewish religion and culture.

V

Scholem thought that the Sabbatian crisis and the antinomianistic and nihilistic attitudes present among its eighteenth-century believers were directly instrumental in opening Jewish culture to European enlightenment and that the

Jewish enlightenment movement of the eighteenth and nineteenth centuries was to some extent the result of the Sabbatian upheaval. [18] Scholem's reasoning was unlike that of other
historians who believed that Jews always craved to be integrated into the culture around them, that they were prevented from doing so because of the discrimination and persecution of the Jews by the non-Jewish authorities and
communities. He believed that in the seventeenth century
the Jews were not interested in and had no ambition to become part of European culture, even if they had the opportunity. In order for this integration to occur, progress had to
be made not only toward the emancipation of the Jews, but
also the wish to emerge from the walls of the ghetto had to
be evoked from within Jewish culture itself.

According to Scholem, the Sabbatian crisis caused the walls
of the Jewish cultural ghetto to be broken from within. Old
certainties, the belief in eternal Jewish values which were
superior to non-Jewish ones, were weakened in the face of the
Frankist nihilistic phenomenon and the existence of a secret
Jewish messianic underground within Judaism. The unfamil-
iar sense of freedom which Sabbatian antinomianism brought
forth, and the doubts it cast concerning the eternity of the
commandments of the Torah, opened new vistas for Jewish
intellectuals. This internal crisis within the Jewish world
opened the eyes of Jews to events in the outside world. When
the movement toward lifting the legal prohibitions which
had kept Jews locked within the ghetto began in Europe, the
opportunity was seized by Jewish intellectuals to cross the
lines and create the Jewish enlightenment movement. There
is no doubt that Jewish historiography will study exhaus-

tively the questions of enlightenment and Sabbatianism that Scholem raised, because of their far-reaching historical consequences for the understanding of modern Jewish history. Is Jewish culture to be viewed as self-oriented and self-sufficient because of the historical circumstances in the Middle Ages and early modern times, which prevented Jews from studying European languages, going to European universities, and accepting the cultural norms of the non-Jewish world around them? Or should it be understood as a culture developed by Jews in order to sustain them in their sense of their special historical mission, which is separate and independent of the cultural trends around them? Is the cultural ghetto the result only of external oppression, or was there an element of choice and national preference in the closed world of Jewish ethics, homiletics, *halakhah,* and kabbalah?

Scholem believed that the image of Judaism waiting impatiently for the approach of emancipation in order to leap into the outstretched arms of German and French enlightenment was not historically substantiated. He believed that the Jews were motivated by drives inherent in their own culture, and that the major developments in Jewish thought were caused by needs springing from the heart of Jewish fate and its understanding of its own mission and message to the world. Sabbatian theology, which cast doubts on the most basic and eternal elements of Jewish self-image, weakened the self-sufficiency of Jewish religion and culture and made it possible for some intellectuals of the age to seek answers outside the ghetto walls. Scholem saw Sabbatianism, not the French revolution and emancipation in Europe, as the watershed between the Jewish Middle Ages and modern times. He be-

325

lieved that Jewish history was to be understood by events within Judaism, rather than by historical developments outside of it.

NOTES

1. On the term "Ba'al Schem," see Gershom Scholem, *Kabbalah* (Jerusalem: Keter, 1974), pp. 310–12. See also G. Scholem, "The Historical Image of R. Israel Ba'al Shem Tob" (Hebrew), *Molad,* 18 (1960–61), pp. 335–56 (enlarged version in G. Scholem, *Devarim Be-Go* [Tel Aviv: Am Oved, 1976], pp. 287–324). See also G. Scholem, "The Two First Testimonies on the Relations between Chassidic Groups and the Ba'al Shem Tob" (Hebrew), *Tarbiz,* 20 (1949), pp. 228–40. Other historical studies of Scholem's on Hasidism were included in *Devarim Be-Go,* pp. 325–60.

2. First published in Kopust, 1815. Two modern editions worthy of note are S. A. Horodezsky, ed., *Shivhei ha-Besht* (Berlin, 1922); J. Mondschein, *Shivhei ha-Ba al Shem Tob: A Facsimile of a Unique Manuscript, Variant Versions and Appendices* (Jerusalem, 1982). For an English translation, see *In Praise of Ba'al Shem Tob,* translated by D. Ben-Amos and J. Mintz (Bloomington: Indiana University Press, 1970). Concerning an early edition in Yiddish, see A. Yaari, "Two Basic Editions of *Shivhei ha-Besht*" (Hebrew), *Kiryat Sefer,* 39 (1964), pp. 249–72, 394–407, 552–62.

3. See G. Scholem, "Die Lehre von 'Gerechten' in der jüdischen Mystik," *Eranos Jahrbuch,* 27 (1958), pp. 237–97. [English translation of the first part, "The Doctrine of the Righteous in Jewish Mysticism," was published in *The Synagogue Review,* 34 (1960), pp. 189–95.] See also G. Scholem, "Devekuth, or Communion with God," *Review of Religions,* 14 (1949–50), pp. 115–39 (reprinted in G. Scholem, *The Messianic Idea in Judaism* [New York: Schocken, 1971], pp. 203–26).

4. G. Scholem, *Major Trends in Jewish Mysticism,* 3rd rev. ed. (New York: Schocken, 1954), pp. 325–50.

5. See B. Z. Dinur, "The Beginnings of Hasidism and Its Social and Messianic Elements" (Hebrew), in *Be-Mifneh ha-Dorot* (Jerusalem: Mosad Bialik, 1955), pp. 82–227.

6. *Ben Porat Yosef* (Koretz, 1781).

7. See esp. Martin Buber, *Be-Pardes ha-Ḥasidut* (Tel Aviv: Davir, 1945).

8. See Isaiah Tishby, "The Messianic Idea and Messianic Trends in the Growth of Hasidism" (Hebrew), *Zion,* 32 (1967), pp. 1–45.

9. G. Scholem, "The Neutralization of the Messianic Idea in Early Hasidism," *Journal of Jewish Studies,* 20 (1969), pp. 25–55 (reprinted in G. Scholem, *The Messianic Idea in Judaism,* pp. 176–202).

10. There was a Hasidic immigration to the land of Israel soon after the Besht's death, in 1764, led by R. Nahman of Horodenka, and another major one in 1773, led by R. Menahem Nahum of Vitebsk and R. Abraham of Kalisk, which enhanced the establishment of Hasidic communities in Safed and Tiberias. See I. Halperin, *The Hasidic Immigration to Palestine during the Eighteenth Century* [Hebrew] (Jerusalem: Schocken, 1946).

11. Buber's collection of Hasidic tales was published in German under the title *Die Erzählungen der Chassidim,* 2 vols. (Zürich: Manesse Verlag, 1949). [English translation by Olga Marx, *Tales of the Hasidim,* 2 vols. (New York: Schocken, 1947–48).]

12. This has been studied with great insight by R. Schatz in her essay "Man's Relation to God and World in Buber's Rendering of the Hasidic Teaching" (Hebrew), *Molad* 144–45 (1960). [English version in P. A. Schilpp and M. Friedman, eds., *The Philosophy of Martin Buber* (La Salle, Ill.: Open Court, 1967).]

13. M. Buber, *Die Geschichten des Rabbi Nahman,* rev. ed. (Köln: Jacob Hegner Verlag, 1955). [English translation by M. Friedman: *The Tales of Rabbi Nachman* (New York: Horizon Press, 1956).]

14. Scholem's bibliography was published in a separate booklet, *Quntras ʾEleh Shemot Sifrei R. Nahman vesifrei talmidov vetalmidei talmidov* (Jerusalem: Azriel, 1928). See the supplement to this list in *Kiryat Sefer,* 6 (1930), pp. 565–70.

15. See G. Scholem, *The Messianic Idea in Judaism,* pp. 176–202.

16. Scholem's only study on Bratzlav Hasidim is the bibliography he compiled (see above, n. 14). He did not accept the notion of a marked messianic element in the teachings of R. Nahman as discussed in recent studies on the latter. See J. Weiss, *Meḥqarim be-Hasidut Braslav* (Jerusalem: Mosad Bialik, 1974); M. Piekarz, *Hasidut Braslav* (Jerusalem: Mosad Bialik, 1972); J. Dan *The Hasidic Story* [Hebrew] (Jerusalem, 1975), pp. 132–87. See also A. Green, *Tormented Master: A Life of Rabbi Nahman*

of Bratslav (University, Ala.: University of Alabama Press, 1979), pp. 182–220.

17. It is important to emphasize that the opponents of Hasidism were no less devoted to the kabbalah than were the Hasidim—perhaps even more. They did not tend to popularize the kabbalah as much as the Hasidim, but their rabbis, beginning with their leader, the Gaon Elijah of Vilna, were noteworthy scholars in kabbalah. The attitude towards the kabbalah was not an issue in the controversy between Hasidim and their opponents.

18. See G. Scholem, "Redemption Through Sin," in G. Scholem, *The Messianic Idea in Judaism,* pp. 78–141.

INDEX

Aaron ben Samuel of Baghdad, Rabbi, 94-95

Abraham Abulafia, Rabbi, 188, 195-97

Abraham bar Hijja, Rabbi, 104, 130-31

Abraham ben David, Rabbi, 149-50, 172, 175, 231

Abraham ben Eliezer ha-Levi, Rabbi, 249

Abraham ibn Ezra, Rabbi, 104

Ahimaaz Scroll, 94

Akiba, Rabbi, 53, 54, 58, 62, 63, 129

Al ha-Azilut ha-Semalit (Rabbi Isaac ha-Cohen), 190-93

Allegory, symbolism and, 162–64

"Alu le-Shalom" (Gershom Scholem), 17

Anthropomorphism, Ashkenazi Hasidism, 106-11

Asher ben David, Rabbi, 176

Ashkenazi Hasidism, 40, 92-119; anthropomorphism and, 106-11; divine glory in, 107-11; divine revelation and, 106-11; ethics in, 111-16; *Hekhalot* mysticism and, 95-98; Jewish philosophy and, 102-6; kabbalah and, 117-19; martyrological

attitude in, 113-14; penitence in, 115-16

Avodat ha-Kodesh (Rabbi Meir ibn Gabbay), 240, 250

Azriel of Gerona, Rabbi, 153, 175-76

Badey ha-Aron (Rabbi Shem Tob ibn Gaon), 234

Bahir, 86, 127-42; Catharist movement and, 135-36; dating problems, 130-33; divine emanations in, 133-36; feminine power in, 136-39; gnostic character of, 133-42; good and evil in, 139-40; parables in, 137-39; *shekhinah* in, 136-39; sources of, 132-33

Bahya ben Asher of Saragossa, Rabbi, 233

Bahya ibn Paqudah, Rabbi, 166

Beginnings of the Kabbalah, The (Gershom Scholem), 127-28

Benjamin, Walter, 8

Bibliographia Kabbalistica (Gershom Scholem), 11, 16

Brith Menuha, 236

Buber, Martin, 316, 317-19

Catharist movement, *Bahir* and, 135-36

Chmelnitzki massacres, 293
Christian kabbalah, 237-39
Commandments, in kabbalah, 167-69
Communion with God, in kabbalah, 170-72
Cosmogony: in *Hekhalot* mysticism, 52; in *Merkabah* mysticism, 52
Cosmology: in *Hekhalot* mysticism, 52; in *Merkabah* mysticism, 52
Creation, interpretation of, in kabbalah, 160-62

David ben Judah he-Hasid, Rabbi, 232
Dinur, Ben Zion, 315-16
Divine emanations, in *Bahir*, 133-36
Divine glory, in Ashkenazi Hasidism, 107-11
Divine revelation, Ashkenazi Hasidism and, 106-11
Dobrushka, Moshe, 13-14
Donmeh, Jewish-Moslem sect of the, 296, 300

Eleazar ben Judah of Worms, Rabbi, 93, 96, 97, 98-102, 104, 105, 108, 109, 110, 112, 113, 114, 115, 117, 118, 135
Eliezer ben Hyrkanus, Rabbi, 57, 82
Elishah ben Avuyah, 62
Eliyahu de Vidas, Rabbi, 255
Emunah veha-Bitahon, ha (Rabbi Jacob ben Sheshet), 176
Enoch literature, *Hekhalot* mysticism and, 41
Ethics, in Ashkenazi Hasidism, 111-16
Etz Hayyim (Rabbi Hayyim Vital Clippers), 257
Evil and good, in *Bahir*, 139-40

Exile, image of, in Lurianic kabbalah, 279
Expulsion of Jews from Spain, 244-49

Feminine power, in *Bahir*, 136-39
Flavius Mithridates, 238-39
Frank, Jacob, 13-14, 305-6
Frankist movement, 304-6
From Berlin to Jerusalem (Gershom Scholem), 4-5

Galya Raza, 249
Gerona circle, 172-73
Ginat Egoz (Rabbi Joseph Gikatilla), 197
Gnosticism, origin of, 44-45
Gnostic literature: *Hekhalot* mysticism and, 41-46; *Merkabah* mysticism and, 41-46
Gnostics of Castile, 189-94
God, communion with, in kabbalah, 170-72
Godhead, 154-56
Good and evil, in *Bahir*, 139-40
Graetz, Heinrich, 41, 46, 57, 147, 148

Hai Gaon, Rav, 81, 86
Hakarat Panim ve-Sidrey Sirtutin, 51
Harba de-Moshe, 51
Hasdai Crescas, Rabbi, 235
Hasidic stories, as historical source, 317-19
Hasidism, 313-26; messianism and, 315-17; Zen Buddhism and, 318-19
Havdalah de-Rabbi Akiba, 51
Hayyim Vital Clippers, Rabbi, 256, 257-59, 264
Hebrew Book of Enoch. See Sefer Hekhalot
Hegyon ha-Nefesh (Rabbi Abraham bar Hijja), 130

Hekhalot literature, 39
Hekhalot mysticism, 40, 49-53; Ashkenazi Hasidism and, 95-98; cosmology in, 52; Enoch literature
and, 41; gnostic literature and, 41-
46; Judaism and, 46-49; mystical
process in, 52-53; physiognomy in,
51-52
Hekhalot Rabbati, 48, 51, 52-55, 59-
61, 82, 129
Hekhalot Zutarti, 48, 51, 52-55, 58-
60, 82, 193
Hochmat ha-Nefesh (Rabbi Eleazar of
Worms), 104
Holy chariot: in *Hekhalot* mysticism,
49-50; in *Merkabah* mysticism, 49-
50
Homunculus, 66, 97, 104

Idra Raba, 207
Idra Zuta, 207
Isaac Abravanel, 248
Isaac ben Todros, Rabbi, 233
Isaac ha-Cohen, Rabbi, 190-93
Isaac ibn Latif, Rabbi, 234
Isaac Luria Ashkenazi, Rabbi, 256-58
Isaac of Acre, Rabbi, 223, 233
Isaac Sagi Nahor, Rabbi, 87, 150,
161, 170, 172-73, 175
Isaiah ha-Levi Horowitz, Rabbi, 255
Ishmael ben Elishah, Rabbi, 53, 54,
60, 61
Islam, 82
Israel Alnaqawa, Rabbi, 237
Israel ben Eliezer, Rabbi, 313-14
Italy, kabbalah in, 237-39
Iyyun circle, 173-74

Jacob ben Sheshet, Rabbi, 176, 233
Jacob Berav, Rabbi, 251, 252
Jacob Emden, Rabbi, 307-9
Jacob Frank, 305-6

Jacob ha-Cohen, Rabbi, 188, 189
Jacob ha-Nazir, Rabbi, 175
Jacob Joseph of Polonoi, Rabbi, 315
Jellinek, Adolf, 128
Jewish Gnosticism (Gershom Scholem),
57
Jewish history, chronology of Middle
Ages in, 287-88
Jewish-Moslem sect of the Donmeh,
296, 300
Jewish mysticism, beginnings of, 38-
66
Jewish philosophy, Ashkenazi Hasid-
ism and, 102-6
Jewish pietism, in Germany. *See* Ash-
kenazi Hasidism
Jewish rationalism, kabbalah and,
147-49, 151-57
Joachim of Fiore, 301
Johanan Alemano, Rabbi, 238-39
Jonathan Eibschutz, Rabbi, 307-9
Joseph Alkabetz, Rabbi, 255
Joseph ben Shalom Ashkenazi, Rabbi,
231
Joseph ben Uzziel, 110
Joseph dela Reina, Rabbi, 249
Joseph Gikatilla, Rabbi, 188, 197-98,
204
Joseph ibn Tabul, Rabbi, 257, 264
Joseph ibn Waqar, Rabbi, 234
Joseph Karo, Rabbi, 252-53
Joseph Taitazak, Rabbi, 250, 255
Joseph Ya'abetz, Rabbi, 248
Joshua ibn Shueib, Rabbi, 233
Judah ben Barzilai, Rabbi, 88, 130-
32
Judah ben Samuel ben Kalonymus the
Pious, Rabbi, 93, 98, 100-101,
104,105, 108, 109, 110, 112,
113, 114, 117
Judah ha-Levi, Rabbi, 80, 88, 105,
157

Judah Hayyat, Rabbi, 240
Judaism: *Hekhalot* mysticism and, 46-49; *Merkabah* mysticism and, 46-49

Kabbalah: Ashkenazi Hasidism and, 117-19; commandments in, 167-69; early, 147-80; interpretation of creation in, 160-62; Jewish rationalism and, 147-49; Lurianic, 259-80; prayer in, 174-78
Kabbalistic symbol: nature of, 157-65; philosophical term and, 158-59
Kaf ha-Ketoret, 249
Karaitic literature, 40
Keter Shem Tov (Rabbi Shem Tob ibn Gaon), 233-34
Kitvey Yad be-Kabbalah (Gershom Scholem), 11
Ktav Tamim (Rabbi Moses Taku), 105
Kurzweil, Baruch, 24
Kuzari (Rabbi Judah ha-Levi), 88

Lieberman, Saul, 47, 57, 58
List of Kabbalistic Manuscripts at the National and University Library in Jerusalem (Gershom Scholem), 16
Lurianic kabbalah, 259-80; as conservative force, 275-80; image of exile in, 279; messianic message of, 278-79; mythology, 260-80
Lurianic mythology, Nathan of Gaza and, 291-92

Ma'ayan ha-Hochmah, 82
Magic: in *Hekhalot* mysticism, 50-51; in *Merkabah* mysticism, 50-51
Maimonides, 105, 149, 151, 235, 251, 252, 300
Major Trends in Jewish Mysticism (Gershom Sholem), 9, 21, 22, 39, 77, 95, 308, 315

Martyrological attitude, in Ashkenazi Hasidism, 113-14
Masechet Azilut, 128
Meir ben Shimeon of Narbonne, Rabbi, 177
Meir ibn Gabbay, Rabbi, 240, 250
Menachem Recanati, Rabbi, 232
Menachem Ziyuni, Rabbi, 117, 232
Menorat ha-Maor (Rabbi Israel Alnaqawa), 237
Merkabah literature, 39
Merkabah mysticism, 49-53; cosmology in, 52; gnostic literature and, 41-46; Judaism and, 46-49; mystical process in, 52-53; physiognomy in, 51-52
Messianism: Hasidism and, 315-17; heretic. *See* Sabbatian movement
Metatron, 53, 61, 62, 81, 189
Middle Ages, chronology of, in Jewish history, 287-88
Midrash ha-Ne'elam, 205-7
Milhemet Mitzvah (Rabbi Meir ben Shimeon of Narbonne), 177
Mishneh Torah (Maimonides), 105, 149
Moreh Nevuchim (Maimonides), 105
Moses Alsheich, Rabbi, 250
Moses of Burgos, Rabbi, 153, 189
Moses Cordovero, Rabbi, 253-56, 262
Moses de Leon, Rabbi, 188, 198
Moses Narboni, Rabbi, 235
Moses Taku, Rabbi, 105-6
Mystical process: in *Hekhalot* mysticism, 52-53; in *Merkabah* mysticism, 52-53

Nachmanides, 152, 172
Nahman of Bratzlav, Rabbi, 318
Nathan of Gaza, 195, 288-309; Lurianic mythology and, 291-92

Nehunia ben ha-Kanah, Rabbi, 53-54, 60, 129-30, 236
Neumark, David, 148
Nevuat ha-Yeled, 249
Numerical harmony, 100-102
Numerical structure, of prayer, 99-102

Or Yaqar (Rabbi Moses Cordovero), 253
Or Zarua (Rabbi Moses de Leon), 198
Otiot de-Rabbi Akiba, 141
Otzar ha-Kavod (Rabbi Todros Abulafia), 192

Parables, in *Bahir*, 137-39
Pardes Rimonim (Rabbi Moses Cordovero), 253-54
Penitence, in Ashkenazi Hasidism, 115-16
Physiognomy: in *Hekhalot* mysticism, 51-52; in *Merkabah* mysticism, 51-52
Pico della Mirandola, Count, 128, 239
Pirkey de-Rabbi Eliezer, 82
Prayer: in kabbalah, 174-78; numerical structure of, 99-102; sytem of intentions in, 102

Ra'aya Mehemna, 205, 231-32
Rabbinic ordination, Safed school of kabbalah and, 250-52
Rashba circle, 233-35
Rationalism, kabbalah and, 147-49, 151-57
Ravad. *See* Rabbi Abraham ben David
Raza Rabba, 128, 134
"Redemption Through Sin" (Gershom Scholem), 11, 14, 20, 21
Reshit Hochmah (Rabbi Eliyahu de Vidas), 255

Reuchlin, Johannes, 239
Reuyot Yehezkel, 54
Roqueah (Rabbi Eleazar of Worms), 105

Saadia Gaon, Rav, 57, 85, 103, 105, 106, 107-8, 131, 140
Sabbatai Zevi, 195, 288-309; conversion to Islam, 295-99
Sabbatian movement, 286-309; spread of, 292-95
Safed school of kabbalah, 244-80; rabbinic ordination, 250-52
Samael, 82-83
Samuel ben Kalonymus, Rabbi, 93
Samuel ibn Tibbon, Rabbi, 105
Sar shel Torah, 51
Sar Torah, 82
Scholem, Gershom: biography, 4-32; as historian, 2-3; study of bibliography, 16-17
Schweid, E., 28, 29
Seder Rabba de-Bereshit, 52
Sefer ha-Emunot (Rabbi Shem Tov ben Shem Tov), 235
Sefer ha-Ḥayim, 109
Sefer ha-Hezyonot (Rabbi Hayyim Vital Clippers), 258
Sefer ha-Iyyun, 173-74
Sefer ha-Kanah, 235-36
Sefer ha-Maggid (Rabbi Joseph Karo), 252
Sefer ha-Meshiv, 249
Sefer ha-Orah (Rabbi Jacob ha-Cohen), 189-90
Sefer ha-Peliah, 235-36
Sefer ha-Razim, 51, 54
Sefer Hasidim, 93, 112, 114, 115-16, 118
Sefer ha-Temunah, 194-95, 301
Sefer Hekhalot, 52-53, 61
Sefer Ma'arechet ha-Elohut, 240

Sefer Yezirah, 52, 63-66, 79, 87-89, 100, 131
Sefer Zerubavel, 290
Shaarey Kedushah (Rabbi Hayyim Vital), 256
Sha'arey Orah (Rabbi Joseph Gikatilla), 197
Shabatai Donolo, Rabbi, 83-84, 88
Shekhinah, in *Bahir,* 136-39
Shem Tob ben Abraham ibn Gaon, Rabbi, 233-34
Shem Tov ben Shem Tov, Rabbi, 235
Shimeon bar Yohai, Rabbi, 60, 205, 226
Shir ha Yihhud, 104
Shiur Komah, 48, 52, 53, 55-56, 58-60, 62, 83, 110, 134
Shivhey ha-Besht (Rabbi Israel ben Eliezer), 314
Shlomo Molcho, Rabbi, 253
Shlomo Shlumil of Dreznitz, Rabbi, 259
Shnei Luhot ha-Berit (Rabbi Isaiah ha-Levi Horowitz), 255
Shulhan Aruch (Rabbi Joseph Karo), 252
Sifra de Zeniuta, 207
Sodei Razaya (Rabbi Eleazar ben Judah of Worms), 96, 98-102
Solomon ben Abraham Adret, Rabbi, 233-35
Solomon ben Gabirol, Rabbi, 88
Song of Songs, 55, 56, 57

Spain, expulsion of Jews from, 244-49
Studies in the History of Kabbalistic Literature (Gershom Scholem), 17
Symbolism, allegory and, 162-64

Third Enoch. See *Sefer Hekhalot*
Tikuney ha-Zohar, 205, 232
Tishby, Isaiah, 316-17
Todros Abulafia, Rabbi, 192
Tomer Devorah (Rabbi Moses Cordovero), 255
Torah de-azilut, 301-4
Transformation of souls, in *Bahir,* 140-41

Ursprung und Anfänge der Kabbala (Gershom Scholem), 22

Yalkut Reuveni, 117
Yesod Mora (Rabbi Abraham ibn Ezra), 104
Yohanan ben Zakkai, Rabbi, 59

Zaddik, 320-21
Zen Buddhism, Hasidism and, 318-19
Zohar, 203-26; authorship, 203-4; composition, 205-7; divine world structure, 208-12; good and evil, 214-17; Man's role, 217-22; pseudepigraphical nature, 222-26; sexual symbolism, 212-13